About This Book

The field of coaching is booming! While this is a great step forward, it also means that too many people claiming to be "experts" are jumping on the coaching bandwagon. We, and publisher Pfeiffer, think it's time to disseminate best practice so that it becomes the norm. Based on our success with the highly acclaimed first edition of Coaching for Leadership, we are certain that we are best qualified to perform this important task.

With almost 25,000 copies sold, Coaching for Leadership is easily the most successful leadership coaching book in Pfeiffer history—as well as one of the top five general Pfeiffer coaching titles of all time. It is an invaluable and timeless compilation of theory and thoughts from some of the world's best thinkers and has become a key resource for individuals, leaders, practitioners, and teachers involved in the burgeoning field of executive coaching. As Warren Bennis said, "It's the single best collection of writing and writers on executive coaching. It's really become a 'must have' for the library of all coaches."

Due to the great success of the first edition of the book, Pfeiffer has commissioned us to update and expand Coaching for Leadership. This new and revised book, Coaching for Leadership: The Practice of Leadership Coaching from the World's Greatest Coaches, focuses its messages on two key audiences. The first is the rapidly growing number of executives who are reaching retirement and aspire to become executive coaches. The second new audience is the corporate HR department, which is now faced with new challenges in understanding and managing a coaching intervention. It delivers the well-researched best practices of the world's finest coaches and includes updated versions of some of the articles published in Coaching for Leadership as well as many entirely new articles.

About Pfeiffer

Pfeiffer serves the professional development and hands-on resource needs of training and human resource practitioners and gives them products to do their jobs better. We deliver proven ideas and solutions from experts in HR development and HR management, and we offer effective and customizable tools to improve workplace performance. From novice to seasoned professional, Pfeiffer is the source you can trust to make yourself and your organization more successful.

Essential Knowledge Pfeiffer produces insightful, practical, and comprehensive materials on topics that matter the most to training and HR professionals. Our Essential Knowledge resources translate the expertise of seasoned professionals into practical, how-to guidance on critical workplace issues and problems. These resources are supported by case studies, worksheets, and job aids and are frequently supplemented with CD-ROMs, websites, and other means of making the content easier to read, understand, and use.

Essential Tools Pfeiffer's Essential Tools resources save time and expense by offering proven, ready-to-use materials—including exercises, activities, games, instruments, and assessments—for use during a training or team-learning event. These resources are frequently offered in loose-leaf or CD-ROM format to facilitate copying and customization of the material.

Pfeiffer also recognizes the remarkable power of new technologies in expanding the reach and effectiveness of training. While e-hype has often created whizbang solutions in search of a problem, we are dedicated to bringing convenience and enhancements to proven training solutions. All our e-tools comply with rigorous functionality standards. The most appropriate technology wrapped around essential content yields the perfect solution for today's on-the-go trainers and human resource professionals.

 Essential resources for training and HR professionals

www.pfeiffer.com

COACHING FOR LEADERSHIP, SECOND EDITION

The Practice of Leadership Coaching from the World's Greatest Coaches

Marshall Goldsmith and
Laurence S. Lyons, Editors

A Wiley Imprint
www.pfeiffer.com

Library of Congress Cataloging-in-Publication Data
Coaching for leadership : the practice of leadership coaching from the world's greatest coaches / Marshall
Goldsmith and Laurence Lyons, editors.—2nd ed.
    p. cm.
  Includes bibliographical references and index.
  ISBN-13: 978-0-7879-7763-4 (alk. paper)
  ISBN-10: 0-7879-7763-2 (alk. paper)
  1. Executives—Training of. 2. Leadership—Study and teaching. 3. Mentoring in business. 4. Business
consultants. I. Goldsmith, Marshall. II. Lyons, Laurence.
  HD30.4.C63 2006
  658.4'07124—dc22

Acquiring Editor: Matthew Davis
Director of Development: Kathleen Dolan Davies
Developmental Editor: Sarah MacArthur
Production Editor: Dawn Kilgore
Editor: Rebecca Taff
Manufacturing Supervisor: Becky Carreño
Printed in the United States of America
Printing 10 9 8 7 6 5 4 3 2 1

CONTENTS

Foreword

You have in your hands a powerful tool. It is the collective thinking of the very best thought leaders in executive coaching. You have the opportunity to be stimulated by the innovators who have forged their way in coaching excellence with little guidance. These creative thinkers have practiced and matured their own coaching art over time and in this book share their best and most applicable experiences.

Reading this book will give you the chance to digest the thinking of academic practitioners who have seen this field emerge and have studied its effect on leaders (as well as those they lead) around the globe. You have here a window into lessons learned from implementing corporate coaching initiatives from the very practitioners who launched them and are now willing to share their stories. And, if you utilize this treasure trove well, you have a chance to further build your own individual perspective into this (not-so-new-anymore) field.

I personally know most of the authors in this book. I've read their previous works and been an avid fan of many. (That's what you get with age!) I know that they are serious about their craft and passionate about their desire to show you their unique lens on the world of coaching. Read carefully, ponder on what they suggest. But know also that this story does not end here.

I've never defined myself as someone squarely in the midst of the leadership coaching movement. And like many readers, I've marveled at the huge array of individuals who have hung up the proverbial shingle and declared themselves to be. . . "a coach."

I've also marveled at the equally vast number of people who have spent countless hours in intensive certification programs even though they have been coaching all of their professional lives.

There is no doubt that executive coaching is indeed needed and a new development approach. My practice has always centered on development. For me, it naturally follows that those who lead others must themselves learn to coach. That is part of development. Throughout my experience, I have found that all the best leader-developers at one time had someone to show them their own special growth edge: they can tell you their stories quite easily for such experience gets indelibly marked.

I've had the good fortune to be the recipient of executive coaching myself. I remember being skeptical, but my desire to become a better leader for my own organization overcame my initial reluctance. I am glad for that. In return I have also become a better liver of my own life. I've gained on both counts and continue to learn each time I allow myself to press that "pause button" and remain open to the question of how to do something differently.

As we move into an era when talent in our organizations has more choice than ever before, we will need leaders who can attract, engage, develop, and retain the best of the best. This book will help you to coach others to do just that. Today's leaders simply need all the help they can get. Bravo to all who offer to develop that skill to leaders, and to all who deploy those initiatives in organizations. Enjoy reading!

Beverly L. Kaye
April 2005

"This book is dedicated to our mentor, coach, and role model, Dick Beckhard. Dick was a man who made the ideas in this book come to life. We will always be grateful for all that he did for us, for our field, and for the world."

PREFACE TO THE SECOND EDITION

It is happening. Executive coaching is exploding. The hope expressed in the first edition of this book is being accomplished.

The Practice of Leadership Coaching is the name we have given to this second edition of *Coaching for Leadership: How the World's Greatest Coaches Help Leaders Learn*. It builds on the success of the original work, acclaimed by many authorities as the definitive text on executive coaching. The original work, written as our subject was dawning, has to date inspired well in excess of twenty thousand English-speaking readers; it has since become available in a further four languages.

When Matthew C. Davis, senior editor at Pfeiffer, commissioned this new work, he most likely expected to receive lightly updated scripts culled to appeal to the important emerging audiences he had identified. We have surpassed this ambition. Readers of the first edition will not be surprised at the approach we have taken in producing this latest work. We remain committed to the research approach. So we went back to our authors and asked how they would like to present their ideas, now that our subject has moved on. Once again, their response was amazing.

The book you now hold is more like a separate volume than a second edition. It expounds a well-accepted leadership practice, not a rapidly emerging bright idea. This book contains fourteen brand new chapters; another ten chapters have been significantly revised. We include new detailed case studies, which we know are highly valued by our readers. We are deeply grateful to all our authors for sharing our motivation, and to the leading companies who have been so generous in sharing their experiences.

Our audiences are expanding. This indicates an expansion of needs beyond a mere growth in numbers. We hope in this edition to address those emerging needs. We have expanded and updated our book to include two clearly important groups. The first is the rapidly growing number of executives who are reaching retirement and aspire to become executive coaches.

Within the next five years, it is likely that more than 30 percent of U.S. executives will be retiring*. In Canada, where the retirement rate of executives is nearly 40 percent, "executive failure" is estimated at a staggering 50 percent. In this context, the possibility of growing the skills of developing leaders makes an attractive corporate investment. Perhaps uniquely, executive coaching has the potential to satisfy this need to up-skill incumbent young leaders. The necessary supply of experienced leadership talent clearly exists, albeit in retirement. A fantastic opportunity has opened up to those leaders who are "officially" retired and are thinking about executive coaching as a "second career." Our authors have much to say to them.

The second emerging audience consists of people in Human Resouce departments who are now addressing the challenge of introducing and managing coaching programs. We have included case studies to demonstrate what has worked in particular instances. We suggest that coaching is better seen as a change management program than a training activity. We hope that the collective views throughout this book give HR sponsors a sense for the coaching opportunity and an indication of the different approach that it requires.

Our book delivers the well-researched best practices of the world's finest coaches to those entering and studying this exciting field. By "best practice" we do not mean that we asked our authors to research different approaches and then select a benchmark. As a matter of fact, we want to discourage our readers from simply copying something that worked for someone else somewhere else. We share with our audience—practitioners, leaders who are transitioning from line manager to executive coach, and HR sponsors—the distilled principles of best practice and an understanding of where and how to apply these principles.

We believe this book to be an invaluable contribution to the growing field of coaching, and we are sure you will find the authors' insights, practices, and experiences useful as you navigate the global business environment.

Coaching is the better way.

What to Expect from *The Practice of Leadership Coaching*

Our book begins by explaining and defining its subject, coaching, and then leads into the essential parts of the coaching process, the strategy of executive coaching as a

*DDI, Executive Resource White Paper, 2002.

change activity, and finally case studies and core applications—in other words, how executive coaching works in the real world. Of course, you may read the chapters in any order. Just pick a subject that you are interested in and find your author. Each article is valuable in its own right and can easily stand alone from the rest.

Book Outline

The articles in Part One, Foundations of Coaching, of *The Practice of Leadership Coaching* build the foundation for our book. These chapters comprise the engine that drives subsequent chapters. In this section, the authors triangulate their topic against coaching. Coaching is the backdrop for each discussion and the main mechanism for change is management. Laurence S. Lyons leads the section with his chapter, "The Accomplished Leader." This chapter sets the stage for the rest of the book, giving invaluable insight into executive coaching and its value in organizations. In Chapter Two, "Coaching and Consultation Revisited: Are They the Same?," Edgar H. Schein sets forth critical descriptions of coaching and consulting, comparing the two and defining their differences. Paul Hersey and Roger Chevalier reveal how Situational Leadership® provides the necessary structure to guide executive coaches in working with their clients in Chapter Three, "Situational Leadership and Executive Coaching." Marshall Goldsmith concludes this foundational section with the updated version of his classic piece, "Coaching for Behavioral Change," which describes his tried-and-true process for behavioral change.

Part Two of our book, Building Blocks, is comprised of articles that discuss the essential parts or key themes of the coaching process. This is the section that tells you how to make executive coaching work and how to build it into your organization. Leading this section is a chapter by Marshall Goldsmith entitled, "Try Feed*forward* Instead of Feedback." In it, Marshall discusses the fundamental problem of feedback, which is that it focuses on the unchangeable *past*. He provides us with a definition and plan for using *feedforward*, looking at the infinite variety of opportunities that can happen in the future, as a supplement to feedback. In his chapter, "Making Coaching Work: Ten Easy Steps," Marc Effron reveals how leaders can use simple questioning tools to help build effective, successful coaching programs within their organizations. Richard J. Leider discusses the essential differences between the success and failure of an organization. In his chapter, "Leading on Purpose: What Do You Care About?," he traces the reasons for how well the leaders engage their followers and provides a process for connecting to employees. In their chapter, "Coaching for Effective Action: A Core Leadership Process," Victoria A. Guthrie and John R. Alexander describe the coaching model used at the Center for Creative Leadership, which emphasizes personal development as a stimulant for taking effective action. Joe Folkman explains the importance to the success of any leader of giving and receiving feedback in his chapter, "Coaching Others to Accept Feedback." In the last chapter of this section, "Selling Up Is Leading Up," John Baldoni and Marshall Goldsmith tout the importance of and tell us how to persuade our leaders—those who don't have to listen, but often should!

Part Three, Leading Change, imparts strategies developed to function in the context of a changing global business environment, an environment in which boundaries are always pushed. These strategies make use of executive coaching as a change activity critical to the survival of leaders and organizations. Heading this section is "Coaching at the Heart of Strategy," by Laurence S. Lyons. This chapter sets the stage for the rest of the section by defining what executive coaching is and what it can do for an organization. In his chapter, "Crossing Over: Making the Transition from Executive to Executive Coach," Brian Tracy reveals how and why executives might transition to becoming executive coaches. David Noer follows with his chapter, "Surviving the Transition from Line Manager to Executive Coach," which explains some of the benefits and pitfalls of making such a career change. "Coaching Business Leaders" by Richard Gauthier and David Giber attends to the fundamentals of setting up and preparing a coaching plan with measurable objectives harnessed to the development goals of the organization. In their chapter, "Coaching and Culture: The Global Coach," Michel Moral and Pamela Warnock advocate the significance of cultural awareness as an essential component of executive coaching that can lead to success or failure in the multicultural business context. Jim M. Kouzes and Barry Z. Posner define leadership as a relationship in their chapter, "When Leaders Are Coaches." "Coaching the Coaches," written by David Ulrich, illustrates an important philosophy of coaching: "Coaching does not mean doing for others, but means helping others to get things done." The last chapter of this section is written by Marshall Goldsmith and Kelly Goldsmith. The article entitled "Why Coaching Clients Give Up and How Effective Goal Setting Can Make a Positive Difference" helps us understand how coaches can keep their clients interested and involved in achieving the goals they set for themselves.

Part Four, Applications, is the final section of this book. It is all about applying what we know about executive coaching in the real world. In this section, we take a look at some core applications and some valuable case studies. In his chapter, "Case Study: Coaching for Change at Aventis," Laurence S. Lyons discusses the nature of coaching, before giving an in-depth account of how coaching worked at Aventis. In their chapter, "The Experience of Siemens in Spain," Marta H. Williams, Carlos J. Paulet, and Rebeca Arroyo outline the leadership evolution at Siemens, with particular attention paid to the innovative use of coaching and 360-degree feedback. Kevin D. Wilde describes the part coaching played in the merger of two well-known competitors in his chapter "The General Mills & Pillsbury Merger." In "The Agilent Technologies Story: Coaching Across the Enterprise," Brian O. Underhill, Dianne Anderson, and Robert A. Silva give an account of the development and implementation of Agilent's APEX (Accelerated Performance for Executives) executive coaching program. Marshall Goldsmith supplies us with a futuristic look into the world of coaching in his chapter, "e-Coaching: Using the New Technology to Develop Tomorrow's Leaders." In her classic piece, "Career Development: Anytime, Anyplace," Beverly Kaye reveals that contemporary organizational practices rely heavily on managers' abilities to get the most from their employees, and to do so must devote time to employees' critical developmental needs. R. Roosevelt Thomas, Jr., explores how leaders and managers of an increasingly diverse workforce may offer coaching to those whose attributes and behaviors differ from their own. He then addresses the impact of diversity on the coaching process in his chapter, "Coaching in the Midst of Diversity." In our book's final chapter, "Coaching Executives: Women Succeeding Globally," Nancy J. Adler defuses the myths about women in the global workforce by bringing a broader perspective to each executive's unique position, organization, and industry.

We hope you enjoy this new volume. We hope you will gain more understanding of coaching as it grows to meet with our changing times. We believe coaching can have an incredibly dramatic impact on leaders and organizations, and it is our sincere wish that you find within these pages a theory, method, and strategy to apply coaching within your own organization, or with the executives of organizations that you coach.

Marshall Goldsmith   Laurence S. Lyons
Rancho Santa Fe, California   Reading, England
May 2005

PREFACE TO THE FIRST EDITION

Motivation: Toward a Better Way

Every so often—perhaps once in a lifetime—we have a chance to anticipate a radical and pervasive change that is truly fundamental in nature. This book exists because we are at this very moment at the pinnacle of such change in the world of work. With the passage of every business day, yesterday's "management" approach becomes less relevant while we struggle to find a better way.

Peter Drucker's "knowledge worker" is replacing the factory worker at such a rate as to become today's stereotypical worker. The flatter, shamrock organization typified by Charles Handy is evolving as modern networks are becoming as familiar as traditional pyramids. Whereas in the past we were taught how to work with managers, now we must ask: How can we learn to work with peers?

Ideas stemming from Edgar Schein's "process consulting" are escaping from the closed professional consulting world to reach a much wider group of practitioners—that growing number of people doing all sorts of work who now recognize themselves as leaders. Business is going global. Work is more turbulent and stressful. The "job for life" has disappeared, thus challenging each individual to take care of career and personal development—paradoxically at a time when organizational memory, knowledge, and learning are becoming more valuable and sought after. Consumers are pressing for products that deliver more value and continue to demand more service. Even the "office" is redefining itself in new places, allowing us to work at all times of the day as technology offers to make our style of work more flexible. The "better way" must somehow accommodate all these major shifts and offer some answers to the really hard questions.

We were motivated to write this book because we could see that a number of individuals and organizations had found a better way. At a time when managers were being urged to re-engineer the processes of their businesses, we noticed that some organizations were making even greater strides by focusing on people. Their approach is coaching. It is far too easy to dismiss coaching as yet another technique in the management toolbag. The editors see coaching quite differently. For us, a leadership attitude is essential if individuals and organizations are to flourish in the new business world: good coaching offers both dialogue and etiquette, which together provide the structure and process in which leadership can work well. For us, coaching is the style of choice that rehumanizes the modern worker.

The goal of the editors, then, was simply to bring together the thinking of the world's greatest coaches at a critical time when leaders and managers need to learn about good coaching. This need has been met in this book with tested guidelines that promote responsible and effective coaching. We feel we have a duty as a progressive group to articulate our experiences, ideas, theories, and practices into one book that consolidates and positions the coaching subject into mainstream leadership and management topics.

Our Audience

Naturally, there are many audiences for this book. Those who already recognize themselves as leaders will find valuable reference material to help develop and improve their own leadership style. All those who see themselves as "managers" will find here a route along which to explore and experiment in leadership activities. Our book is for those who sponsor coaching, those who provide or receive coaching, the designers of coaching programs, and anyone who will integrate coaching into his or her own personal style whenever relating to others in the workplace.

Our Authors

We did not expect to write this book alone. At the outset it was clear that we needed to consolidate the thoughts, experiences, and insights of the world's greatest coaches and thinkers on management and leadership. We feel that their generosity in contributing chapters and their enthusiasm toward this ambitious project has validated our own beliefs about the importance of coaching. We take this opportunity to thank our authors warmly, for their willingness to share, for their perseverance in keeping to deadlines, for working with us on making changes to their chapters, and for their unanimous encouragement and support. Their response has built this book into a unique collection of chapters offering an entry point into our subject to readers from all backgrounds.

We have read and edited all the chapters. In areas where we have found different authors writing about the same idea, we have tried to adjust the language so that the same word or expression in one place will refer to the same idea in another place, in a uniform way throughout the book.

We have been editors, never censors. While we have diligently applied a uniformity of language, we have deliberately avoided any insistence on a uniformity of ideas beyond a commitment to coaching. Ours is an emerging subject in which specific situations can be as important as tested techniques in determining outcomes. Practice concepts that today might appear to us as ambiguous, paradoxical, or even contradictory will compete in the real world of experience; they will synthesize, and our collective thinking will make progress into the future.

Our Subject

In order to describe our subject area, we make a few general comments. There is something fundamental about coaching that enables it to fit into organizations of all kinds. Coaching is a behavioral approach of mutual benefit to individuals and the organizations in which they work or network. It is not merely a technique or a one-time event; it is a strategic process that adds value both to the people being coached and also to the bottom line of the organization.

Coaching establishes and develops healthy working relationships by surfacing issues (raw data gathering), addressing issues (through feedback), solving problems (action planning), and following through (results)—and so offers a process in which people develop and through which obstacles to obtaining business results are removed. Coaching can also be looked at as a peer-to-peer language expressed in a dialogue of learning.

Coaching is transformational. Through a behavioral change brought about in individuals, a leader may transform the organization and gain commitment. Coaching can offer a new propellant to organizational change. In coaching, people are offered the chance to align their own behavior with the values and vision of the organization. By helping people understand how they are perceived when they are out of alignment—and then putting these individuals back into alignment, one person at a time—coaching can make real impact and build healthy organizations—top-down, and from the grass roots up.

As to a formal definition of "coaching," how it relates to "leadership," and questions such as the difference between coaching and "mentoring," or whether the "sports metaphor" is appropriate—here we have let our authors speak for themselves. Of course, each of us has a personal view, and we take the opportunity to share this in our own individual chapters, which open the book.

Our Hope

Our hope is that, through the reading of this book, the reader will gain an understanding of the importance of coaching as a preferred and tested route to achieve leadership; the dramatic impact that can be achieved through coaching; why managers need to develop into leaders; and how coaching fits in with other techniques and approaches (consulting, therapy, organizational development, and so forth).

You will gain a thorough grasp of how—and for whom—coaching should be applied in your own organization and in your career, and also how to perform in your role as a coach, a person being coached, a sponsor, or as a buyer or supplier of a coaching service. Last, you can return to this reference work when you need to see how the world's top forty-five leading professionals have successfully responded to difficult coaching problems and successfully applied their own ideas in diverse situations.

Ultimately it is you—our reader—who we hope will complete the quest of this book by bringing good coaching practice into the world of work for the benefit of all.

May 2000

ACKNOWLEDGMENTS

We are especially grateful for the outstanding work done by Sarah McArthur. Sarah is largely responsible for all of the work "behind the scenes" that was necessary to put this book together. She has a unique gift of being able to combine an incredible knowledge of the language with the people skills needed to work with thought leaders around the world.

We would like to thank the authors for their inspiring and thoughtful contributions, as well as the editorial and production staff at Pfeiffer, especially Matt Davis, Kathleen Dolan-Davies, and Dawn Kilgore, for their diligence and care of this essential second edition of *Coaching for Leadership*.

We would also like to acknowledge Alyssa Freas for her contribution to *Coaching for Leadership*, which helped lay the foundation for this second volume.

ABOUT THE EDITORS

Marshall Goldsmith is a world authority in helping successful leaders achieve positive change in behavior: for themselves, their people, and their teams. He is a co-founder of Marshall Goldsmith Partners, which, in alliance with Hewitt Associates, provides coaching for leaders around the world.

Dr. Goldsmith has recently been named by the American Management Association as one of fifty great thinkers and leaders who have impacted the field of management over the past eighty years. He has been described in *The Wall Street Journal* as one of the top ten executive educators; in the *Economist* as one of the most credible thought leaders in the new era of business; in *Forbes* as one of five most-respected executive coaches; and in *Fast Company* as America's preeminent executive coach. His work has been featured in a *Harvard Business Review* interview, *New Yorker* profile, and *Business Strategy Review* (London Business School) cover story.

Dr. Goldsmith has a Ph.D. from UCLA and is an adjunct professor at Dartmouth's Tuck School of Management. He has been asked to teach in executive education programs at Michigan and the Wharton School. He is one of a select few consultants who have been asked to work with over seventy major CEOs and their management teams.

He is co-editor or author of eighteen books, including *The Leader of the Future* (a *Business Week* best seller); *Global Leadership: The Next Generation;* and *The Art and Practice of Leadership Coaching.* Six of his books have been rated as most popular in their field by amazon.com. Harvard Business School has chosen five of his books to be its *Working Knowledge* recommended books. Contact: www.marshallgoldsmith.com; marshall@marshallgoldsmith.com.

Laurence S. Lyons (www.lslyons.com) is an accomplished coach, consultant, public speaker, and author. A former technical director at Digital Equipment Corporation, he has been described as a "leading authority on business transformation" by Henley Management College, where he is a member of the associate faculty and founding research director of the Future Work Forum.

Dr. Lyons is regarded as a pioneer in the field of executive coaching; he has coached hundreds of senior and high-potential executives in organizations in the United States and across Europe. Many of his personal coaching clients are to be found in *Who's Who.*

He specializes in the design, introduction, and implementation of large-scale executive coaching and change management programs to support personal learning, team development, cultural shift, and organizational change.

Dr. Lyons is the founding director of The Metacorp Group, whose clients include Aventis (Frankfurt), BBC, BT (Benelux), British Airways, Deutsche Bank, Equant (Paris), Unilever (Madrid), Lufthansa, Oracle (Nordic), PricewaterhouseCoopers, and WH Smith.

Dr. Lyons holds a Ph.D. and MSc from Brunel University and the CIM (diploma in marketing). He is an invited member of the *Leader to Leader Institute* Thought Leaders Forum (formerly the Drucker Foundation).

Dr. Lyons's coaching work has been featured in *The Times* (London), and he has been interviewed on BBC National Radio 4. His website www.lslyons.com contains many of his published articles and book extracts. Contact: www.lslyons.com; lslyons@lslyons.com.

PART ONE

FOUNDATIONS OF COACHING

Personal success merely brings achievement. Helping others succeed confers genuine accomplishment. Passion for "success through others"—the common aspiration of the consultant, counselor, and coach—is a source of synergy and a hallmark of leadership.

Only an accomplished leader leaves a social legacy. Having "made his mark" on the organization, he leaves behind talented people who will in turn make their mark into the future. For this to come about, the accomplished leader will have made time to pass on learning to others.

This idea was taught by Dick Beckhard whose motto—"we have a duty to pass on our learning"—was a deep source of inspiration for this book. The practice of leadership coaching has much to offer the person being coached. Inescapably, it offers the coach an opportunity to become accomplished as a leader.

CHAPTER ONE

THE ACCOMPLISHED LEADER

Laurence S. Lyons.

A leader becomes complete only after giving something back.

The Sheraton Hotel at Brussels airport is a short walk from the terminal building, making it a popular meeting place for the affluent traveler. Those adventurous enough to explore beyond the spacious restaurant level will find a secluded café frequented by the business jet-set. Chuck, a dapper fifty-something, confidently saunters in, immediately searching out a quiet corner. The plush atmosphere evokes a feeling of opulence and a sense of power. This is the life.

Chuck has arrived early, so finds time to reflect. Surely twenty-five years' experience in the corporate world amply qualifies him for this imminent encounter. Chuck has worked in small businesses and in huge corporations. He was once a line manager responsible for a department of six-hundred people. He has done major tours of duty in operations, finance, and customer service. In one posting, Chuck served as a deputy regional manager. Chuck has experienced the thrills and spills of mergers from both sides. Chuck has lived the corporate life, and Chuck has survived.

In his time, Chuck has come across many difficult situations and plenty of challenging people, each providing some new learning experience. An alumnus of the "hard knocks" school of management, he has acquired a sharp taste for reality. Chuck knows how much damage is done daily by organizational politics and mindless rules. He has seen great ideas get quashed, and under-spent budgets wastefully squandered at year-end. Chuck is mature now, and has learned how to play the corporate game. Chuck understands—and often correctly predicts—organizational outcomes that are completely counter-intuitive to the man in the street. Chuck speaks the language of management. Chuck is able to think as a leader. Chuck has much to offer; today he is ready to give something back, to pass on his learning.

Remembering that this will be his very first face-to-face meeting in his new role as an independent business coach, he opens his briefcase and again reads his notes. . . .

Soon, Chuck is to meet Susan, a fast-track executive currently running the marketing department at a blue chip. In her early thirties, Susan has ambitions to work in public relations before moving to some more senior position, maybe one day to go onto the board. In their phone conversation last week, Susan told Chuck that she does not get on well with her boss and has recently been passed by for promotion. Susan suspects she is hitting a "glass ceiling." Susan directs the work of fourteen marketing communications and program people, and seems to have only a vague idea about the work or personality of her peers.

A careful observer sitting in the lobby might notice Chuck lightly biting his bottom lip while contorting his eyebrows. He is now deep in thought: *How do I start to make sense of Susan's story? What do I really know about marketing or glass ceilings? What should we talk about? Where should I take this? What good can I do?* And, more acutely: *What damage might I do?* As Chuck ponders these grave matters, he realizes that deep down he is just a tiny bit worried.

We'll leave Chuck in suspended animation, anticipating Susan's arrival at the hotel. *Painting by numbers* won't effectively guide their conversation because Chuck does not know what gambit Susan might bring. Chuck's strength lies in his ability to be responsive to Susan, to follow the needs of his client. To help him in this, Chuck needs general orientation, not specific advice. How should Chuck define the area of his work? How should he deal with his own lack of familiarity with some of Susan's situations? How can Chuck play to his strengths? He does not realize it yet, but Chuck is in great shape. What he badly needs right now is a good theory.

A Clear Focus on Coaching

Now would make an excellent time for Chuck to focus his thoughts on what he is meant to be doing. In the conversation yet to take place, Chuck will follow Susan into many and varied topics. As coach, Chuck will at times touch on career planning; he may borrow techniques from personal counseling; he will sometimes process-consult. He will always bring his own experience and knowledge into the room. Yet at all times it is *executive coaching* that must remain at the forefront of his efforts. A commitment to *coaching* places Chuck's work squarely within a learning context. The client is always an *executive*, so Chuck works exclusively within an organizational setting.

Executive coaching is about helping clients gain benefit from learning in an organizational setting. Ranging from the development of general personal skills, to helping Susan figure her way out of a tight corner, all that Chuck does as coach is in pursuit of that end. Chuck's impact will be determined by his ability to transform organizational situations into realistic learning challenges matching the immediate needs of his client. Supremely importantly, *How the client now thinks* and *How the client might think differently* will be key components of that project.

Requisite Variety

Different people prefer different learning styles. This makes it extremely important for Chuck to offer Susan a choice of learning approach. As manager, Chuck himself may be able to get easily from *A* to *C* via *B*. As coach, his task is not to escort Susan to *his* intermediate comfort-point *B*; rather he should help Susan find her own path to *C*. Or, indeed, find an even better destination.

At work here is the systems concept of *equifinality* permitting a variety of personal styles, any of which may be applied to a given situation, to meet the same learning or business objective. Such choice is vital to ensure that each and every step in Susan's learning program respects her personal values. It is only freedom of choice that allows Susan to remain true to herself. She must never feel that her quest to become a leader is forcing her to mimic a style that is distasteful to her, or make her adopt noxious behavior that she would recoil from seeing in others. Her ability to design her own authentic "Susan" style will bolster Susan's feeling of comfort with herself and with her coaching program. She may at times test an unfamiliar tactic; while doing so she must never be asked to compromise her integrity of action.

At the root of designing such a learning strategy lies the coach's ability to deeply understand "the organization," how it works, and the different ways in which a client may survive, win, and prosper within it. Fortunately, this is an area where Chuck can claim to be something of an expert. Good coaches do more than point out an executive's faults. They best help their clients by encouraging them to play to strengths. It is no different for Chuck, one of whose strengths is his expert understanding of *organizational dynamics* absorbed from his exposure to the corporate world. This is a skill he must leverage when making the transition from manager to executive coach.

Thinking Like a Theorist

An effective manager-turned-coach thinks like a theorist; acts like a researcher; never gives advice.

Theory can be that dry stuff found in textbooks. Alternatively a good theory inspires and stimulates action. Theory is capable of doing many useful things. It helps focus our attention on what is important when it encapsulates useful ways we have found in which to view our world. Theory can help get us quickly to the point. Theory helps us discover hidden connections; it helps us remember what otherwise we might forget. Theory may be the only thing we can cling to when we have little reliable data at hand. For coaches, who are behavioral practitioners in an imperfect world, a good theory is simply shorthand for good practice.

Theory truly comes alive when it helps practitioners tackle practical problems. While waiting for Susan in the freeze-frame action at the hotel, it is this more vibrant type of theory that Chuck definitely needs. Chuck may believe he is simply looking for some tested theory to help guide him along his new coaching path. Theories and models abound; simply collecting them is largely a sterile activity. Chuck adds value only when he helps his client. He will only start to do that and make real progress as a coach when he comes to understand that in his new job he has *become* a theorist. A theorist is someone who admits to not knowing and who is prepared to begin by making an informed guess as to cause and effect in a problem situation.

Learning by Theory

There are many parallels between Chuck's work and that of a scientist. Both pick up the theorist's work and conduct experiments in the real world from which learning results.

As a coach, Chuck must be clear about his role and know the boundaries of his work. He must be able to crystallize what he already knows and have the ability to transfer his insight. His deliverable will always be a learning opportunity. Of course, this is far from saying that Chuck will always have the right answers. Chuck's perspective on a situation will never constitute more than a candidate hypothesis which may have to share the stage with several competitors. As always, the client must herself select between approaches and choose an appropriate way to learn. The best Chuck can hope to do is question and inform Susan based on his experience.

Chuck is concerned that some of Susan's presenting issues seem to be outside his immediate experience. For one thing, he has never personally encountered a glass ceiling. The good news for Chuck in his conversations with Susan is that although he may come across subject matter with which he is totally unfamiliar, as a former manager he is well qualified to analyze what counts—the patterns of situations and relationships he is likely to find. Even better news for Chuck is that as he is now a coach not a manager, his role is all about learning systems: this positively prohibits him from giving any content advice. Shifting a gear into the theoretical level is just what Chuck needs to help keep him honest.

Chuck knows that very soon he will hear Susan's story. He is preparing himself to draw out and organize Susan's ideas. He considers for a moment the far-ranging scope that this conversation will likely have. During today's little chat, Chuck must expect to exert considerable influence over the lives of Susan, those close to her, and others in and around the organization for which she works.

Chuck feels it important to shed any prejudices and false assumptions that may be in play—in his own mind, as well as in Susan's. He feels a deep sense of listener responsibility and realizes that he will need to discipline himself in the way he chooses to receive Susan's story. Chuck does not want to contaminate or judge that story. He will succeed by assuming a research style, or, in more familiar management terms—by conducting a friendly audit. Today, Chuck will say little, and instead concentrate his efforts on building rapport while simply *listening to the music.*

Susan's Story

Susan has proven herself to be an exceptional marketing professional. Susan has the experience of growing and leading an excellent team. She has reached a career stage where the perceptions of her by peers in other functions have become critical to her advancement in the company. To be credible at her present level, it is important for Susan to express herself in terms of broader business ideas. To remain strong, Susan must demonstrate that she can think strategically and orchestrate the political dimensions of her role.

Susan's regional boss wants to combine the marketing and public relations departments locally, and can see economies in doing so. But Susan works in a matrix organization in which her marketing boss wants to keep these functions separate. His logic for this is that PR audiences and market sectors need very different handling, different skill sets, and different kinds of people to engage them. It also happens to be the case that the alternative would mean a smaller marketing empire.

Susan remains loyal to both camps and therefore has pursued only timid policies that are controversial to neither manager. This has caused her some personal frustration. For as long as this issue remains unresolved, it also harms the business. While Susan treads water, the business remains sub-optimal: resources are duplicated; motivation stays low; productivity inevitably suffers. For as long as such ambiguity in her position persists, Susan's long-term future as a leader is at risk.

The political situation causing this stress is a form of organizational madness, even though it is constructed solely out of rational positions taken by interested parties. Susan needs to succeed in the face of and despite this madness. As is often the case, many of the tools she needs are closer to hand than she realizes. Susan needs to become more politically astute, to play to her strengths and capitalize on her proven knowledge of marketing. She needs a coach to help her see how easily she could apply her existing know-how to promote *herself* in the company—in the same way her marketing team promotes the company.

Systems Change Agent

At any time the coach may appear to be talking to one individual person but in reality he is always—in some sense—in dialog with the entire client system. Shortly, Susan will tell Chuck about her situation. We do not yet know what they will say. But we know it is likely that, as a result, Susan will be doing some things differently tomorrow. Susan may ask her bosses new questions; she may try out new responses in familiar situations; she may even create totally new situations in which to initiate new dialog. Susan may start to investigate the feasibility of integrating two departments by floating a few probing questions.

Today's conversation is going to extend far beyond the hotel walls. Its ripples will be felt by Susan's bosses and others. With thoughtful preparation and presentation, Susan has an opportunity to impress her peers and inspire her direct reports along the way, as she makes progress in learning how to address the structural dilemma she faces.

Chuck will speak to Susan yet engage her whole organization. And Chuck will do even more than that. He will influence Susan's career beyond this corporation. He will expand the skills Susan employs in her personal life too. Chuck has become an agent of change in a set of complex systems, and he carries a heavy burden of responsibility.

Theoretical Foundations

Thinking in a Corporate Setting

The most basic concept in executive coaching is how a person thinks in a corporate setting. It is the degree to which this concept is developed by the coach that makes any coaching intervention impactful. A good theory distinguishes itself by offering a working model that captures a sufficiently rich corporate description for the job in hand.

Depending on circumstances, Chuck or Susan might use this model in different ways. Chuck reflects on his own thought processes to better understand how he thinks as a manager; in this case Chuck becomes the model's subject. In another application, Chuck employs this model with Susan as the subject, the aim here to unravel Susan's thinking towards the supposed glass ceiling. Then again, in their conversation the pair considers how Susan's work colleagues regard Susan, now placing her managers, direct reports, peers, or customers under the lens at the center of the model. Chuck and Susan have the option to collect *feedback*, to populate their current model with data, to ignite a more public learning process. When a coach is present, some model for *thinking in a corporate setting* is at work whether we are aware of it or not.

No single discipline holds a monopoly on thinking about thinking. Sharing our common interest in the topic of thinking, psychology and philosophy, each has something to offer for coaching theory. Both contribute insights to help us understand *how the client thinks*. These contributions only become valuable to executive coaching clients, however, when they are set in a management context that directs practical action towards business results. It is primarily the job of the coach to help the client translate insight into action within their specific corporate setting.

We might observe that a certain executive thinks fast. Indeed, this may be very important where the objectives of coaching are purely behavioral: there is a potential danger that colleagues who think at only the normal rate may get left behind. This situation is grist for the mill for the middle-manager behavioral coach who may suggest trying out new techniques for "bringing the audience along."

Thinking Deeply

At senior levels in the organization the application of coaching tends to shift focus into the strategic and political arenas. Here, these same words *how the client thinks* should be understood to extend their meaning to include whatever rational, social, attitudinal, emotional, interest-centered, planning, goal-directed, or any other aspects of *thinking* may be relevant so that useful coaching work can get done.

Suppose Susan tells Chuck she has "engaged" participants in her new marketing project by writing them a memo. Chuck has seen this memo and agrees it contains logical, impressive, compelling and elegant arguments, the correctness of which seems indisputable. Susan is surprised that none of the recipients has taken any notice whatsoever.

The problem here is that Susan thinks about engagement in purely rational terms. Her *thinking* about engagement does not yet extend to recognize the importance of her personal presence or the power of an appeal to her colleagues' own interests. To usefully engage she must articulate the link between her pet project and the greater good of the business; rewards to shareholders, benefits to customers, contribution towards a better life on the planet. For her, *engagement* means giving a rational explanation: this is how Susan now thinks.

The challenge for Chuck is to explore how Susan might think differently. Modeling Susan's thinking, Chuck will extend the idea of *thinking* to include any important attitudinal components in play. Susan lacks confidence in inspiring her peers. She harbors feelings of restraint when there is a need for her to stand up to her line manager. Then again, Susan may have some genuine blind spot of which she is totally unaware. She may have a phantom obstacle she needs to expunge: a glass ceiling, perhaps.

Chuck finds it useful to say that all of this has to do with how Susan "thinks" in a corporate setting. Insight into Susan's thinking provides Chuck with an essential building block for designing her learning program.

Rich Description

Sometimes we use words such as *think* to include other factors that are more commonly described by separate words. Another example is *process,* which may simply mean a mechanistic repetitive set of actions. Equally, we may use the word to denote a complete system that has knowledge of its purpose, the structure, and culture in which it operates, and even has the ability to adapt itself to change. In one sense, a whole business could be described simply as a process.

When theorists choose to extend the meaning of a word in this way, far beyond the regular face-value dictionary definition, they are using *rich description*. Rich description can open new horizons to expand the extent of a coach's impact. For the client, too, it offers a useful choice about how to think in a given situation. If Susan were to use a rich description of the word *audiences* in her conversations with her managers, she would have at her disposal a vocabulary highly conducive to integrating the work of marketing and PR in her region.

Acting Like a Researcher

As a coach, Chuck will spend a lot of time involved in research. A researcher is someone who, when presented with a tangle of information, will first sift out what is important and then go on to formulate new questions. These research questions seek to uncover what might be important yet currently unknown. With its focus on learning in an organizational setting, the research aspect of executive coaching will often have as its objective the discovery of perspectives to assist the client's personal development. Susan benefits from finding out the extent to which her credibility as a leader will improve were she to properly engage her peers and inspire her bosses.

Chuck needs to be more that just a regular researcher; he must be forensic and meticulous when looking at evidence. In today's conversations with Susan, all data comes from a single source—Susan. Quality data will likely be scarce, especially as Susan has some blind spots. While it may be safe for Chuck to assume Susan's reporting of her own experience is totally genuine, any data describing Susan's environment—including any perceptions held about her by work colleagues—will be largely unsubstantiated. In truth, from today's exchange alone, Chuck may have little verifiable information to work with.

Tentative Solutions

Given the high degree of risk in Chuck's raw material—reliable information—we might allow him to pause for a moment and rejoice that he has become a theorist. With a paucity of data, any coach is in real danger of making a serious mistake through incorrect inference. It is in such a situation that theory excels. Chuck's insight into real-world organizations contains exactly the theory he needs to help bridge gaps in data and make his intervention more robust. Chuck brings to the conversation a large number of theories and research questions grounded in the experience of real organizational life. Chuck uses story-telling to bring prototype models into his conversation with Susan.

Client Learning

The research that Chuck will engage in will always be of the *pure* kind. This again keeps him at the theoretical end of his partnership with Susan, whose role is to do all the hard work. It is Susan as client who will be interacting with her work system by raising new questions with peers and bosses. After all, the learning must be experienced by Susan, not Chuck.

Reaching Out

Chuck may find he does not have access to Susan's stakeholders. Susan will periodically return to future coaching sessions with stories that relate interactions with work colleagues from which theories will get built and refined. This coaching approach can be extremely effective in highly charged political situations; when the executive is new in post and so is "unknown" to colleagues; and in other cases where supporting data cannot reasonably be collected. This does not mean that involving more people in data gathering is necessarily better. Triangulating data from multiple sources brings its own problems.

Challenge vs. Validation

Like many amateur coaches, Chuck is in danger of becoming evangelical, insisting his client *changes for the better.* Chuck zealously wants to make Susan a "better" executive, and to do this he thinks he must *challenge* her to instantly address some perceived weakness indicated by the feedback. It is possible he will feel the need to say: *"Susan, I know you think you are an excellent listener. But I have here the feedback from twelve of your direct reports who completely disagree with you. Now, should we get started on improving your listening skills?"* There are many useful techniques for achieving this, such as leaving pauses in the conversation to allow people the opportunity to seek clarification.

Chuck will not make such an elementary mistake. Chuck, who thinks like a theorist and acts like a researcher, asks: *"Susan, they say you don't listen; why might they think this?"* Susan responds that during the past six months, as well as running the marketing department in Europe, she has been representing the company in secret merger discussions, reporting directly to the CFO. These talks take place frequently, involving specialist consultants from the Big Five, together with teams of attorneys, accountants and technical experts, all of whom take up residence across discreetly separated suites at a top Beijing hotel. The consequential volume of travel and follow-up work placed on Susan is monumental. Susan says that she is aware her team might feel alienated but insists she is not allowed to tell them why.

Instead of immediately looking for compensating behavior, a researcher first questions source and context. An expert coach will *validate* raw data. Chuck will be interested to know what was happening when Susan's feedback was being collected, and whether anything unusual might have been going on at that time. A research approach wins the day. Suggesting to Susan that she should fix her listening problem by taking long breaths between sentences would not have been helpful.

How Chuck Came on the Scene

Joe is the management accountant responsible for, among other things, approving expenditure in Susan's company. A few months ago, he made his first serious mistake. Joe almost bounced Thelma's budget. Thelma is Vice President, Human Resources. Thelma is a no-nonsense executive with attitude. Joe's email had asked Thelma to produce a *return on investment* justification for her coaching program. Joe reasoned that management is responsible for investing shareholders' money, and shareholders are entitled to know what they should expect in return. *Where is the bottom-line benefit?* Joe had questioned in his email. The answer, *that the bottom line will be there,* was not the one he had expected, or indeed was prepared for.

Instead of replying with a curt email, Thelma sensibly invited Joe to her office. Joe was prompt. As Thelma was running behind schedule that day, her personal assistant told Joe he could wait in her office, which he did.

When she eventually arrived, Thelma offered her apologies, announcing with a knowing smile that she was exactly ten minutes and twenty-two seconds late. She had unexpectedly stopped off to fit a replacement watch battery. Joe suspected that Thelma's accurate time-check was her way of making sure she was getting good value for money from her recent purchase, a quality Joe highly admires in a budget holder. Little did he know that in a very short time he would be back in his office wondering what had happened.

"You asked me to estimate the return on investment for our coaching program, so let's start there. As an investment the RoI from this program would simply be an increase in share price. In my experience, investors tend to like that. So I guess that settles *that* question. Our investor relations people tell us that share price is strongly related to analysts' confidence in the quality of management. Coaching is the method we're using here to grow our management quality and translate it into tangible business impact.

"As I remember, your standard accounting paperwork doesn't ask for the most fundamental measure of success that's relevant here—the protection and enhancement of share price. Until it does, how can I be expected to properly respond?"

Thelma beamed. Joe tried to say something, but was cut short.

"But that's not the point. By asking for RoI, you're telling me you haven't yet understood what we're dealing with here, Joe. We're not justifying our *Coaching for Leadership* program as an investment. Make no mistake, this program is an unavoidable expense; we won't safely achieve this year's plan without it. That's why your request for a return on investment figure is technically meaningless."

During the short pause that followed, Joe scribbled something on his multi-column legal pad. To Thelma, who admittedly was reading upside down, it seemed to resemble a cartoon character, but she could not be totally certain about that.

"Moreover, you should be aware that the relevant asset has already been acquired. It's in place right now. And this planned expenditure on it has already been implicitly justified at corporate level by the main board. Frankly, further justification seems unnecessary."

For some reason, at just that moment, Joe had unexpectedly become aware of the existence of his Adam's apple, but was unable to say why. He had so many questions; he did not know which to ask first. He did not get the chance.

"You look confused, so let me explain. The asset in question is the senior management team, our regional board. Corporate expects us to carry out a program of work, plus whatever unexpected change the world might throw at us—over the coming year. Our success in this as a business is not negotiable. Indeed, as a board we have a responsibility to do whatever is necessary to give ourselves the best chance of achieving our objectives. The coaching program resources that responsibility.

"It strengthens our bottom line by squeezing out the risk of missing it."

Joe repeated that last sentence to himself slowly inside his head. Thelma paused to give Joe time to take this in, then smiled broadly, her face now full of reasonableness. Conspiratorially, she continued:

"Look around. We have members who are new to the board, and with the recent re-organization we have people on the board who will need to work together in totally new ways this year. We also have aggressive sales targets, growth targets, and an extremely turbulent business environment which may include making a local acquisition. We are running this coaching program to make sure the people we have in place are given the best chance to be as effective as the business needs them to be in doing all this. It's simply the 'soft' part of our business plan that has already been agreed and signed-off. I am only sorry we didn't start all this earlier.

"Yes, it is true that there are some choices to be made. Of course we'll be prudent. The key to getting all this right lies in the design of our HR program which we've framed as a change initiative. We've put a lot of effort into that. Naturally only suitably qualified coaches will get anywhere near our top talent. For high potentials like Susan we've found an individual named Chuck who may fit the bill perfectly. For the senior management team, we want a heavyweight coach to work closely with the entire regional board. Given the strategic challenges and degree of change we're facing this year, we've decided to get a very experienced coach at the top end of the range. Of course, I'll copy you on the figures as soon as I have them all.

"Joe, I appreciate your taking a personal interest in this. I know that direct share price enhancement and bottom-line risk reduction may not be the typical benefits you normally recognize in our regional cost center budget. But our business has to recognize exactly that. If we've learned anything from our experience of *business process re-engineering* it's that soft factors drive hard results. We have a board who strongly believes in that maxim, and in response to that, we in HR have built a robust plan to achieve those hard results today and protect our talent well into the future.

"The senior management team is a corporate asset, even though you may not see it as an accounting asset. Yet it still needs nourishment. This new approach will make us a stronger company. That's what this coaching program is really all about. This is how modern companies look at senior coaching programs.

"Well, I guess that just about covers everything. It was so good for us to talk today rather than to simply exchange paperwork. I am a great believer in cross-functional co-operation like this. Joe, I want you to know how much I value your support. Thank you so much for taking the time to see me today."

As Joe was leaving, Thelma locked his gaze, smiled, and then lovingly looked down at one of her personal assets—the diamond-studded Rolex Cellini Quartz sparkling on her wrist. "Nobody will balk about paying a fair price for a replacement battery," she said. Then, looking directly into Joe's eyes with the slightest hint of a wink: "But who'd want to propose owning an expensive watch that can't correctly tell the time?"

In an era when HR is striving to find ways to add strategic value to the business, it is leaders such as Thelma who hold out a blazing beacon to lighten up a path. And, as Joe will attest, its brilliant flame has the power to cauterize as it goes along its way.

The Hybrid Coach

We have become familiar with the consultant as an external agent of change or as someone responsible for helping managers develop the purely technical aspects of their business, such as marketing or operations. More recently, working with individuals and teams, the behavioral coach has emerged as a practitioner in the development of the social fabric of the organization. Today's executive coach is a hybrid of these prototypes and whose playground is the management of an entire socio-technical business system. As such, he or she must be adept in engaging the mesh of political-behavioral and strategic-philosophical components of the organization.

The modern corporation has awakened to realize that a business does not exist in splendid isolation. Far beyond its functions of simple economic exchange, the corporation is today regarded from those outside as having its place in society and its role in the world. Those managers who inspire co-workers by linking the immediate task at hand to their personal development and to the greater purpose of their enterprise are among the new breed of corporate leaders. And those coaches able to foster this sense of *purposeful connectedness* by inducing inspiration in the minds of leaders are truly coaching for leadership.

Back at the hotel, Susan enters the lobby. Chuck has returned the notes to his briefcase alongside his well-thumbed copy of *Practice of Leadership Coaching.* Chuck is prepared. He will succeed today and into the future. With more experience, Chuck will go on to coach more-senior individuals; to work across an entire management team; and even to accept the hardest coaching contract of all: coaching clients across organizational levels within the same team. In that very challenging context, he will advance his capability. Chuck has the potential to one day be among those few able to offer coaching as a highly effective results-oriented conflict dissolution alternative, reaching way beyond brute confrontation and sub-optimal mediation.

Chuck is focused, oriented, and ready. That's partly because Chuck is well-read in the subject of coaching. It helps a lot that Chuck brings a track record as a solid line manager. These factors go a long way in explaining how Chuck will so easily succeed in his inaugural coaching assignment. Chuck will excel, to one day become a truly great coach. For in the deep recesses of his heart and embedded within the very fabric of his approach to life, he is a leader.

In a few weeks, Susan proclaims her first success as a coaching client; she is beginning to make her mark in the organization. Only now is Chuck certain to have truly given something back: he has started to pass on his learning. Susan's breakthrough gives him an especially deep sense of achievement. He also has the feeling that something fundamental has changed. Then the awesome self-realization dawns: Chuck is an accomplished leader.

◆ ◆ ◆

Laurence S. Lyons (www.lslyons.com) is an accomplished coach, consultant, public speaker, and author. A former technical director at Digital Equipment Corporation, he has been described as a "leading authority on business transformation" by Henley Management College, where he is a member of associate faculty and Founding Research Director of the Future Work Forum.

Dr. Lyons is regarded as a pioneer in the field of executive coaching; he has coached hundreds of senior and high-potential executives in organizations in the United States and across Europe. Many of his personal coaching clients are to be found in *Who's Who.*

Dr. Lyons holds a Ph.D. and MSc from Brunel University and the CIM Diploma in Marketing. He is an invited member of the Leader to Leader Institute Thought Leaders Forum (formerly Drucker Foundation). Contact him at lslyons@lslyons.com.

CHAPTER TWO

COACHING AND CONSULTATION REVISITED

Are They the Same?

Edgar H. Schein

Before addressing the question in this title, it is important to note that coaching in various forms reached epidemic proportions in the 1990s and continues to flourish. I rarely run into a trainer or consultant nowadays who does not claim that most of his or her business is coaching, most typically "executive coaching." As this trend continues, if coaching becomes a mainstream activity of all kinds of helpers, it becomes all the more important to understand the socio-psychological dynamics of this complex process. In my forty-five or so years of consulting with various kinds of organizations, I have often found myself in a coaching role, sometimes with the explicit request to play that role, sometimes inadvertently or by default. I never thought of coaching as such a discrete activity with such unique dynamics, but it is now time to confront and describe those dynamics.

"Coaching" as an option arises under one of two conditions: (1) When a client defines the situation as one in which he or she wants individual help to work on a personal issue, in which case the resulting process can be likened to counseling or therapy, or (2) When a manager asks someone to take on a coaching role to work with an individual to improve job performance or to overcome some developmental deficiencies, in which case the resulting process can be likened to indoctrination or coercive persuasion.[1] Both of these situations can also arise with groups or larger organizational units, as when a process consultant helps a group to solve some problem defined by the group, or when a consultant is asked to "help" a group to learn some new processes or adopt some new values that the larger organization has imposed. As a consultant I have found myself working simultaneously with several members of the client system in an individual counseling role while, at the same time, working with broader group and organizational issues that would not be described as coaching per se but that involve elements of indoctrination along with elements of education. From this point of view the consultant's job is at times much broader than the coach's in that the client system is defined as more than the sum of the individual coaching projects that members may engage in (Schein 1999b).[2]

Although coaching is often defined as working with an individual based on the athletic analogy, one can imagine coaching a group, or an organizational unit, or perhaps even a whole organization. In sports, the coach is usually in a direct supervisory role, whereas in organizational coaching the coach is typically a staff member or outsider. If the CEO is being coached on how to improve her relationship to the board or on matters of company strategy, one could argue that any behavior change on her part influences the entire organization. But if a middle manager is being coached on how to make himself more effective and promotable, the connection to organizational effectiveness is more remote. What this suggests is that the degree of overlap between coaching and consulting depends on (1) who initiated the request for coaching, (2) who is being coached, (3) in what role he is being coached, and (4) on what issues he is being coached.

Before analyzing each of these issues, let us examine the interpersonal process that is involved in what we call "coaching." To begin, what is the *essential* difference between indoctrination, training, education, and coaching? All of these processes involve an agent of the society, occupation, or organization trying to change (improve?) the behavior of a target person. What is *implied* in coaching that is different from the other three types of interaction is (1) that the coach does not *necessarily* have in mind a predetermined direction or outcome, (2) that the coach does not have arbitrary power over the target person, and (3) that the target person volunteers and is motivated to learn. If the organization "imposes" a coach and a predetermined direction of learning, then by definition we are dealing with indoctrination, not coaching. It is only coaching if the coach asks the client in what areas he or she wants to improve and works strictly to help the client to help him- or herself. In other words, coaching as it is broadly used nowadays is an intrinsically ambiguous process in terms of its goals. An organization can ask a coach to help a manager perform better against certain company standards, but in that process the coach may find that the person is a real misfit and might work with the person to help him or her leave the organization (even though the company has footed the bill). As we will see, this distinction between working for the organization and working for the individual mirrors closely the distinction I have made between expert consulting and process consulting, and the distinction between indoctrination and therapy.

In my previous analyses of consulting I have emphasized the need to distinguish three fundamentally different roles that the consultant can play in any client relationship: (1) the provider of expert information, (2) the diagnostician and prescriber of remedies, and (3) the process consultant whose focus is on helping the client to help herself.[3] In all of these roles, and that would include coaching, the overarching goal is to be *helpful* to the immediate client, and to be mindful of the impact of interventions on the larger client system and the community.

I have argued that the consultant must move among these roles constantly, but she must *always* begin in the process mode in order to find out in what way her expertise or diagnostic insight and prescription might be helpful. To gain this insight she has to build up enough of a "helping relationship" to stimulate the client to reveal what is really the problem and what kind of help is really needed. And we know from both therapeutic and consulting experience that clients are notoriously reluctant to reveal what is really bothering them until they have a feeling that the consultant is really trying to help.

In the case of organizational consulting, a further complication is that the consultant will never understand the culture of the client system well enough to make accurate diagnoses or provide workable prescriptions.[4] In organizational consulting, therefore, the consultant and client must become a team that jointly owns the consequences of all diagnostic and remedial interventions, even though it must remain clear that it is the client who owns the problem and is ultimately responsible for the solution. The consultant enters into what amounts to a therapeutic relationship with the client system to facilitate in any way possible the improvement of the situation as the client defines it.

Clearly, coaching can then be thought of as one kind of intervention that may be helpful to clients under certain circumstances. In that context I think of coaching as being a set of behaviors on the part of the coach (consultant) that helps the client to develop a new way of seeing, feeling about, and behaving in situations that are defined by the client as problematic. And in that setting, the same issue surfaces of when the coach should be an expert who simply shows the client how to do it, a diagnostician and prescriber who figures out why the client is having a given problem and suggest remedies of various sorts, or a process oriented "therapist" who helps the client to gain insight into his situation and to figure out for himself how to improve his own behavior. The balance and timing of these roles would, of course, depend on whether the coaching was requested by the client or suggested by others in the organization, what organizational role the client is in, and the nature of the problem that the client reveals.

Who Initiates the Coaching Relationship?

Initiated by the "Boss"

One major source of initiation is when someone higher in an organization "suggests" that someone lower get some coaching to overcome some deficiency that is perceived to limit the person's effectiveness or career potential. A common version of this is to mandate that a person's performance appraisal is to be done by the 360-degree method, where feedback is collected from superiors, peers, and subordinates. It is then assumed that an outside coach is needed to go over the data with the person being assessed, because the discussion would be too threatening if conducted by the boss. If the "problem" is primarily defined by the boss, the issue then arises of whether or not the coach is expected to report back to the boss on progress or whether the coaching remains an entirely private matter between coach and client.[5]

If the coach is expected to report back, we are dealing with a situation that may be called "coaching," but is really training or indoctrination. In that case, the "coach" is basically working for the boss, even though the coach may claim to be trying to help the individual. In such a situation, the coach should probably function as expert, diagnostician, and prescriber, because the desired behavioral outcome is defined by someone other than the client being coached. The client's basic choice is whether or not to enter the relationship at all and whether or not to make an effort to learn the new behavior and way of seeing things. If the new behavior and way of seeing things happens to fit the client's own developmental potentials, the outcome could be beneficial for both the organization and the individual. All too often, however, what the client is expected to learn does not fit his or her personality, so either failure or short-run adaptations without long-run changes are the result. From a consulting point of view this whole scenario is risky, because there are too many ways it can fail—the boss not seeing the initial situation accurately, the boss not communicating the need clearly or the consultant not understanding what is really wanted, the individual not willing or able to be "trained," or the individual making a surface adaptation without any real change.

However, there is an alternative way that the boss can initiate the process that is more likely to be successful. The boss can outline to the coach (consultant) what the problem is as she sees it, but not expect to have reports back and to license the coach to be therapeutic if that seems appropriate. In other words, in this scenario, the boss should be prepared for the coaching to result in an outcome that might not be organizationally expected but might be good for the individual client's development. The coaching may even lead the individual client to recognize a mismatch and subsequently to leave the organization. If that is an acceptable outcome from the point of view of the boss, then the coach can try to focus entirely on helping the individual to help herself and to make truly developmental interventions. In that instance, the boss is in effect playing a consulting role as well in trying to be helpful to the individual. As we will see below, this issue interacts that of what the coaching is about. Does the boss want to help the individual develop in a broad sense or does the boss want the individual to learn a particular point of view or set of competencies that are organizationally relevant, for example, learn how to use a new computerized budgeting system.

Initiated by the Individual

Any time a member of an organization goes to an outsider or staff insider for some kind of help there is the potential in the relationship for coaching or individual counseling/therapy. Helping the individual becomes the primary agenda. In that situation, the outcome is not prescribed by the organization in any way and the issues may have very little to do with organizational problems. This kind of coaching/consulting then merges with what any of us face when someone seeks our help—do we tell them what to do, do we privately diagnose the situation and come up with prescriptions, or do we engage in a period of building the relationship in order to find out how best to be helpful?[6] This issue occurs within the family all the time, between friends, between parents and children, teachers and students and is, therefore, a generic human process that needs to be learned by all of us. The ability to do this kind of individual coaching/consulting should be part of any adult's repertory of skills. The basic principle that governs this process is to establish a relationship first through process consultation and only when the client's needs are clear shift to an expert or diagnostic role.

Who Is Being Coached?

How the coaching/consulting relationship evolves will depend on the rank and organizational position of the person being coached. Sociologically, the higher a person's status, the more sacred one is as a social object, and the more care one must take in maintaining appearances. If coaching the CEO or a high-ranking executive, the coach must be able to be in a peer or even superior relationship or the client may simply not listen or may even be offended by the idea of engaging in the relationship. Given the potential sensitivities of high-ranking executives, it becomes especially important for the coaching to begin in the process mode to ensure that a helping relationship is built before any guidance, advice, or prescriptions are offered.

If the coach is clearly superior in rank or status, a different dynamic will be active—the client may actively seek and expect expert advice. The risk in giving it is that it will not fit the personality or total situation of the client and will therefore be ignored or unconsciously subverted. The subordinate cannot really say to the higher ranking or higher status coach that she does not understand or agree with what is offered, or that she has already tried that and it did not work, etc. So even though the temptation to become the instant expert coach is tremendous in this situation, it must be sternly resisted. The coach, to be effective, must engage in open-ended inquiry to establish an equilibrated helping relationship before he or she can determine what kind of help is needed.

If the coach is a status peer, there still remains the problem that the client may feel "one down" for having a problem, for having been singled out for coaching. In western cultures it is not OK to need help; it implies some lack, some inability to help oneself to solve one's own problems. Here too the helper coach must build the relationship first, especially if the coaching involves fairly face-threatening personal issues.

In What Role Is the Client Being Coached?

The key distinction here is whether the client is dealing with a problem that is personal or is seeking help in his or her role as an executive. A personal issue might be how to learn some new skills, such as becoming computer competent or developing a more strategic outlook in order to be promotable to a higher level; an organizational issue might be how to learn to manage the executive team better in order to improve the organization's strategy process, how to learn to think more like a marketer, because the future of the organization lies in better marketing, or how to learn the new computerized budgeting and accounting system on which the future of the organization depends.

If the person is in an individual development role, the same ideas apply as those mentioned above. A helping relationship must be built first, and then the coaching can proceed as appropriate. If the person is in an organizational role, the issue is more complex because the client is now the organization, not just the individual being coached. Suppose, for example, that the CEO wants to be coached on how to get more out of his team, how to get them to compete more for his job, and how to drive their own subordinates harder. How does the coach/consultant decide whether this is an appropriate goal given that it might hurt others lower down in the organization? How does the coach/consultant deal with the situation if she feels that this would be the wrong strategy for the organization to pursue? If the coach is outside the organization, he can walk away from such conflicts, but if he is part of an internal staff or HR organization he cannot. It is at points such as these that coaching and consulting part ways. As a coach the person might have to go along with what the client wants and become a trainer/indoctrinator; as a consultant, even as an internal consultant, he must consider the needs of the larger client system and, if necessary, challenge the CEO's goals.

One might suppose that a similar issue can come up with personal coaching in that the coach might disagree with the learning goals that the client articulates. The goals can then be negotiated between client and coach. However, if those goals have been set by others in the organization, then the coach is bound to them even if the client is not. That is again the indoctrination or "coercive persuasion" scenario in which many coaches de facto find themselves. As a consultant, the helper can "push back," but as a coach the implication is that the organization decides what is needed and the coach's job is to help individuals get there.

What Is the Actual Goal of the Coaching?

Coaching as training or indoctrination covers everything from helping people to learn a new computer system to helping people broaden their whole outlook on what the company is doing. Our most familiar version is, of course, athletics, where the coach helps a person to improve his golf or tennis stroke by observing, diagnosing, providing feedback, demonstrating, and setting training routines and targets. The goal is chosen by the client, but the coach functions as an expert and trainer, often being quite coercive in that process. Such coaching can also involve broader goals, as in the previously cited case of having a coach go over the results of a 360-degree feedback process with the client who has been assessed. In a case that Flaherty cites throughout his book, the goal is how to broaden an executive's outlook so that he can become promotable to a higher level in his company.[7]

My own assumption is that, for any of these goals, from the most concrete skill development to the most abstract reshaping of basic mental models, one will not succeed without establishing a *helping relationship* first. This is relatively obvious in the more abstract personal arenas, but it is often overlooked in skill development coaching. I notice, especially in coaching people on the use of computers, that the coach quickly falls into the expert or doctor mode and "instructs" without any sensitivity to the problems the learner is experiencing. No such coach has ever asked me what my problems were in dealing with the computer or what my learning style is. We jump in with instructions and I find myself struggling, resisting, and not learning.

On the organizational side, this distinction has an important counterpart. Are we talking about coaching on mission, strategy, and goals, or are we talking about coaching on the means, measurement, and remedial processes the organization uses to accomplish its goals.[8] I think coaches are much more sensitive to the needs of the client in the mission and goals area because those are more abstract. When it comes to coaching on the means and processes, coaches quickly become "trainers" and forget to build helping relationships. This tendency to become experts may account for the poor implementation of many programs, such as new computer systems, re-engineering, quality circles, total quality programs, and 360-degree feedback programs. If the learners are not involved in designing their own learning and if they do not have a relationship with the coach in which they are comfortable, they will not learn to the level that the organization expects and needs. To avoid this, coaches must become skilled process consultants as well.

Conclusion

Coaching is a sub-set of consultation. If coaching is to be successful, the coach must be able, like a consultant, to create a helping relationship with his or her client. To create such a helping relationship, it is necessary to start in a process mode, which involves the learner/client, which identifies what the real problems are that need to be worked on, and which builds a team in which both the coach and the client take responsibility for outcomes. How the coaching relationship develops then varies according to who initiated the process, the status differential between coach and client, whether the client is working an individual or organization problem, and whether the content of the coaching concerns organizational mission and goals or organizational process and means. In each of these situations, the coach should have the ability to move easily between the roles of process consultant, content expert, and diagnostician/prescriber. The ultimate skill of the coach, then, is to assess the moment-to-moment reality that will enable him or her to be in the appropriate role.

Paradoxically, indoctrination and coercive persuasion do not work when the target person or group does not have a relationship with the coach, but can work very well if such a relationship has been created by involving the learner at least in the process of learning. Whether or not one wants to call this process "coaching" depends on how broadly one defines coaching. What one calls it matters less, however, than understanding the psychological and social dimensions of the different kinds of relationships that can exist between a coach and a client.

Notes

1. Schein, E. H. (1969). *Process consultation: Its role in organization development.* Reading, MA: Addison-Wesley.
   Schein, E. H. (1999a). Empowerment, coercive persuasion and organizational learning: Do they connect? *The Learning Organization, 6*(4), 163–172.
2. Schein, E. H. (1999b). *Process consultation revisited: Building the helping relationship.* Reading, MA: Addison-Wesley-Longman.
3. Schein, E. H. (1969). *Process consultation: Its role in organization development.* Reading, MA: Addison-Wesley.
   Schein, E. H. (1987). *Process consultation, Vol. II: Lessons for managers and consultants.* Reading, MA: Addison-Wesley.
   Schein, E. H. (1988). *Process consultation, Vol. I: Its role in organization development* (2nd ed.). Reading, MA: Addison-Wesley.
   Schein, E. H. (1999b) *Process consultation revisited: Building the helping relationship.* Reading, MA: Addison-Wesley-Longman.
4. Schein, E. H. (1999c). *The corporate culture survival guide.* San Francisco: Jossey-Bass.
   Schein, E. H. (2004). *Organizational culture and leadership* (3rd ed.). San Francisco: Jossey-Bass.
5. Flaherty, J. (1999). *Coaching: Evoking excellence in others.* Boston: Butterworth-Heinemann.

6. Schein, E. H. (1999b). *Process consultation revisited: Building the helping relationship.* Reading, MA: Addison-Wesley-Longman.

7. Flaherty, J. (1999). *Coaching: Evoking excellence in others.* Boston: Butterworth-Heinemann.

8. Schein, E. H. (2004). *Organizational culture and leadership* (3rd ed.). San Francisco: Jossey-Bass.

◆ ◆ ◆

Edgar H. Schein is Sloan Fellows Professor of Management Emeritus and continues at the Sloan School part-time as a senior lecturer. He is also the founding editor of "Reflections" the *Journal of the Society for Organizational Learning,* which is devoted to connecting academics, consultants, and practitioners around the issues of knowledge creation, dissemination, and utilization.

Professor Schein has been a prolific researcher, writer, teacher, and consultant. Besides his numerous articles in professional journals, he has authored fourteen books, including *Organizational Psychology, Career Dynamics, Organizational Culture and Leadership, and Process Consultation Vol. 1 and Vol. 2, Process Consultation Revisited,* and *The Corporate Culture Survival Guide.* He wrote a cultural analysis of the Singapore Economic Development Board entitled *Strategic Pragmatism* and has published an extended case analysis of the rise and fall of Digital Equipment Corporation entitled *DEC Is Dead; Long Live DEC: The Lasting Legacy of Digital Equipment Corporation.* He was co-editor with the late Richard Beckhard of the Addison-Wesley Series on Organization Development, which has published over thirty titles since its inception in 1969.

Professor Schein's consultation focuses on organizational culture, organization development, process consultation, and career dynamics, and among his past and current clients are major corporations both in the United States and overseas.

CHAPTER THREE

SITUATIONAL LEADERSHIP AND EXECUTIVE COACHING

Paul Hersey and Roger Chevalier

Executive coaching requires exceptional leadership and questioning skills to be effective. At no point is leadership more important than in assisting clients in defining their performance issues and identifying the underlying causes.

In this chapter, we will show how Situational Leadership® provides the needed structure to guide executive coaches in working with their clients. We will add an Executive Coaching Guide® to further elaborate on the process. A model for gap and cause analysis will then be added, followed by sample questions that can be used to assist executive coaches as they guide their clients as they work together to improve organizational performance.

Situational Leadership

Situational Leadership gives executive coaches the guidance they need as they work with their clients. The underlying principle in Situational Leadership is that executive coaches should adjust their leadership styles to their client's readiness level (ability and willingness) to perform a given task. Leadership is the amount of task behavior (direction) and relationship behavior (support) given by a leader. (See Figure 3.1.)

To be effective, executive coaches must adjust the way in which they lead their clients based on their level of readiness for each task that they are expected to perform. Executive coaching is a unique application of the principles of Situational Leadership that guides executive coaches as they work with their clients.

FIGURE 3.1. SITUATIONAL LEADERSHIP.

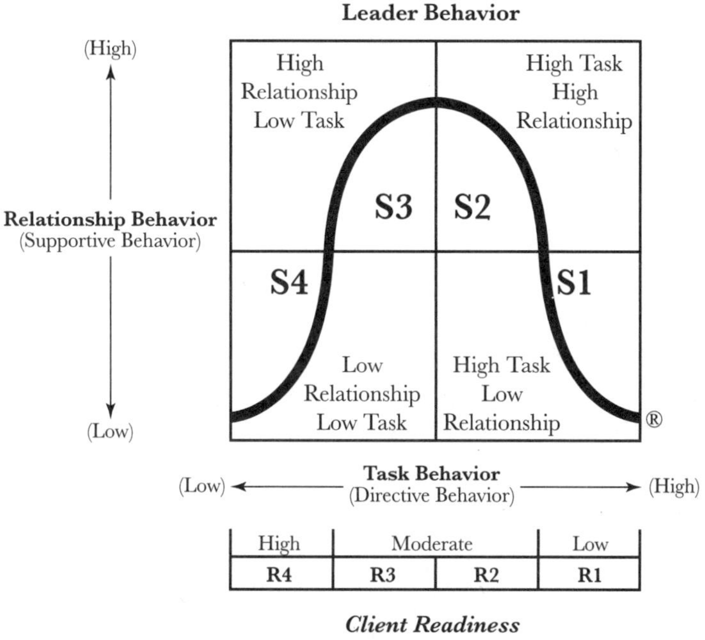

Leader Behavior

(High)

High Relationship Low Task	High Task High Relationship

Relationship Behavior
(Supportive Behavior)

S3   S2

S4   S1

Low Relationship Low Task	High Task Low Relationship

(Low)   ®

(Low) ◄——— **Task Behavior** (Directive Behavior) ———► (High)

High	Moderate		Low
R4	R3	R2	R1

Client Readiness

The lowest readiness level (R1) for an individual or group is described as not willing and not able to do a given task. The appropriate leadership style (S1) is that of providing high amounts of task behavior (direction) and low amounts of relationship behavior (support). The next readiness level (R2) is described as willing but not able. The appropriate leadership style (S2) is that of high amounts of both task and relationship behavior.

The next readiness level (R3) is described as able but unwilling in that the individual lacks confidence or commitment. The appropriate leadership style (S3) is that of high amounts of relationship behavior and low amounts of task behavior. The highest readiness level for a group or individual to do a given task is willing and able (R4). The appropriate leadership style is that of low amounts of both relationship and task behavior.

The Situational Leadership model provides a framework from which to diagnose different situations and prescribes which leadership style will have the highest probability of success in a particular situation. Use of the model will make executive coaches more effective in that it illustrates the connection between their choice of leadership styles and the readiness of their clients. As such, Situational Leadership is a powerful tool for executive coaches to use in working with their clients.

The Executive Coaching Guide

The Executive Coaching Guide® is a performance aid that describes a process that is used in formal interviewing, counseling, and coaching situations. The guide is divided into two phases that focus on assessing the client's readiness and then choosing an appropriate leadership style. The first phase uses Situational Leadership Styles 4, 3, and 2 to prepare, open the lines of communication, and diagnose the client's readiness level for the tasks necessary to be successful.

When the executive coach is not working with the client, the client perceives a Style 4. The client continues to perceive low amounts of direction and support as the executive coach prepares for the coaching session by reviewing relevant materials, such as records from their previous meeting and setting goals for the session.

At the beginning of the meeting, the executive coach moves to a Style 3, increasing support by building rapport, by opening up the lines of communication, and by reinforcing positive performance or potential. In this step the executive coach works to assess how the client sees the overall situation by asking open-ended questions.

The executive coach then moves to Style 2 to focus the discussion with direct questions to gain further insight into the client's current problem areas. For each task that is critical for the client's success, the executive coach must assist the client in defining performance gaps and identifying underlying causes. The executive coach must also assess the client's readiness (ability and willingness) level for dealing with each performance issue so that the coach can choose the best style with which to intervene.

The assessment phase is described in Figure 3.2.

After assessing the client's readiness for each issue, the executive coach selects the appropriate leadership style based on the client's readiness level for each performance issue from the diagram in Figure 3.3. As is the case with the Situational Leadership Model, the performance issue must be clearly defined before a readiness level can be determined.

FIGURE 3.2. ASSESSMENT PHASE.

Assessment of Client Readiness		
S4: Prepare ➡	**S3: Assess** ➡	**S2: Diagnose**
Low Relationship Low Task	High Relationship Low Task	High Task High Relationship
1. Research the client, organization, and industry. 2. Review records of previous meetings. 3. Set goals for the session; develop a strategy.	1. Build rapport, trust, and personal power. 2. Begin the session with open-ended questions. 3. Identify the client's performance issues.	1. Focus discussion with direct questions. 2. Define performance gaps and underlying causes. 3. Assess readiness and select leadership.

FIGURE 3.3. HIGH PROBABILITY INTERVENTION.

S4: Follow-Up ◄	S3: Reinforce ◄	S2: Develop ◄	S1: Prescribe
Low Relationship Low Task	High Relationship Low Task	High Task High Relationship	High Task Low Relationship
1. Document session in client's record. 2. Follow through on all commitments. 3. Monitor progress and prepare for next	1. Reinforce the process used the progress made. 2. Reinforce self-worth and self-esteem. 3. Encourage, support, motivate, and empower.	1. Discuss ways to improve performance. 2. Reach agreement on best course of action. 3. Guide, persuade, explain, and train.	1. Present alternative courses of action. 2. Identify the best course of action. 3. Inform, describe, instruct, and direct.
Selection of Leader's Style Matched to Client			
Able and Willing or Confident	Able but Unwilling or Not Confident	Unable but Willing or Confident	Unable and Unwilling or Not Confident
R4	R3	R2	R1

Clients can be at several different task relevant readiness levels for the different issues. Once the readiness level is decided, the corresponding high probability leadership style is chosen to begin the intervention. After the initial intervention, if the client responds appropriately, the executive coach then moves to the next style to further develop the client. The selection of the high probability intervention style is shown in the diagram that follows.

If the client is unable and unwilling or insecure (R1), initially use a Style 1 (Prescribe) to inform, describe, instruct, and direct. If the client is unable but willing or confident (R2), initially use a Style 2 (Develop) to explain, persuade, guide, and train. If the client is able but unwilling or insecure, initially use a Style 3 (Reinforce) to encourage, support, motivate, and empower. After making the initial intervention, move through the remaining styles to Style 4 (Follow-Up) to monitor progress and prepare for the next session.

The Executive Coaching Guide in Figure 3.4 is a performance aid derived from the Situational Leadership Model and describes the process used to develop people. The executive coaching process follows a pattern that typically includes varying the amount of direction and support given clients as the executive coach prepares, assesses, diagnoses, prescribes, develops, reinforces, and follows up.

The assessment phase is critical to the coaching process in that the executive coach must prepare, assess, and diagnose prior to making the actual intervention. In effect, the executive coach must "earn the right" to intervene. All too often executive coaches intervene without taking the time to truly assess the client's readiness. While the initial intervention style is chosen based on the client's readiness for a given task, the goal is to develop the client by using successive leadership styles as the executive coach moves from prescribe to develop, to reinforce, and then to follow-up.

FIGURE 3.4. EXECUTIVE COACHING GUIDE.

Assessment of Client Readiness			
S4: Prepare ➡	**S3: Assess** ➡	**S2: Diagnose**	
Low Relationship Low Task	High Relationship Low Task	High Task High Relationship	
1. Research the client, organization, and industry. 2. Review records of previous meetings. 3. Set goals for the session; develop a strategy.	1. Build rapport, trust, and personal power. 2. Begin the session with open-ended questions. 3. Identify the client's performance issues.	1. Focus discussion with direct questions. 2. Define performance gaps and underlying causes. 3. Assess readiness and select leadership.	
S4: Follow-Up ⬅	**S3: Reinforce** ⬅	**S2: Develop** ⬅	**S1: Prescribe**
Low Relationship Low Task	High Relationship Low Task	High Task High Relationship	High Task Low Relationship
1. Document session in client's record. 2. Follow through on all commitments. 3. Monitor progress and prepare for next	1. Reinforce the process used the progress made. 2. Reinforce self-worth and self-esteem. 3. Encourage, support, motivate, and empower.	1. Discuss ways to improve performance. 2. Reach agreement on best course of action. 3. Guide, persuade, explain, and train.	1. Present alternative courses of action. 2. Identify the best course of action. 3. Inform, describe, instruct, and direct.
Selection of Leader's Style Matched to Client			
Able and Willing or Confident	Able but Unwilling or Not Confident	Unable but Willing or Confident	Unable and Unwilling or Not Confident
R4	R3	R2	R1

Performance Gap and Cause Analysis

The key to the executive coaching process is in asking the right questions in the right order to assist clients in identifying their overall situation, specific performance gaps, and the underlying causes. The executive coaching process is an application of leadership in which the consultant becomes a trusted resource for the client.

The starting point in assisting clients in analyzing performance shortfalls is called gap analysis. The executive coach must lead the client in identifying an individual's or group's present level of performance (where they are) and their desired level of performance (where they'd like to be). The difference between where they are and where they want to be is the performance gap. Another useful step is to identify a reasonable goal, something that can be accomplished in a short time that moves the organization in the direction toward where it wants to be. This should be defined clearly with measures of quality, quantity, time, and cost delineated for the goal.

Once the performance gap has been defined, the next step is to identify the causes. The Behavior Engineering Model (BEM), developed by Thomas Gilbert and presented in his landmark book, *Human Competence: Engineering Worthy Performance,*[1] provided a way to systematically and systemically identify barriers to individual and organizational performance. This model has been recently updated to better assist executive coaches in assisting their clients in identifying causes for performance gaps.[2]

The updated model (Figure 3.5) focuses attention on the distinction between environmental and individual factors that impact performance. Environmental factors are the starting point for analysis because they pose the greatest barriers to exemplary performance. When the environmental supports are strong, individuals are better able to do what is expected of them.

The support given by the work environment is divided into three factors that influence performance: information, resources, and incentives. Information includes communicating clear expectations, providing the necessary guides to do the work, and giving timely, behaviorally specific feedback. Resources include ensuring that the proper materials, tools, time, and processes are present to accomplish the task. Incentives ensure that the appropriate financial and non-financial incentives are present to encourage performance. These apply to the worker, the work, and the workplace.

What the individuals bring to the job include their motives, capacity, knowledge, and skills. Individual motives should me aligned with the work environment so that employees have a desire to work and excel. Capacity refers to whether the worker is able to learn and do what is necessary to be successful on the job. The final factor refers to whether the individual has the necessary knowledge and skills to do a specific task needed to accomplish a project or goal.

The model gives the structure needed to assess each of the six factors: *information, resources, incentives, motives, capacity, and knowledge and skills* that affect individual and group performance on the job. These factors should be reviewed in this order since the environmental factors are easier to improve and have a greater impact on individual and group performance. It would also be difficult to assess whether the individual had the right motives, capacity, and knowledge and skills to do the job if the environmental factors of information, resources, and incentives are not sufficiently present.

Leading with Questions

The executive coach can lead the client with questions to identify the causes of performance shortfalls. Thomas Gilbert published a collection of questions used to assess the state of the six cells in his Behavior Engineering Model. He called these questions

FIGURE 3.5. UPDATED BEHAVIOR ENGINEERING MODEL.

	Information	**Resources**	**Incentives**
Individual	1. Roles and performance expectations are clearly defined; employees are given relevant and frequent feedback about the adequacy of performance. 2. Clear and relevant guides are used to describe the work process. 3. The performance management system guides employee performance and development.	1. Materials, tools, and time needed to do the job are present. 2. Processes and procedures are clearly defined and enhance individual performance if followed. 3. Overall physical and psychological work environment contributes to improved performance; work conditions are safe, clean, organized, and conducive to performance.	1. Financial and non-financial incentives are present; measurement and reward systems reinforce positive performance. 2. Jobs are enriched to allow for fulfillment of employee needs. 3. Overall work environment is positive, where employees believe they have an opportunity to succeed; career development opportunities are present.
	Knowledge/Skills	**Capacity**	**Motives**
Environment	1. Employees have the necessary knowledge, experience, and skills to do the desired behaviors. 2. Employees with the necessary knowledge, experience, and skills are properly placed to use and share what they know. 3. Employees are cross-trained to understand one another's roles.	1. Employees have the capacity to learn and do what is needed to perform successfully. 2. Employees are recruited and selected to match the realities of the work situation. 3. Employees are free of emotional limitations that would interfere with their performance.	1. Motives of employees are aligned with the work and the work environment. 2. Employees desire to perform the required jobs. 3. Employees are recruited and selected to match the realities of the work situation.

The PROBE Model, a contraction of "PROfiling BEhavior."[3] The PROBE model consisted of forty-two questions to be used to assess the accomplishment of any job in any work situation.

Following Gilbert's lead, updated PROBE questions were developed to support the Updated Behavior Engineering Model. In addition to the direct questions that reflect the original PROBE questions, open-ended questions have been added to start the discussion with the client. It is important to start the discussion with an open-ended question so as to keep the client from getting defensive from a series of direct questions.

Updated PROBE Questions

A. Information

Open-ended, exploratory question: How are performance expectations communicated to employees?

Direct, follow-up questions:

Have clear performance expectations been communicated to employees?

Do employees understand the various aspects of their roles and the priorities for doing them?

Are there clear and relevant performance aids to guide the employees?

Are employees given sufficient, timely, behaviorally specific feedback regarding their performance?

Does the performance management system assist the supervisor in describing expectations for both activities and results for the employee?

B. Resources

Open-ended, exploratory question: What do your employees need in order to perform successfully?

Direct, follow-up questions:

Do employees have the materials needed to do their jobs?

Do employees have the equipment to do their jobs?

Do employees have the time they need to do their jobs?

Are the processes and procedures defined in such a way as to enhance employee performance?

Is the work environment safe, clean, organized, and conducive to excellent performance?

C. Incentives

Open-ended, exploratory question: How are employees rewarded for successful performance?

Direct, follow-up questions:

1. Are there sufficient financial incentives present to encourage excellent performance?

2. Are there sufficient non-financial incentives present to encourage excellent performance?

3. Do measurement and reporting systems track appropriate activities and results?

4. Are jobs enriched to allow for fulfillment of higher level needs?

5. Are there opportunities for career development?

D. Motives

Open-ended, exploratory question: How do your employees respond to the performance incentives you have in place?

Direct, follow-up questions:

1. Are the motives of the employees aligned with the incentives in the environment?

2. Do employees desire to do the job to the best of their abilities?

3. Are employees recruited and selected to match the realities of the work environment?

4. Do employees view the work environment as positive?

5. Are there any rewards that reinforce poor performance or negative consequences for good performance?

E. Capacity

Open-ended, exploratory question: How are employees selected for their jobs?

Direct, follow-up questions:

1. Do the employees have the necessary strength to do the job?

2. Do the employees have the necessary dexterity to do the job?

3. Do employees have the ability to learn what is expected for them to be successful on the job?

4. Are employees free from any emotional limitations that impede performance?

5. Are employees recruited, selected, and matched to the realities of the work situation?

F. Knowledge and Skills

Open-ended, exploratory question: How do employees learn what they need to be successful on the job?

Direct, follow-up questions:

1. Do the employees have the necessary knowledge to be successful at their jobs?
2. Do the employees have the needed skills to be successful at their jobs?
3. Do the employees have the needed experience to be successful at their jobs?
4. Do employees have a systematic training program to enhance their knowledge and skills?
5. Do employees understand how their roles impact organizational performance?

Summary

Situational Leadership is a powerful tool for guiding executive coaches in interacting with their clients. The Executive Coaching Guide was derived from the Situational Leadership Model and adds more structure to the leadership process. Since the key interaction between executive coaches and their clients is to identify performance shortfalls and their causes, the Updated Behavior Engineering Model provides the basis for identifying causes by using the Updated PROBE Questions. This group of performance aids provides the needed structure for the executive coaching process.

Notes

1. Gilbert, T. F. (1978). *Human competence: Engineering worthy performance.* New York: McGraw-Hill.
2. Chevalier, R. D. (2003). Updating the behavior engineering model. *Performance Improvement, 42*(5), 8–14.
3. Dean, P. J. (Ed.). (1999). *Performance engineering at work* (2nd ed.). Silver Spring, MD: International Society for Performance Improvement.

◆ ◆ ◆

Paul Hersey is chairman of the Center for Leadership Studies, Inc., providers of leadership, coaching, sales, and customer service training. He is one of the creators of Situational Leadership®, the performance tool of over 10,000,000 managers worldwide and has personally presented Situational Leadership in 117 countries, influencing the leadership skills of 4,000,000 managers in over 1,000 organizations worldwide. He is the co-author of the most successful organizational behavior textbook of all time,

Management of Organizational Behavior, now in its seventh edition, with over 1,000,000 copies in print. Contact: www.situational.com; ron.campbell@situational.com.

Roger Chevalier is Director of Information and Certification for the International Society for Performance Improvement (ISPI). He is responsible for encouraging the use of performance technology with ISPI's 10,000 worldwide members by developing materials for and instructing in ISPI's Institute programs, delivering presentations at professional conferences, establishing partnerships with other organizations, publishing articles, working with authors to publish their books, and evaluating performance improvement professionals applying for the Certified Performance Technologist (CPT) designation.

Previous roles have given him experience in both the private and public sectors. Following a sixteen-year relationship as a trainer and management consultant, he was selected as vice president of Century 21 Real Estate Corporation's Performance Division. He is a former U.S. Coast Guard commander and was recognized by the National Society for Performance and Instruction (NSPI) as Military Trainer of the Year.

As an independent performance consultant, Chevalier specialized in integrating training into more comprehensive performance improvement solutions. His past clients include a wide range of businesses, government agencies, and non-profits. He has personally trained over 25,000 managers, supervisors, and sales people in leadership, coaching, performance improvement, change management, and sales programs.

Chevalier is author of more than thirty articles on leadership, coaching, management of change, and performance improvement published professional and trade journals. Contact: rogerc@ispi.org or rdc@sonic.net. Visit www.ispi.org for more information on the International Society for Performance Improvement.

CHAPTER FOUR

COACHING FOR BEHAVIORAL CHANGE

Marshall Goldsmith

My mission is to help successful leaders achieve positive, long-term, measurable change in behavior. The following process is being used by coaches around the world for this same purpose. When the steps in the process are followed, leaders almost always achieve positive, measurable results in changed behavior—not as judged by themselves, but as judged by pre-selected, key co-workers. This process has been used with great success by both external coaches and internal coaches.[1]

Our "Pay for Results" Behavioral Coaching Approach

Our coaching network (Marshall Goldsmith Partners in collaboration with Hewitt Associates) provides coaches for leaders around the world. All of the behavioral coaches who work with us use the same general approach. We first get an agreement with our coaching clients and their managers on two key variables: (1) what are the key behaviors that will make the biggest positive change in increased leadership effectiveness? and (2) who are the key stakeholders who can determine (six to eighteen months later) whether this change has occurred?

We then get paid only after our coaching clients have achieved a positive change in key leadership behaviors, as determined by key stakeholders.

I believe that many behavioral coaches are paid for the wrong reasons. Their income is a largely a function of "How much do my clients *like me*?" and "How much *time* did I spend in coaching?" Neither of these is a good metric for achieving a positive, long-term change in behavior. In terms of liking the coach, I have never seen a study that showed that clients' love of a coach was highly correlated with their change in behavior. In terms of spending clients' time, my clients are all executives whose decisions often impact billions of dollars, and their time is more valuable than mine. I try to spend *as little of their time as necessary* to achieve the desired results. The last thing they need is for me to waste their time!

Qualifying the Coaching Client

Knowing When Behavioral Coaching Won't Help

Since we use a "pay only for results" process in behavioral coaching, we have had to learn to *qualify* our coaching clients. This means that we only work with clients we believe will benefit from our coaching process.

Have you ever tried to change the behavior of a successful adult who had no interest in changing? How much luck did you have? Probably none! We only work with executives who are willing to make a sincere effort to change and who believe that this change will help them become better leaders. We refuse to work with leaders who do not demonstrate this sincere commitment to personal development.

Some large corporations "write people off." Rather than just fire them, they engage in a pseudo-behavioral coaching process that is more "seek and destroy" than "help people get better." We only work with leaders who are seen as potentially having a great future in the corporation. We only work with people who will be given a fair chance by their management. We refuse to work with leaders who have been "written off."

There are several different types of coaching. We only do behavioral coaching for successful executives—not strategic coaching, life planning, or organizational change. I have the highest respect for the coaches who do this kind of work. That is just not what our network does. Therefore, we *only* focus on changing leadership behavior. If our clients have other needs, we refer them to other coaches.

Finally, I would never choose to work with a client who has an integrity violation. We believe that people with integrity violations should be *fired*, not coached.

When will our approach to behavioral coaching work? If the issue is behavioral, the coaching client is given a fair chance, and he or she is motivated to improve, the process described in this article will almost always work. If these conditions do not exist, this process should not be used.

Involving Key Stakeholders

In my work as a behavioral coach, I have gone through three distinct phases.

In phase one, I believed that my clients would become better because of *me*. I thought that the coach was the key variable in behavioral change. I was wrong. We have recently completed research with over 86,000 respondents on changing leadership behavior.[2] We have learned that the key variable for successful change is *not* the coach, teacher, or advisor. The key variables that will determine long-term progress are the people being coached and their co-workers.

In phase two, I spent most of my time focusing on my coaching clients. I slowly learned that a motivated, hard-working client was more important than a brilliant coach! I learned that the client's ongoing efforts meant more than my clever ideas. My results improved!

In phase three (where I am now), I spend most of my time, not with my coaching clients, but with the key stakeholders around my clients. By my doing this, my clients' results have dramatically improved.[3]

How do I involve key stakeholders? I ask *them* to help the person I am coaching in four critically important ways:

- *Let go of the past.* When we continually bring up the past, we demoralize people who are trying to change. Whatever happened in the past happened. It cannot be changed. By focusing on a future that can get better (as opposed to a past that cannot), the key stakeholders can help my clients improve. (We call this process *feedforward,* instead of feedback.)[4]
- *Be helpful and supportive, not cynical, sarcastic, or judgmental.* As part of our coaching process, my clients involve key co-workers and ask them for help. If my clients reach out to key stakeholders and feel punished for trying to improve, they will generally quit trying. I don't blame them! Why should any of us work hard to build relationships with people who won't give us a chance? If my clients' co-workers are helpful and supportive, they experience increased motivation and are much more likely to improve.
- *Tell the truth.* I do not want to work with a client, have him or her get a glowing report from key stakeholders, and later hear that one of the stakeholders said, "He didn't *really* get better; we just said that." This is not fair to my client, to the company, or to me.
- *Pick something to improve yourself.* My clients are very open with key stakeholders about what they are going to change. As part of our process, our clients ask for ongoing suggestions. I also ask the stakeholders to pick something to improve and to ask my client for suggestions. This makes the entire process "two-way" instead of "one-way." It helps the stakeholders act as "fellow travelers" who are trying to improve,

not "judges" who are pointing their fingers at my client. It also greatly expands the value gained by the corporation in the entire process.[5]

Steps in the Behavioral Coaching Process

The following steps outline our behavioral coaching process. Every coach in our network has to agree to implement the following steps. If the coach follows these basic steps, our clients almost always get better!

1. *Involve the leaders being coached in determining the desired behavior in their leadership roles.* Leaders cannot be expected to change behavior if they don't have a clear understanding of what desired behavior looks like. The people we coach (in agreement with their managers) work with us to determine desired leadership behavior.

2. *Involve the leaders being coached in determining key stakeholders.* Not only do clients need to be clear on desired behaviors, they need to be clear (again, in agreement with their managers) on key stakeholders. There are two major reasons why people deny the validity of feedback: wrong items or wrong raters. By having our clients and their managers agree on the desired behaviors and key stakeholders in advance, we help ensure their "buy in" to the process.

3. *Collect feedback.* In my coaching practice, I personally interview all key stakeholders. The people I am coaching are all potential CEOs, and the company is making a real investment in their development. However, at lower levels in the organization (that are more price-sensitive), traditional 360-degree feedback can work very well. In either case, feedback is critical. It is impossible to get evaluated on changed behavior if there is not agreement on what behavior to change!

4. *Reach agreement on key behaviors for change.* As I have become more experienced, my approach has become simpler and more focused. I generally recommend picking only one to two key areas for behavioral change with each client. This helps ensure maximum attention to the most important behavior. My clients and their managers (unless my client is the CEO) agree on the desired behavior for change. This ensures that I won't spend a year working with my clients and have their managers determine that we have worked on the wrong thing!

5. *Have the coaching clients respond to key stakeholders.* The person being reviewed should talk with each key stakeholder and collect additional "feed*forward*" suggestions on how to improve the key areas targeted for improvement. In responding, the person being coached should keep the conversation positive, simple, and focused. When mistakes have been made in the past, it is generally a good idea to apologize and ask for help in changing the future. I suggest that my clients *listen* to stakeholder suggestions and not *judge* the suggestions.

6. *Review what has been learned with clients and help them develop action plans.* As was stated earlier, my clients have to agree to the basic steps in our process. On the other hand, outside of the basic steps, all of the other ideas that I share with my clients are *suggestions*. I just ask them to listen to my ideas in the same way they are listening to the ideas from their key stakeholders. I then ask them to come back with plans of what *they* want to do. These plans need to come from them, not from me. After reviewing their plans, I almost always encourage them to live up to their own commitments. I am much more of a facilitator than a judge. I usually just help my clients do what they know is the right thing to do.

7. *Develop an ongoing follow-up process.* Ongoing follow-up should be very efficient and focused. Questions such as, "Based on my behavior last month, what ideas do you have for me next month?" can keep a focus on the future. Within six months, conduct a two- to six-item mini-survey with key stakeholders. They should be asked whether the person has become more or less effective in the areas targeted for improvement.

8. *Review results and start again.* If the person being coached has taken the process seriously, stakeholders almost invariably report improvement. Build on that success by repeating the process for the next twelve to eighteen months. This type of follow-up will assure continued progress on initial goals and uncover additional areas for improvement. Stakeholders will appreciate the follow-up. No one minds filling out a focused, two-to-six-item questionnaire if they see positive results. The person being coached will benefit from ongoing, targeted steps to improve performance.

The Value of Behavioral Coaching for Executives

While behavioral coaching is only one branch in the coaching field, it is the most widely used type of coaching. Most requests for coaching involve behavioral change. While this process can be very meaningful and valuable for top executives, it can be even more useful for high-potential future leaders. These are the people who have great careers in front of them. Increasing effectiveness in leading people can have an even greater impact if it is a twenty-year process, instead of a one-year program.

People often ask, "Can executives *really* change their behavior?" The answer is definitely yes. If they didn't change, we would never be paid (and we almost always get paid). At the top of major organizations even a small positive change in behavior can have a big impact. From an organizational perspective, the fact that the executive is trying to change anything (and is being a role model for personal development) may be even more important than what the executive is trying to change. One key message that I have given every CEO I coach is: "To help others develop, start with yourself!"

Notes

1. For a study on the effectiveness of this process with internal coaches in GE Financial Services, see "Leveraging HR: How to Develop Leaders in 'Real Time,'" in *Human Resources in the 21st Century*, M. Effron, R. Gandossy, & M. Goldsmith (Eds.). New York: John Wiley & Sons, 2003.
2. "Leadership Is a Contact Sport," H. Morgan & M. Goldsmith, in *strategy+business*, Fall 2004.
3. This process is explained in more detail in "Recruiting Supportive Coaches: A Key to Achieving Positive Behavioral Change" in *The Many Facets of Leadership*, M. Goldsmith, V. Govindarajan, B. Kaye, & A. Vicere (Eds.). Upper Saddle River, NJ: Prentice Hall, 2003.
4. "Try Feed*forward*, Instead of Feedback" originally published in *Leader to Leader*, Summer 2002.
5. For a great description of the impact of co-workers' focusing on their own improvement, read "Expanding the Value of Coaching: from the Leader to the Team to the Organization" in *The Art and Practice of Leadership Coaching*, H. Morgan, P. Harkins, & M. Goldsmith (Eds.). New York: John Wiley & Sons, 2004.

◆ ◆ ◆

Marshall Goldsmith has recently been named by the American Management Association as one of fifty great thinkers and leaders who have impacted the field of management over the past eighty years. He has been described in *The Wall Street Journal* as one of the top ten executive educators; the *Economist* as one of the most credible thought leaders in the new era of business; *Forbes* as one of five most-respected executive coaches; and *Fast Company* as America's preeminent executive coach.

Dr. Goldsmith has a Ph.D. from UCLA and is an adjunct professor at Dartmouth's Tuck School of Management. He has been asked to teach in executive education programs at Michigan, MIT, and the Wharton School. He is one of a select few consultants who have been asked to work with over seventy major CEOs and their management teams.

Dr. Goldsmith is co-editor or author of eighteen books, including *The Leader of the Future* (a *Business Week* best seller), *Global Leadership: The Next Generation*, and *The Art and Practice of Leadership Coaching*. Contact: www.marshallgoldsmith.com/; marshall@marshallgoldsmith.com.

PART TWO

BUILDING BLOCKS

CHAPTER FIVE

TRY FEED*FORWARD* INSTEAD OF FEEDBACK

Marshall Goldsmith

Providing feedback has long been considered to be an essential skill for leaders. As they strive to achieve the goals of the organization, employees need to know how they are doing. They need to know whether their performance is in line with what their leaders expect. They need to learn what they have done well and what they need to change. Traditionally, this information has been communicated in the form of "downward feedback" from leaders to their employees. Just as employees need feedback from leaders, leaders can benefit from feedback from their employees. Employees can provide useful input on the effectiveness of procedures and processes and as well as input to managers on their leadership effectiveness. This "upward feedback" has become increasingly common with the advent of 360-degree multi-rater assessments.

But there is a fundamental problem with all types of feedback: it focuses on a *past*, on what has already occurred—not on the infinite variety of opportunities that can happen in the future. As such, feedback can be limited and static, as opposed to expansive and dynamic.

Over the past several years, I have observed more than ten thousand leaders as they participated in a fascinating experiential exercise. In the exercise, participants are each asked to play two roles. In one role, they are asked provide feed*forward*—that is, to give someone else suggestions for the future and *help as much as they can*. In the second role, they are asked to accept feed*forward*—that is, to listen to the suggestions for the future and *learn as much as they can*. The exercise typically lasts for ten to fifteen minutes, and the average participant has six to seven dialogue sessions. During the exercise participants are asked to:

- Pick one behavior that they would like to change. Change in this behavior should make a significant, positive difference in their lives.
- Describe this behavior to randomly selected fellow participants. This is done in one-on-one dialogues. It can be done quite simply, such as, "I want to be a better listener."
- Ask for feedforward—for two suggestions for the future that might help them achieve a positive change in their selected behavior. If participants have worked together in the past, they are not allowed to give ANY feedback about the past. They are only allowed to give ideas for the future.
- Listen attentively to the suggestions and take notes. Participants are not allowed to comment on the suggestions in any way. They are not allowed to critique the suggestions or even to make positive judgmental statements, such as, "That's a good idea."
- Thank the other participants for their suggestions.
- Ask the other persons what they would like to change.
- Provide feedforward—two suggestions aimed at helping them change.
- Say, "You are welcome" when thanked for the suggestions. The entire process of both giving and receiving feedforward usually takes about two minutes.
- Find another participant and keep repeating the process until the exercise is stopped.

When the exercise is finished, I ask participants to provide one word that best describes their reaction to this experience. I ask them to complete the sentence, "This exercise was. . . ." The words provided are almost always extremely positive, such as "great," "energizing," "useful," or "helpful." The most common word mentioned is "fun!"

What is the last word that most of us think about when we receive feedback, coaching, and developmental ideas? Fun!

Ten Reasons to Try Feedforward

Participants are then asked why this exercise is seen as fun and helpful as opposed to painful, embarrassing, or uncomfortable. Their answers provide a great explanation of why feedforward can often be more useful than feedback.

1. *We can change the future. We can't change the past.* Feedforward helps people envision and focus on a positive future, not a failed past. Athletes are often trained using

feedforward. Racecar drivers are taught to "Look at the road, not the wall." Basketball players are taught to envision the ball going in the hoop and to imagine the perfect shot. By giving people ideas on how they can be even more successful, we can increase their chances of achieving this success in the future.

2. *It can be more productive to help people be "right" than prove they were "wrong."* Negative feedback often becomes an exercise in "let me prove you were wrong." This tends to produce defensiveness on the part of the receiver and discomfort on the part of the sender. Even constructively delivered feedback is often seen as negative, as it necessarily involves a discussion of mistakes, shortfalls, and problems. Feedforward, on the other hand, is almost always seen as positive because it focuses on solutions.

3. *Feedforward is especially suited to successful people.* Successful people like getting ideas that are aimed at helping them achieve their goals. They tend to resist negative judgment. We all tend to accept feedback that is consistent with the way we see ourselves. We also tend to reject or deny feedback that is inconsistent with the way we see ourselves. Successful people tend to have very positive self-images. I have observed many successful executives respond to (and even enjoy) feedforward. I am not sure that these same people would have had such a positive reaction to feedback.

4. *Feedforward can come from anyone who knows about the task. It does not require personal experience with the individual.* One very common positive reaction to the previously described exercise is that participants are amazed by how much they can learn from people they don't know! For example, if you want to be a better listener, almost any fellow leader can give you ideas on how you can improve. They don't have to know you. Feedback requires knowing about the person. Feedforward just requires having good ideas for achieving the task.

5. *People do not take feedforward as personally as feedback.* In theory, constructive feedback is supposed to "focus on the performance, not the person." In practice, almost all feedback is taken personally (no matter how it is delivered). Successful people's sense of identity is highly connected with their work. The more successful people are, the more this tends to be true. It is hard to give a dedicated professional feedback that is not taken personally. Feedforward cannot involve a personal critique, since it is discussing something that has not yet happened!

6. *Feedback can reinforce personal stereotyping and negative self-fulfilling prophecies.* Feedforward can reinforce the possibility of change. Feedback can reinforce the feeling of failure. How many of us have been "helped" by a spouse, significant other, or friend who seems to have a near-photographic memory of our previous "sins" that they share with us in order to point out the history of our shortcomings. Negative feedback can be used to reinforce the message, "This is just the way you are." Feedforward is based on the assumption that people can make positive changes in the future.

7. *Face it! Most of us hate receiving negative feedback, and we don't like to give it.* I have reviewed summary 360-degree feedback reports for over fifty companies. The items "provides developmental feedback in a timely manner" and "encourages and accepts constructive criticism" almost always score near the bottom on co-worker satisfaction with leaders. Traditional training does not seem to make a great deal of difference. If leaders got better at providing feedback every time the performance appraisal forms were "improved," most should be perfect by now! Leaders are not very good at giving or receiving negative feedback. It is unlikely that this will change in the near future.

8. *Feedforward can cover almost all of the same "material" as feedback.* Imagine that you have just made a terrible presentation in front of the executive committee. Your manager is in the room. Rather than make you "relive" this humiliating experience, your manager might help you prepare for future presentations by giving you suggestions for the future. These suggestions can be very specific and still delivered in a positive way. In this way your manager can cover the same points without feeling embarrassed and without making you feel even more humiliated.

9. *Feedforward tends to be much faster and more efficient than feedback.* An excellent technique for giving ideas to successful people is to say, "Here are four ideas for the future. Please accept these in the positive spirit that they are given. If you can only use two of the ideas, you are still two ahead. Just ignore what doesn't make sense for you." With this approach almost no time is wasted on judging the quality of the ideas or proving that the ideas are "wrong." This "debate" time is usually negative; it can take up a lot of time, and it is often not very productive. By eliminating judgment of the ideas, the process becomes much more positive for the sender, as well as the receiver. Successful people tend to have a high need for self-determination and will tend to accept ideas that they "buy" while rejecting ideas that feel "forced" upon them.

10. *Feedforward can be a useful tool to apply with managers, peers, and team members.* Rightly or wrongly, feedback is associated with judgment. This can lead to very negative unintended consequences when applied to managers or peers. Feedforward does not imply superiority of judgment. It is more focused on being a helpful "fellow traveler" than an "expert." As such, it can be easier to hear from a person who is not in a position of power or authority. An excellent team-building exercise is to have each team member ask, "How can I better help our team in the future?" and listen to feedforward from fellow team members (in one-on-one dialogues).

Summary

In summary, the intent of this article is not to imply that leaders should never give feedback or that performance appraisals should be abandoned. The intent is to show how feedforward can often be preferable to feedback in day-to-day interactions. Aside from its effectiveness and efficiency, feedforward can make life a lot more enjoyable. When managers are asked, "How did you feel the last time you received feedback?" their most common responses are very negative. When managers are asked how they felt after receiving feedforward, they reply that feedforward is not only useful, it is fun!

Quality communication—between and among people at all levels and every department and division—is the glue that holds organizations together. By using feedforward—and by encouraging others to use it—leaders can dramatically improve the quality of communication in their organizations, ensuring that the right message is conveyed and that those who receive it are receptive to its content. The result is a much more dynamic, much more open organization—one whose employees focus on the promise of the future rather than dwelling on the mistakes of the past.

◆ ◆ ◆

Marshall Goldsmith has recently been named by the American Management Association as one of fifty great thinkers and leaders who have impacted the field of management over the past eighty years. He has been described in *The Wall Street Journal* as one of the top ten executive educators; the *Economist* as one of the most credible thought leaders in the new era of business; *Forbes* as one of five most-respected executive coaches; and *Fast Company* as America's preeminent executive coach.

Dr. Goldsmith has a Ph.D. from UCLA and is an adjunct professor at Dartmouth's Tuck School of Management. He has been asked to teach in executive education programs at Michigan, MIT, and the Wharton School. He is one of a select few consultants who have been asked to work with over seventy major CEOs and their management teams.

Dr. Goldsmith is co-editor or author of eighteen books, including *The Leader of the Future* (a *Business Week* best seller), *Global Leadership: The Next Generation,* and *The Art and Practice of Leadership Coaching.* Contact: www.marshallgoldsmith.com/; marshall@marshallgoldsmith.com.

CHAPTER SIX

MAKING COACHING WORK

Ten Easy Steps

Marc Effron

This year in executive coaching is shaping up to be a lot like last year. Companies will waste millions of dollars on poorly planned, questionably effective, and largely unaccountable coaching processes. High-potential leaders will lose the opportunity to change a few critical behaviors and accelerate their careers. Line executives will roll their eyes at another costly and highly touted human resource initiative that achieves nothing. Human resource leaders will wonder how a process with such promise could go so awry. Yes, it's going to be another stellar year for executive coaching.

All sarcasm aside, the description above likely rings true to many leadership development and human resource professionals. As someone who has managed coaching processes within major corporations and who now coaches senior executives worldwide, I've seen significant amounts of time, money, and political capital consumed in pursuit of coaching nirvana. The increased focus on coaching as a leadership development tool has caused many firms to build their own coaching programs, often without the rigorous thought processes and clear action plans that could help ensure success.

There is a better way. By answering some fundamental questions before you start, you will be able to design, manage, and attain significant results from the coaching process in your organization. Answering these questions will ensure that you've thought through the factors that drive the program's success and the objections your senior executives may raise. The ten questions in this article address the areas where I most frequently see coaching programs derail. If you can answer all ten, you're likely to realize the benefits of a well-designed process. Anything less than eight is a red flag that more thought is needed before moving forward.

Question 1: What Is the Company's Strategy?

The purpose of executive coaching (and all leadership practices) should be to align leaders' behaviors with what's required to realize the business strategy. Leaders who are able to demonstrate behaviors that are supportive of that strategy should, on average, deliver superior results. This means that the behaviors you expect from your leaders, which are those you coach them toward developing, should relate directly to the business strategy. You may feel you've already identified these behaviors through your leadership competency model. I'd challenge you to look again.

Most attempts at leadership competencies end up with a thoughtfully developed but all too generic list of behaviors that could just as easily support your competitor's strategy. Coaching leaders in these areas may increase some baseline leadership capabilities, but it won't create any competitive advantage. With my clients, I use a tool called the Strategic Leadership Matrix (SLM) to help them develop leadership competencies that support their specific business strategies and provide clear direction for coaching. (See Figure 6.1.) The SLM begins with the fundamental and well-validated concept that people perform best when their personal characteristics "fit" with their environment.[1] The question is, what causes leaders to fit or not fit?

Through my research and consulting, I have found that two factors account for most of that fit: the business strategy and the degree of change in the environment. In other words, the more closely aligned your leaders' personal characteristics and capabilities are with the business strategy and the amount of change in your business, the more successful they are likely to be. The SLM allows you to analyze how closely a leader "fits" with your business.

On the SLM, the two factors are placed into a two-by-two matrix.

The Strategy factor can be expressed as ranging from an aggressive Growth Strategy (a company focused on revenue growth through marketing, sales, innovation, new product development. Think Amazon.com) to a Return Strategy (a company seeking to extract bottom-line earnings by being the lowest cost provider of goods or services, focused on removing costs from the business and finding synergies. Think Wal-Mart). Most strategies fit at some point along that strategy continuum, and most leaders, due to their past experiences and their core personalities, will be most successful at a select part of that continuum as well. In other words, they will "fit" with some strategies and not fit with others.

FIGURE 6.1. THE STRATEGIC LEADERSHIP MATRIX.

Transformational Change

Transformational Change means that fundamental changes are occuring in the
industry or company (a major technology shift, large acquisition, financial crisis).
Transformational Change situations require great leadership.

Return Strategy
A company pursuing a *Return Strategy* has a dominant focus on cost reduction, process improvement, efficiencies—items leading to earnings growth. It will compete on the basis of its ability to be more efficient than its rivals.

Growth Strategy
A company pursuing a *Growth Strategy* has a dominant focus on sales, marketing, product development—items leading to revenue growth. At the extreme, growing the top line is more important than growing the bottom line.

Leaders will need: Vision, decision making, financial acumen, managing change, risk management, cost control	**Leaders will need:** Vision, speed, aggressiveness, risk taking, managing change, driving sales, innovation
Leaders will need: Risk management, process management, financial acumen, cost control, rule orientation, task focus	**Leaders will need:** Speed, aggressiveness, process management, risk taking, planning, task focus

Transactional Change

Transactional Change is the underlying amount of change experienced in all
businesses. Incremental changes requires sound general management, but not
great leadership.

Copyright © Marc Effron, 2005.

The SLM also incorporates and applies the Change factor, which acknowledges that some companies are going through Transformational Change (large mergers, industry consolidations, huge growth challenges), while others are simply experiencing the typical ups and downs of any business, which dictate more gradual Transactional Change. Some leaders are transformational leaders capable of leading through the upheaval in that environment and they will "fit" best at the top of the scale. Others are better at managing day-to-day challenges and will be most successful at the Transactional (or incremental) Change end of the scale.

Identifying the types of leaders you need is as simple as mapping on this graph where your business is today and where it will be in three or four years. The implications for the types of leadership capabilities you will need in the future are spelled out in the SLM. What does this have to do with coaching? Your challenge is to build the leadership characteristics that will help you achieve your business strategy. Coaching is a key component in making that happen.

Question 2: Does Your Senior Team Support Coaching?

Your CEO and senior team need to see coaching as a legitimate way to accelerate the performance of high-potential leaders. Their support will help secure enough funding for coaching and, more importantly, will ensure that they support the efforts of those being coached. When I find senior executives who don't support coaching, it's usually because they fail to see the return on investment. They may have seen prior coaching programs not deliver the changes expected or they may simply be looking for a solid metric to prove coaching's effectiveness.

To convince them, your best approach is to create a coaching business plan (you can use these ten questions as a template) and present it to them with a comprehensible way to measure performance. In this plan, be clear about who will be coached and why and how you will be able to measure their success (how we will know whether someone has changed). If you haven't used coaching in your organization before, suggest starting with one high-potential individual to test the process. Ideally that individual would be a member of senior management who would become an advocate of the process through his or her experience. If, despite your best efforts, your senior team doesn't support using coaching to accelerate performance, you need to decide whether it's worth the risk to move ahead anyway or if it's better to develop leaders in another way.

Question 3: Who Will Participate and Who Will Decide?

While every leader can benefit from coaching, most companies have a limited budget for the process. The decision of who receives those few dollars is a critical one. Many of my clients reserve coaching for high-potential employees, those who have been specifically identified as the top 10 percent of all leaders through their performance management or succession planning process. Using only high-potentials helps ensure that there is a consistent criteria for selection, rather than individual managers nominating their favorite direct reports to participate. If you don't specifically identify a high-potential group in one of these processes, you should identify a few criteria that you can use to screen potential participants. A few suggestions would include:

- Those at a director level or above. (More junior employees can probably benefit from less personalized development activities.)
- Those with meaningful potential to advance. (Does this person have the potential to move up two levels in the organization, or one level if he or she is a VP or above?)
- Those who want to change. (It's interesting how many people are assigned coaches without ever being asked whether they want to change. If they are not genuinely interested in changing their behaviors, why would you invest in their development?)

Question 4: What Coaching Methodology Will You Use?

This question is rarely considered when starting a coaching process, because many human resource professionals aren't aware of their choices. But this is a key question since there are two fundamental approaches to coaching, psychological and behavioral, and our experience (and some great research[2]) shows that one is meaningfully more effective than the other.

The psychological approach seeks to understand the "why's" of behavior, looking for personality type or personal experience issues that cause an individual to act in a specific way. While it doesn't qualify as therapy, it usually includes some use of psychological assessments, ranging from the relatively straightforward (FIRO-B, Myers-Briggs) to the more complex (16PF, California Psychological Inventory). These tools are used to help the coachee better understand why he or she behaves as the basis for helping him or her change. The psychological approach often places the coach at the center of the coaching relationship as the person who is primarily responsible for change.

The behavioral approach believes that how we behave is largely a consequence of our interactions with friends, family, and co-workers over time. The behaviors we engage in are the ones that have been either rewarded in these interactions or at least not significantly dissuaded. Some of these behaviors may be beneficial early in a leader's career, but become derailing behaviors as he or she advances (for example, personal attention to detail, which is great for project managers, not as great for CEOs).

Behavioral coaches investigate which behaviors should change by interviewing the people with whom the coachee frequently works. Behavioral coaches believe that new behaviors will develop through the same process as the leader's current behaviors. The leader will try a new behavior, receive reinforcement if it's done right, try it again, get reinforcement, ad infinitum until the new behavior replaces the old one.

Behavioral coaches don't deny that we are all born with certain natural attributes or that we might have had some tough experiences that shaped how we interact with others. They simply believe that you can only change your behavior by changing your behavior, not by trying to understand "why." As Marshall Goldsmith, well-known executive coach, says, "When you're over fifty, blaming Mom and Dad is weak."[3] Behavioral coaches put the coachee at the center of the relationship, since the coachee is the only one who can change his or her behaviors. The coach is seen as the process facilitator, not as the person responsible for changing behaviors.

While behavioral coaching may seem counterintuitive, the research cited earlier involving more than 80,000 people clearly shows that the behavioral approach (at least using the methodology created by Marshall Goldsmith and that I use with my clients), delivers measurable results. There is no similarly comprehensive research that proves psychological coaching actually changes behavior.

Question 5: Are You Interested in Feedback or Coaching?

A number of very well-respected, highly successful organizations provide services that you may think of as coaching. Some of these organizations provide week-long offsite sessions during which leaders engage in various exercises within a small team and take assessment tests, receiving feedback from their teammates and a counselor about their behaviors during these sessions. These sessions may include 360-degree feedback from their actual direct reports as well. Others offer traditional assessment centers with "in-box" exercises and other tools that are observed by a counselor and on which the leader is provided feedback at day's end. Some of these sessions are followed by formal coaching, but many are not. The primary value of these exercises is feedback. They provide the participants with a thorough understanding of their behaviors, albeit in an artificial setting. In many cases, the burden of applying these lessons is left to the participant.

Coaching involves gathering information about an individual's behaviors (I find that interviews are much more helpful than surveys) and setting specific, measurable, behavioral goals for change. Over six to eighteen months, a coach should work with the individual on a regular basis to help him or her identify opportunities to practice those new behaviors and receive feedback on whether change has occurred. The process should end with a final assessment (quantitative, as described in Question 6) of whether the change goals have been achieved.

Both feedback and coaching offer benefits, but be sure you understand exactly what results you're expecting before you launch the program.

Question 6: What Is Your Success Measure?

This one's easy. The only success measure for coaching is whether the coachee has positively changed his or her behavior. If there are clear goals for change, it's easy to measure whether someone has improved over time. The same individuals who provided the coach with input at the start of the process on the coachee's behavior should provide input at the end of the process. The "mini-survey" process developed by Marshall Goldsmith is taken on a quarterly basis. This process uses a +3 to −3 scale to both track improvement and also to provide assessors a chance to reflect on how the coachee's behaviors have changed. Without this periodic opportunity for them to consider this, they may not realize that the coachee is making progress.

Question 7: How Long Is the Coaching Process?

A coaching process must have both defined goals and a defined time period. The ideal time period allows enough time for behaviors both to change and to be reinforced. While change often comes rapidly when high-potential leaders are coached, it's too easy to slip back into the original behaviors if the new behaviors aren't reinforced over time. Twelve months is usually enough time to ensure both change and reinforcement. If any assignment stretches more than eighteen months, you should question why change hasn't occurred. In these cases, either the goal is too aggressive, the coach isn't facilitating the process properly, or the coachee isn't making the effort to change.

Question 8: Who Will Your Coaching Provider Be and Why?

Answering Questions 1 through 7 will help narrow down the choice of coaching providers, but a number of key questions remain. Think not only about the first assignment but the possible assignments that follow. What are your needs for the following?

- *Global reach:* If you might need coaches in more than one region of the world, do you want to be able to use the same firm? If so, does the firm have offices in the locations you need or will there be travel involved?
- *Performance guarantees:* Some coaches offer a "don't pay until change occurs" promise. Clients are billed at the end of a coaching assignment and only if the client measures positive change in the coachee's behaviors. What level of performance guarantee would you like the coach or coaching firm to provide? How will you know whether the firm is successful?
- *Dedicated coaches or networked:* Some coaching firms have full-time coaches who are employees of the company. Others use an independent network of coaches they use as needed. There are advantages and disadvantages to each arrangement. If you can only select from a small, dedicated network, you may not find the level of experience or specialty you'd like. If you use a network, it may be more challenging to receive consistent quality across multiple assignments.
- *Cost:* You need to feel comfortable that you are receiving value for your investment in coaching. Coaching providers are available from $5,000 to $175,000 per assignment, and, as with anything else, you get what you pay for. Your mid-level managers don't necessarily need a coach with the same experience that your CEO does, so it's OK to pay $20,000 at one level and $80,000 or more for a senior executive coach. Whether the coach offers a performance guarantee should factor into this decision as well, since guaranteed results should be worth more than "hoped for" results.

Question 9: How Personally Involved Will You Be in the Coaching Process?

While the details of the coaching conversations should be considered confidential, that doesn't mean that you should be removed from the process. You should require a summary of the assessment report at the start of the assignment and ask for at least quarterly updates from the coach. Updates should tell you whether the coachee is advancing toward his or her goals and any other facts that would be helpful to you.

Anything the coach finds that is unethical or illegal during this process should be mentioned to you immediately.

Question 10: How Will You Use the Findings from Coaching to Benefit the Organization?

Larger-scale coaching projects give you the opportunity to use the coaching feedback to improve the overall process of developing leaders. Look at the feedback to see whether key themes emerge across participants. Do the coachees have any negative behaviors in common? If so, how can you screen for those behaviors during recruiting or develop courses or other interventions that will address them before they become issues? Which behaviors do coachees find most difficult to change? It could be that cultural or other organizational issues are making it more difficult to change certain behaviors. How can you help everyone in the organization by addressing these shared issues?

While few practices can deliver the return on investment possible with coaching, the potential benefits can only be realized through a well-planned and well-executed process. Human resource and leadership development leaders need to consider the choices available to them and which fit best with their organization and their goals. Answering these ten questions before your next foray into coaching will provide you with a markedly better chance at success.

Notes

1. Edwards, J.R. (1991). Person-job fit: A conceptual integration, literature review, and methodological critique. *International Review of Industrial and Organizational Psychology, 6,* pp. 283–357.
2. Goldsmith, M., & Morgan, H. Leadership is a contact sport: The "follow-up" factor in leadership development. *Strategy+Business,* September 2004.
3. Goldsmith, M. Conversation: Behave yourself. *Harvard Business Review,* October 2002.

Marc Effron is global practice leader for Hewitt Associates' Leadership Consulting Practice. He coaches senior executives at Global 500 companies, including the world's largest banks and multi-industry corporations. Effron uses the Goldsmith behavioral coaching methodology exclusively.

Effron co-authored *Leading the Way,* co-edited *Human Resources in the 21st Century,* and has written articles in *The Change Champions Field Guide, Leading Organizational Learning,* and *The Practice of Leadership Coaching* (2005). He is a frequent speaker to business groups and conferences throughout the world. He is widely quoted on leadership issues, including in recent articles in the *New York Times, Asian Wall Street Journal, Business Week, The Economist,* and *HR Executive.* Contact: marc@effrons.com.

CHAPTER SEVEN

LEADING ON PURPOSE

What Do You Care About?

Richard J. Leider

It's no revelation that many leaders today are overwhelmed with busyness. They are being challenged from every direction. So why do some leaders prosper whereas others do not?

We can speculate at length why some falter or fail due to *external* reasons—failure to execute or failure to innovate. Yet another essential difference between success and failure today can be traced to *internal* reasons—to how well leaders engage the hearts and souls of their followers. One sure test of leadership today is whether a leader has engaged followers. Engaged people are simply more productive.

What Does It Take to Engage People Today?

What does it take to engage people today? What does it take to inspire people to rally around a common purpose? First, it takes purpose-driven leadership. One big difference between the success and the failure of leaders can be traced to their purpose—how effectively they connect people to a larger mission. Purpose usually accompanies greatness in anything, and it is largely responsible for the engagement found in high-performing teams and organizations.

So a primary role of leaders today is to answer the question many of their followers are asking: "Why should I care?" Leaders must first look in the mirror and answer this question for themselves. They must be clear that leadership is earned from the inside out. Honest engagement comes through asking oneself (and answering) the tough purpose questions first.

During my thirty-plus years as an executive coach, I have been continually impressed with the courage that effective leaders have for holding up the mirror to look inside themselves. They understand that the soft aspects of leading are as important as the hard ones.

Leading on Purpose

Back in the good old days of predictable work values and patterns, a leader could say, "This engagement stuff's not for me. I'm going to keep on doing what's always worked." This choice no longer exists for most leaders, as they are caught in a struggle to engage talented workers. Leaders who have enjoyed years of predictable growth are now struggling to engage true talent. The old social contract is broken, forever. No leader today can promise employment or security in exchange for engagement.

Leaders today are going to have to be *discoverers*. The discoverers who created this nation had no maps, no guides. It was just their vision and courage. Some made it, but many did not. If the futurists are right, this means that for the foreseeable future we'll be continually discovering, too. We'll have to take on greater leadership risks without maps. We'll have to learn to engage talent *as we lead them into new territories toward greater purposes.*

Effective leaders today have a strong sense of their essence. They have true purpose; they know what they care about. Robert K. Greenleaf, in his book *Servant Leadership,*[1] urged leaders to go "beyond conscious rationality" and to go into the "uncharted and unknown" to lead from within. Our *purpose* is our mission or the reason we were born; it is the central quality or essence that comes out in our leadership and it is always larger than we are. It inspires us, of course, but it is also the quality that serves and leads others.

Greenleaf said, "Serving and leading are still mostly intuition-based concepts." He believed that self-insight is "the most dependable part of the true servant." By finding and fulfilling the purpose deep within us, we can meet Greenleaf's criteria for servant-leaders: "Those served grow as persons." To lead on purpose, we must be willing to look inside—to understand our underlying substance and to lead from it.

Why Should I Follow You?

Today's talent doesn't blindly follow. They are educated, street smart, globally wise, and aware of their options. Their engagement on the job is dependent on the trust they have in their leaders. They are hungry for purposeful leadership—leaders who care. They know their leaders do not have all the answers, so they want an essential conversation to help create their futures together.

Let's assume for a few minutes that you have been asked to interview your new leader. What would *you* want to know about him or her as a leader? Assume you know the basics of the person's résumé: work history, age, family, and so forth. What would you ask?

Purposeful leadership demands essential conversations. Conversation relies on trust. In his book *Principle-Centered Leadership,*[2] Stephen Covey notes that our heritage was governed by the "character ethic," which valued principles such as keeping promises, being honest, and exercising courage. Character is the "why" of "Why should I follow you?" Far too many leaders today have emphasized the "personality ethic" by focusing on projecting a certain image and using the right phrases. In doing so, they have mistakenly focused too much on the *form* and not enough on the *essence* of leadership. They have lost their character, and they have lost people's full engagement.

Character comes from the inside out. It can be summed up in the words of an Anglican bishop found inscribed on his tomb in Westminster Abbey:

"When I was young and free and my imagination had no limits, I dreamed of changing the world. As I grew older and wiser, I discovered the world would not change, so I shortened my sights somewhat and decided to change only my country. But, it too seemed immovable. As I grew into my twilight years, in one last desperate attempt, I settled for changing only family, those closest to me, but alas, they would have none of it. And now as I lie on my deathbed, I suddenly realize, if I had only changed myself first, then by example I would have changed my family. From their inspiration and encouragement I would then have been able to better my country and, who knows, I may have even changed the world."

Who You Are Comes Before What You Do

Form does not create trust. The response of others to one's form depends on the degree to which one's *essence* is also present.

Essence lies beneath the surface, at a leader's core. Essence is our underlying substance: our purpose, values, and courage. When we discover our essence and learn to lead with it, then leading becomes a courageous discovery process into purposeful futures.

A key to courageous leadership is to address the question of "who we are" *before* the question of "what we do." When we focus on the *who* question before the *what* question, we discover our purpose as leaders.

The Power of Purpose

An essential question for leaders to ask themselves today is: "What do I care about?" Care creates conditions of engagement. When we lead from what we care about, trust is built. When we integrate who we are with what we do, our followers sense and are inspired by the power of our purpose.

FIGURE 7.1. THE LEADERSHIP MIRROR.

When was the last time you stepped back and looked into the mirror? When was the last time you challenged your old answers and ways of doing things and looked for the underlying substance of your leadership?

Answer the following questions and score yourself on a scale from 1 to 7. A "1" implies a definite "no" to the question. A "2" or "3" implies an infrequent articulation or use, "4" implies sometimes, a "5" or "6" implies a frequent articulation or use, and "7" implies a definite "yes." Put your answers in the boxes provided.

1. Do I have clear values as a leader? ☐
2. Do my followers recognize my values through key actions that I demonstrate? ☐
3. Am I clear on my leadership strengths? ☐
4. Am I engaged in self-development efforts that focus on my strengths? ☐
5. Do I have a clear sense of my purpose as a leader? ☐
6. Do I leave my leadership legacy daily? ☐
7. Do I have a clear point of view about what it means to lead? ☐
8. Do those around me understand my point of view about leadership? ☐
9. Do I have a vision for what I'd like to accomplish as a leader? ☐
10. Do my followers know my vision because I communicate it to them? ☐
11. Do I take time for leadership reflection? ☐
12. Do I have a personal "board of directors" with whom to share reflections? ☐
13. Do I have written personal leadership goals? ☐
14. Do I take action on my leadership goals? ☐

The Power of Purpose Quiz above is a first step to help us discern what we care about. In filling out the questionnaire, it is important to dig below the surface and to look deeply into the mirror.

Talented people instinctively seek a work environment where they know that they will have a full voice in matters of consequence. They seek a workplace where they don't feel constricted, where they don't have to check themselves at the door. Such a work environment lets them breathe life into their gifts and passions. If they don't find an environment that feeds their hearts and souls, all they're left with are paychecks, and that's not enough for most people today.

We may think that leading on purpose is an unaffordable luxury in a tough business environment. But "caring" is a thriving skill. Talented performers care about their customers, colleagues, and the organization's thriving. They yearn to use their core strengths on things they truly care about. Put purpose-workers up against people who simply work for status and a paycheck, and who do you think will win?

FIGURE 7.2. SCORING AND INTERPRETATION.

QUESTIONS

	1		3		5		7		9		11		13	
7	•	•	•	•	•	•	•	•	•	•	•	•	•	•
6	•	•	•	•	•	•	•	•	•	•	•	•	•	•
S 5	•	•	•	•	•	•	•	•	•	•	•	•	•	•
C O 4	•	•	•	•	•	•	•	•	•	•	•	•	•	•
R E 3	•	•	•	•	•	•	•	•	•	•	•	•	•	•
2	•	•	•	•	•	•	•	•	•	•	•	•	•	•
1	•	•	•	•	•	•	•	•	•	•	•	•	•	•
		2		4		6		8		10		12		14

QUESTIONS

When leaders lead on purpose, they aren't motivated exclusively by external benefits like money or a job title. They are motivated from within—and stand a far better chance of being effective in their leading and successful in their careers.

Notes

1. Greenleaf, R. K. *Servant leadership: A journey into the nature of legitimate power and greatness.* New York: Paulist Press, 1977.
2. Covey, S. *Principle-centered leadership.* New York: Summit Books, 1990.

◆ ◆ ◆

Richard Leider is a pioneer in executive coaching. His specialization is helping executives discover the power of purpose. *Forbes* and other media have repeatedly cited him as one of the top coaches in the world. Founder and chairman of The Inventure Group, he is a best-selling author and speaker to thousands of people worldwide each year. His clients include many of the world's leading organizations. He is the author of seven books, including three best-sellers. His work has been translated into fifteen languages. *Repacking Your Bags, The Power of Purpose,* and *Whistle While You Work* are considered classics in the career development field. His newest book, *Claiming Your Place at the Fire,* has been touted as "the defining" book on the new retirement. Along with his professional pursuits, Leider leads yearly Inventure Expedition walking safaris in East Africa. Believing passionately that each of us is born with a purpose, he is dedicated to coaching executives and their teams to discover the power of purpose. Contact: www.inventuregroup.com.

CHAPTER EIGHT

COACHING FOR EFFECTIVE ACTION

A Core Leadership Process

Victoria A. Guthrie and John R. Alexander

As the demand for executive coaching increases, an accompanying proliferation of different philosophies, styles, and coaching specializations has occurred. Coaching now focuses on a range of client needs, such as transition and career issues, health and fitness, entrepreneurship, small business, family-owned business, financial coaching, and, of course, executive and corporate coaching. The challenge for professionals is to carefully match the appropriate philosophy or style to the specific needs of the individual being coached, to spend sufficient up-front time articulating the purpose and outcomes of the coaching process, and to align the organization's needs and expectations with the readiness of the coachee.

Over the past fifteen years, one approach at the Center for Creative Leadership (CCL) that we've found to be consistently effective is the coaching model that emphasizes personal development as a stimulant for taking effective action. This technique has allowed us to offer a sustained, focused coaching experience to a relatively large, diverse pool of managers and executives as part of an extended leadership development process.

This model is a specialized form of coaching that emphasizes learning, personal development, and effective action in a specific leadership situation. It was conceived in the late 1980s as a way to enhance and reinforce leadership development for executives and managers. The idea was to move beyond a one-time training event and create a process that would enhance an individual's ability to take effective actions in his or her real-life leadership situation—learning on the job as he or she interacted with employees and worked through challenges.

Role of Coaching for Effective Action

Jim had just accepted a new assignment within his company. He felt well-prepared for his new post because, as a supervisor for the preceding seven years, he had been "steeped in the authoritarian style of the organization." The entire group he worked with had spent their careers in this environment, so it felt easy for Jim to pick up the ball and run with it.

However, things changed as he moved into his new job, and he quickly got the message, "We do things differently here now." He spent the next three years working an average of seventy to ninety hours per week; he gave up nine of the twelve weeks of vacation he had earned. The workforce was very young; he saw them as inexperienced, but willing to try anything and work hard.

For Jim, the definition of success on the job had changed. His previously effective leadership style and processes were failing him, but he didn't know what to change or how to change. Jim wanted insight into how he might become more effective in his new environment.

We knew from our research and experience with executives like Jim that leadership development takes place over time and requires ongoing assessment, challenge, and support. Our clients, from corporate executives to entrepreneurs, told us they needed more real-time, real-world leadership development to enable them to manage the complexity and turbulence of today's work environments.

One client articulated the needs of many: "We want development experiences that go beyond awareness and move to action, that go beyond teaching heads to moving feet."

To meet this need, we designed multi-session programs, typically taking place over a six-month period, which addressed specific, individual leadership challenges. Within that framework, we believed the ongoing support of a coach would be vital during, between, and following the developmental experience. Thus, the Process Advisor (PA) framework was created, which, in turn, became the precursor to our current coaching model.

The term Process Advisor was carefully chosen as we began to define the coaching intent. Process, defined as a natural phenomenon marked by gradual changes that lead toward a particular result, was at the core of our development technique that emphasizes future action.

Just as important, we wanted the role to be a blend of advocate, partisan, and adherent. We found that "advisor" was the best word to combine the support, assistance, fidelity, loyalty, and help in keeping something going. Thus, the PA would be a key learning partner who would help individuals determine the best course of action in their current work situations. The linking of a process over time with learning and taking action served as the prototype of our contemporary coaching model and our current cadre of coaches.

Seven Key Competencies of the Coaching for Effective Action Relationship

Coaching, by any name, is complex; however, we identified seven key competencies that guide the coaching for effective action relationship. Both the effective action coach and the person being coached must:

1. Deal effectively with interpersonal relationships;
2. Think and behave in terms of systems;
3. Approach decision making from the standpoint of tradeoffs;
4. Think and act with flexibility;
5. Maintain emotional balance by coping with disequilibrium;
6. Clarify and maintain the sense of purpose; and
7. Be able to learn how to learn.

In this coaching model, successful coaches come from a variety of backgrounds, such as clinical psychology, organizational change, career development and counseling, and management or leadership development; but all have a thorough understanding of human development and adult learning processes, and all have the ability to surface and work through challenges and issues.

Typically, the coaching recipients are experiencing some form of personal or professional turbulence, such as downsizing, new management, culture or job change, or health, family, or psychological problems; and they are seeking ways to adapt or cope. In this context, the coaches are process experts who are able to aid coachees in taking the actions or making the personal changes necessary to be more effective leaders. As one coaching recipient explained, "The coach helped me visualize needed changes and showed me how to focus on the where and how of accomplishing my goal."

Although personal styles may vary, coaches for effective action are carefully trained to work within the focused objectives of the program and the coaching recipient's specific challenges. Yet, like any coach, they must remain flexible to deal with the dynamics that evolve as new information is introduced. An effective action coach provides the coaching recipient the discipline and support for the implementation of change but recognizes the impact of specific work and personal situations on the development process.

Successful and beneficial coaches for effective action also possess motivation to teach others, keen observation skills, the ability to understand the advisee, ways to sense personal issues underlying the situation, and a strong desire to help others grow and change.

As with any form of coaching, the most effective coaches view coaching for effective action as an integral part of their work, not as a sideline role. They work with two to three coachees from several programs for a six-month period. Their work is done through a set number of phone conversations, face-to-face meetings, and e-mail exchanges.

During this defined period of time, the coaches provide the opportunity for the coachees to develop their leadership skills and move from "management-by-objectives" thinking to process management thinking.

In the coaching sessions, the coach's major job is to focus the coaching recipient on effective action by asking two key questions:

1. "What does the situation call for from me as an individual, as a team or group leader, and as a contributing member of an organization?"
2. "What is the ideal or purpose I am striving for?"

By clarifying the situation, current needs, and larger goals, the coachee is able to focus on finding new solutions. The effective action coach helps the individual clarify strengths and potential blocks, provides perspective, gives feedback, and inquires and offers support. The coachee determines his or her action plans and developmental needs and evaluates his or her progress and learning.

For example, one coachee had just made a change from a secure job at a local college to a risk-taking entrepreneurial position. Her coach helped her learn that her creativity and global perspective often kept her from examining the small details that were critical to the success of her new business. As a result, she developed a process for addressing the specific needs of the business, even as she worked to expand her leadership and decision-making skills.

"My coach constantly pushed me to the edge of my comfort zone," she reported. "I was cognizant of a gain in confidence, listening skills, and open and honest feedback. I am learning to listen to suggestions for changes in my new entrepreneurial work with increased confidence and receptiveness."

Over time, we have found that, regardless of the specific work environment or challenges, the individual outcomes often include:

- *Greater Self-Empowerment.* Following the takeover of the company by new management, one executive reported that he "fell from grace and no longer felt like an exemplary leader." [The program and my coach] "helped me figure out a way to adapt my leadership style to changing situations. . . . It helped me get through the anger, the disappointment, and the doubts and empowered me once again to be myself."
- *An Expanded View of Leadership.* "Getting the job done is no longer enough," explained one manager. "I learned how and why to change my personal habits to become a more sensitive leader. Leadership has a new meaning to me now; I certainly see things through a different lens."

- *Greater Focus on Systems-Level Interventions.* Coaching recipients often gain a greater appreciation of forces affecting organizations and their own relevance to the organizations. Kay's organization was in a period of radical change, and she was perceived as being unable to implement the new strategy. With her effective action coach, she developed a plan to develop new skills and behaviors that helped her initiate the changes needed in her department.
- *Improved Understanding of Diverse People and Viewpoints.* Coaching recipients typically gain greater awareness of how differences add strength to teams and organizations. "I learned to reflect with others from diverse backgrounds, new ways of looking at things, and new ways of working with others," noted one coaching recipient.
- *Greater Flexibility.* Coaching recipients learn to visualize individual and organizational possibilities and how to engage others in developing a shared vision. One executive, who attributed his success to "brute force," learned that much of leadership is about developing a personal leadership plan that includes letting others lead, building consensus, connecting with others, and sharing ideals and vision.
- *Commitment to Continuous Learning.* Many coaching recipients see the coaching for effective action process and the use of an effective action coach as just the beginning. In the words of one manager, "My learnings have just begun. I am continuing to learn and grow both as a person and as a professional."

Jim, our overworked, ineffective manager, worked with a coach for effective action through one of our organization's multi-session programs. Jim's coach helped him see his strengths as well as his weaknesses. He recognized his tendency to become reactionary and learned how it was affecting the team he managed. With his coach, he has developed a process to recognize and control this behavior. Jim's colleagues and subordinates further encouraged this change, commenting that he was becoming more effective. Jim committed to further growth and learning. He found a mentor in the organization and discovered a role in which he can be an agent for positive change.

Coaching for Effective Action and Coaching Situations

Over the years that we have been working with this coaching model, the roles coaches for effective action play reflect many, but not all, of the roles typical in a coaching situation.

Coaches for effective action provide process expertise, reflective thinking, feedback, dialogue, accounting, positive reinforcement, counseling, historical reference, and continuity. Effective action coaches do not offer content expertise or focus on specific management skills, nor do they serve as consultants to the business. Coaching for effective action is different from executive coaching, which usually entails one-on-one interaction at senior levels and typically carries a greater sense of urgency for the organization's strategic success.

Coaching for effective action, because of its focus and its combination of face-to-face dialogue and email and telephone work, is a development method that is available to a larger number of people concurrently. As a consequence, we've found it to be an efficient and effective way to extend the benefits of a training and development program.

Coaching for effective action is a developmental relationship process between the coach and recipient in which all information is confidential and remains solely within the relationship. With that in mind, coaches report that coaching for effective action seems less intense than executive coaching. This response may be because it operates within a specified time frame and given structural framework. This framework includes a clearly articulated intent with specific goals of the developmental relationship, a set of competencies to use as reference points, and a focus on the demands of the individual's situation. This dynamic creates an interaction in which the individual selects the situations or issues he or she wishes to work on and, with the guidance of the coach, develops an ongoing action plan.

Coaches themselves stress the assessment, challenge, and support responsibility of coaching for effective action, which expands a typical coaching role. They emphasize the following:

- Coaches for effective action do not need to know all the answers. The foundation of the relationship lies in the coach's ability to understand fully what the situation calls for from the individual, not in competing with the individual for the right answers.
- Coaches for effective action need to remain nonjudgmental. They must establish trust and a strong sense of confidentiality.
- Coaches for effective action need to blend candor with belief in the individual. Less successful coaches tend to be those who flinch or hedge when giving feedback.
- Coaches for effective action must respect and work with the changes the individual decides to make.
- The ongoing relationship and counseling aspect can result in both personal and professional or work-related impact.
- The coach brings reality (feedback); hope (what's possible); and a learning process (structure, steps, stress management), and a safety or holding pattern to the relationship.

The Future of Coaching for Effective Action

Our experience has taught us much of what works and what doesn't work in coaching for development. We know that, to be effective, any model and the coaching for effective action process must:

- Establish a clear development goal;
- Establish key competencies and guiding questions;
- Train, coach, and develop skilled effective action coaches;
- Set specific guidelines on time, frequency of contact, and modes of interaction between advisor and advisee;
- Set specific objectives and expectations for both parties;
- Establish regular contact between process advisor and organizational sponsor;
- Establish a learning community to expand the advisors' knowledge; and
- Build in design evaluation and quality checks to ensure a successful process.

At our organization, we continue to explore and evaluate new ways that our coaching model and effective action process may be used in our programs. For example, the effective action process is an integral part of most customized programs at CCL, and we are continually working with human resource departments to incorporate coaching for effective action into their internal development systems. We are also using technology, such as Internet meetings and online support, to add depth and flexibility to the process. Coaching for Development Surround enables participants to electronically meet and begin working with their coaches prior to attending a program. In addition, we have seen effective results partnering our coaches with executive coaches retained or provided by the client organization. We are experimenting with action-learning coaching processes that include multi-level internal coaching in which senior-level leaders are the coaches for the middle managers. Executive team and project team coaching are also increasingly popular methods. In the latter settings, coaches work with intact teams engaged in action learning projects and help the teams give feedback to each other on what and how they are learning. To maximize the impact of our work, we are disseminating our findings and knowledge through coaching programs and publications.

In addition to its ability to enhance individual growth and development, coaching has become a mainstay for business performance and organizational success. Professional coaching is now used to support and enhance numerous organizational needs, including leadership development and succession planning. For these reasons, the model of coaching for development that emphasizes effective action remains part of the Center's core work. It is a dynamic model informed by our coaching for effective action process and thus enables us to offer a number of approaches, from executive coaching to internal coaching.

The effective action coaches enable leaders and managers to balance between behavioral change to be more effective and continually assessing what the leadership challenge or business situation requires of them. This dynamic process represents our continuing contribution to today's leaders, who are increasingly expected to perform well on the job, in the moment, and to learn and grow while doing so.

◆ ◆ ◆

Victoria A. Guthrie is a senior fellow and director of innovative program initiatives at the Center for Creative Leadership. Her responsibilities include bringing fresh initiatives to the Center's established programs, as well as generative ideas for future program development. Prior to this position, Guthrie headed up the Organizational Leadership Group, which included programs that enabled participants to act on and apply their individual developmental learning in the context of their organizational situations.

She is co-designer of three of the Center's programs: LeaderLab, Leading Transitions, and Leading Creatively. In addition to her leadership role at CCL, she holds teaching roles in all three programs and also designs and conducts client-specific programs for international organizations worldwide.

Guthrie is author of *Coaching for Action: A Report on Long-Term Advising in a Program Context* and co-author of *Training for Action: A New Approach to Executive Development*, "The Lessons of Life at Work: Continuous Personal Development" (*Career Planning and Adult Development Journal*), and two chapters in the Center for Creative Leadership's *Handbook of Leadership Development*: "Developing Leaders with a Feedback Intensive Program" and "The Ability and Willingness to Learn." Contact: guthrie@leaders.ccl.org.

John R. Alexander is president of the Center for Creative Leadership, an international, nonprofit educational institution devoted to behavioral science research and leadership education. Founded in Greensboro, North Carolina, in 1970 by the Smith Richardson Foundation, the Center is today one of the largest institutions in the world focusing on leadership.

Alexander came to the Center in 1990 after an eighteen-year award-winning career as a journalist and newspaper editor. He has received numerous state and national awards for his writing, including the Scripps-Howard Walker Stone Award for editorial writing and first place in editorial writing from the North Carolina Press Association. In 1979, Alexander was a finalist for the Pulitzer Prize in editorial writing. He most recently co-authored "Leading Across Cultures: Five Vital Capabilities," a chapter in the Peter Drucker Foundation's *The Organization of the Future*. Contact: www.ccl.org.

CHAPTER NINE

COACHING OTHERS TO ACCEPT FEEDBACK

Joe Folkman

Possibly the most valuable gift we can receive from another person is honest feedback. Receiving developmental feedback can lead to life-enhancing improvements. And although negative feedback is frequently unappreciated, those who receive it must occasionally be reminded that receiving no feedback at all could be much worse.

Feedback establishes a connection between what we think and what we are seen to do, a measure of the gap between our intentions and how others perceive our actions. In the absence of good feedback, we can never know how our behavior may affect others. We are left on our own to figure out what others think and feel about us.

Many coaching relationships begin by helping those being coached to accept feedback. This article will present four steps that will help you coach others to accept feedback and transform it into positive change.

Step One: Hearing the Feedback

For many people, it is difficult to tell the difference between feedback and noise. One of the most intriguing characteristics of the human body is its ability to filter what we hear. We teach ourselves to pay attention to some noises and to ignore others. As you read this, stop a few times and notice the noises occurring around you.

Today's organizations are full of noise. Voice mail, email, announcements, memos, interruptions, meetings, discussions, and other messages abound in most offices. With such a high volume of noise from incoming information, it becomes impossible to pay attention to every message. To cope, we develop fairly sophisticated mental filters that help us pay attention to some and ignore others.

Coaches play a critical role in helping others hear feedback when it has been ignored in the past. Many who need this coaching were originally hired into important positions because of their clear points of view and strong opinions. As they progressed in their positions, they became confident and tough-minded; they made difficult decisions and moved their organizations forward on issues for which there might not have been 100 percent agreement. These managers needed to develop thick skins, and so they ignored some feedback to accomplish more effectively the jobs they were hired to do.

Often, the peers and direct reports of this group observe that these managers "just don't get it." Within the above scenario, such observations are often correct. Many people teach themselves to ignore the feedback they are given. Similarly, one of my children is often easily distracted by the events going on around him. Occasionally I must place my hands gently on both sides of his face, point his eyes directly at mine, and then talk to him before I am sure he is paying attention and listening effectively. Sometimes coaches must do the same thing, figuratively, for others to genuinely hear their feedback.

Step Two: Accepting the Feedback

We are unwilling to change what we do not believe needs to be changed. Beyond simply coaching people to hear or to become aware of feedback, coaches must help others to accept the feedback provided. If the feedback is not accepted, no change will occur.

It is frequently said of alcoholics that although they are given plenty of feedback, and often demonstrate awareness of the feedback, many initially deny it: "I'm not an alcoholic! I can stop whenever I choose!" When people are in a state of denial, no change or improvement can be made until they can "own" the problem. Part of the acceptance process involves admitting that the feedback received is accurate.

Acceptance means more than a passive acknowledgment of feedback. It means embracing it and believing that the perceptions of others are valid. It is possible to hear, and even believe, feedback from others while continuing to think, "Who cares?" "What do they know?" or "This doesn't really matter." Someone may admit, "I understand that those with whom I work think I'm indecisive," while saying to himself, "If those people only understood the complexity I have to deal with, they might understand that I just take the time to analyze a problem thoroughly before making my decisions." Acceptance means believing that we do, in fact, "have a problem."

Acceptance also means that we understand the feedback and are clear about what the behavior looks like, when the behavior occurs and does not occur, and how the behavior impacts others. Someone who has not fully accepted feedback might say, "I understand that my direct reports would like to be better informed." But someone who is accepting the same feedback would understand, "When I don't keep my direct reports well-informed, they do not spend their time productively and they feel disempowered." Acceptance means understanding how the behavior impacts our personal effectiveness: "My job would be a lot easier, and this project would run more smoothly if people were kept well-informed."

Step Three: Prioritizing

A key to coaching people toward successful change is to focus their efforts on only a few critical behaviors. Trying to change too much inevitably results in changing nothing at all. The 80/20 rule of individual performance helps capture the philosophy of prioritization: 80 percent of our performance comes directly from only 20 percent of our behaviors.

This concept can be used to demonstrate that a few critical behaviors account for the bulk of our performance. The central idea is to focus our efforts on the critical behaviors that leverage that performance.

Those who provide feedback do not typically prioritize it usefully for us. They tell us what may be bothering them and what they observe, and they tend to do it in the order in which these things come into their minds. As a result, when we receive highly negative feedback, we sometimes feel overwhelmed because it indicates problems in every aspect of our behavior. But in reality, poor performance that creates a "halo effect" from just a few critical areas can drag down overall perception. When others are extremely frustrated with us about some aspect of our performance, it is difficult for them to acknowledge that this one behavior is bad while all the other behaviors are good. Instead, they tend to form general impressions and adjust their perceptions about other behaviors to fit those impressions. Thus, poor performance in one critical behavior tends to produce a "negative halo" when providing feedback.

For successful change to occur, we must analyze the feedback we receive and determine those key drivers of our performance. Coaches can identify these critical behaviors and help create dramatic change. Expending great effort to change a behavior that will have little impact on the perceptions of others will not lead to benefit. But if we can change a few *critical* behaviors that leverage our performance, then our focused efforts will help to create a "positive halo effect." Just a few noticeable changes can cause others to change their general impressions.

Here is how to determine the key drivers of performance.

Clarify the Key Objectives or Expectations of the Job

It is impossible to improve performance without establishing clear and specific performance objectives. For many, merely carrying out this activity will help leverage performance. Often, poor performance is the result of unclear expectations ("I didn't know I was expected to do that!") or competing expectations ("I can't manage all the details of this project if I have to take on three projects at the same time!").

Determine Whether Making a Change in a Particular Behavior Would Significantly Improve Overall Performance

For many behaviors, it is not clear how a change would improve performance. In one instance, a manager had received strong feedback about his cynicism. Although the cynicism bothered some people, it was unclear whether changing this behavior would have a substantial impact on the bottom-line performance of the group. So rather than trying to change the behavior, he decided to keep his cynicism private. He determined that involving others in decisions and keeping them informed would have a greater impact on the group's performance.

Find Out Which Behavior the Person Desires to Change the Most

Behaviors for which people have passion, commitment, and a desire to change have a significantly higher probability of being changed. All too often, people try to change behaviors for which their desire to change is low. The inevitable result is that nothing changes. Review the feedback and determine what is easy to change. Finding a "quick win" can provide both momentum for the person making the change and optimism for those who provide feedback and can demonstrate that the person is serious about change. Some behaviors are more difficult to change than others.

Step Four: Making Change Happen

When left alone, many of us approach personal change with great enthusiasm but little planning. Although enthusiasm is important, perhaps even critical, enthusiasm alone is rarely enough. When quizzed about how we plan to carry out a change, we generally answer, "I'll just do it."

Identifying a goof "change lever" can help. When moving a large rock, the more effectively positioned the levers are, the higher the probability that the rock will be moved. Some change approaches work better for some people than for others. The key to increasing the probability that change will happen is to increase the number of levers used and the effort applied to each.

Some Levers of Change

Making the Change Goal Specific. Usually, when we begin a change effort, we start with a general goal. We say we are going to "become a better communicator," "be more sensitive to others," "exert more leadership," "better motivate our direct reports," or (my personal favorite) "become a better person." Although these are all desirable goals, they lack specificity. The problem with general goals is that it is difficult to tell whether we are succeeding or failing, or to know what actions we should take next. To make effective changes, our goals must be specific and must indicate explicit, measurable behaviors. When our goals are specific, it is easier for us and for others to determine whether we are succeeding or failing.

Creating a Clear Vision. I recently took my five-year-old son skiing for the first time. As we began our ski day, I helped him put on his skis and explained to him the basics. The first thing you must learn is the "snowplow," for which you make an upside-down "V" with the skis, which helps you to slow down and to turn.

As I explained the concept to my son, I could see a blank look on his face. On the way to the ski resort that morning, we had seen a snowplow, but it had been pushing a single blade, pointed sideways, along the road. My explanation was not working.

As we got to the top of the hill to begin our first run, I heard a ski instructor ask his student to "make a piece of pizza." The student quickly positioned her skis in exactly the same manner I had tried to explain to my son. I thought to myself, "Now, if there is one thing that my five-year-old is clear about, it is the shape of a piece of pizza." Then I asked my son if he could make a piece of pizza with his skis. The light visibly went on in his eyes.

He replied, "Sure, Dad. Do you want me to make a big piece or a small piece?" Once my son had a clear vision in his mind, it was much easier to learn this new behavior.

Often, we begin our change efforts with only a very vague vision of our ultimate goal. A clear vision:

- *Has a destination.* A vision should describe a place we want to go, not a place we want to avoid. We should be clear not only about what the vision is, but also about what it is not. It is just as important to describe where we are not going as where we want to go.
- *Is visual.* We must be able to picture a vision in our minds. The picture often starts out as a distant object that is not totally clear. Later, as we get closer, the vision becomes more clear.
- *Is simple.* Complex visions are difficult to clarify and often lead people in multiple directions. Simple visions are the most focused and the most compelling.
- *Is challenging, but realistic.* The vision needs to be attainable.

- *Is consistent with our personalities.* Visions that do not connect with us, that require us to be something other than ourselves, do not have the energy to carry us forward.

Obtaining Support from Others.

Persuading other people to support your change effort is potentially one of the most powerful change levers (although many powerful people tend to want to "go it alone"). Enlisting help from others keeps us honest, because others are watching. Others can often help us avoid the traps that lead to problems. For people who have difficulty controlling their anger, several easily observable behaviors often precede its eruption. These behaviors are often discernible to others, but not to the person with the problem. Having another person help us recognize such patterns of behavior can provide a wonderful monitoring device. Eventually, we learn to monitor ourselves.

But enlisting others to help us make changes is often difficult. Some people believe that asking for help diminishes their positions or reputations. One person commented to me, "It's like admitting you have a problem." We sometimes deceive ourselves into believing that other people don't know we have problems. Although a few people might be surprised, most people already know the problems exist. Asking for help allows others to see us as authentic or teachable. As you begin your coaching effort, take the time to identify people whom you can count on for support.

Both hearing and accepting feedback are critical skills that help us to improve our effectiveness. A coach's role in helping others to "get it" is absolutely critical in bringing about such change. Once people can understand and accept the feedback they receive, they should prioritize the issues they plan to change. Although it is difficult to change many things at one time, those who are motivated can create dramatic impact by changing one or two critical behaviors that leverage their performance.

Remember that a change in one critical behavior can generate significantly greater performance than can trying to change five things at once. Coaching people to use different approaches or "levers," such as setting specific goals, clarifying vision, and enlisting the support of others, helps improve the probability of a change occurring.

◆ ◆ ◆

Joe Folkman is president of Zenger-Folkman, an organization that helps companies and individuals deliver extraordinary results through leadership development, assessment, and research. His book, *Turning Feedback into Change®: 31 Principles for Managing Personal Development Through Feedback*, suggests how to use feedback in intelligent ways to bring about genuine and positive change in personal behavior. Folkman and his co-author, Jack Zenger, have written two books on leadership: *The Extraordinary Leader* and *The Handbook for Leaders*. Folkman is also the author of two books on employee surveys: *Making Feedback Work: Turning Feedback from Employee Surveys into Change* and *Employee Surveys That Make a Difference.*

CHAPTER TEN

SELLING UP IS LEADING UP

Coaching Your Manager Can Be Just as Important as Coaching Your Direct Reports

John Baldoni and Marshall Goldsmith

While almost everyone agrees that coaching is a key component of leadership, we often think of applying coaching only with direct reports. However, in some cases we may need to coach our upper management! When this need arises, one key variable usually changes. We have the power to make ultimate decisions with our direct reports; we don't have the power to make ultimate decisions for higher management. When we don't have the power to make a decision, we need to learn how to sell to the people who do.

Jack Smith was a rising executive within General Motors when he had the opportunity to visit Japan and tour some Toyota facilities. To his surprise, Smith discovered that the Japanese automaker needed only half the number of workers to produce its vehicles. In other words, Toyota was twice as efficient in manpower as General Motors. Armed with his findings, Smith made a presentation to GM's executive committee. The committee members disregarded the information, and Smith was shocked by their arrogance. Unfortunately, such hubris would not last for long; General Motors was in the midst of a tailspin that would see it hemorrhage market share and incur huge losses. Ironically, Smith had the last laugh; as CEO he shepherded a turnaround that has seen General Motors regain share and sales.[1]

Failure to Persuade

What happened to Smith has happened to many managers in their careers; their attempts at upward coaching fall on deaf ears. Given the hidebound, top-down culture of General Motors at the time he made his report, likely nothing could have compelled the board to listen to coaching from an underling. Nonetheless, Smith failed to persuade the committee, and his company eventually paid the price. Put another way, Smith could not sell his message. He is not alone. For example, investigations into what went wrong prior to 9/11 reveal a trail of missed opportunities. Field agents in the FBI had identified men of Middle Eastern origin taking flying lessons in sophisticated simulators; their reports were passed up the system, but their bosses took no notice. In testimony to a specially formed investigative committee, Richard Clarke, former anti-terrorist czar for both the Clinton and Bush administrations, itemized his failures to persuade his higher-ups to take action against Al Queda. Sadly for our nation, the field agents and Mr. Clarke were not more effective coaches and salespeople.

One of the most salient characteristics of leadership is the ability to persuade others to follow. Without followers, there can be no leaders. Yet, more and more, especially in large organizations in both the private and public sectors, there is a compelling need to *lead up*. Michael Useem, author of *Leading Up*, writes, "Leadership is a matter of bringing more to the office than we were given, of adding greater value to the company or country that it would achieved without us."[2] Leading up is bringing the leadership point of view to those around you. Leading up is based on one's own sense of personal leadership. That is, it is a commitment buttressed by character, values, and beliefs that is directed toward doing what is good for the organization in order to get things done the right way.

Critical to leading others is the ability to persuade or sell your ideas. To many professionals, the concept of salesmanship is abhorrent. Better to ask them to run down the hallway in their underwear than ask them to *sell* anything! This is a huge mistake that, as we have seen in recent years, has costly consequences. A review of summary 360-degree-feedback results from many different companies shows that an inability to influence up is common among managers in all kinds of organizations. In fact, such an inability was partially accountable for the two NASA shuttle disasters, which occurred decades apart. When managers cannot get their ideas heard by senior leaders, the organization as a whole suffers. Salesmanship is the ability to illuminate your point of view so that others want to get behind it. When the idea or message is rooted within an organization's vision, mission, and values, it needs to be heeded. In other words, selling up is a key component of coaching up.

Taking Stock

Before attempting to sell up, take stock of your idea and how it will benefit your organization. Consider four questions:

1. Is this idea good for the company?
2. Is this idea good for employees?
3. Is this idea good for customers?
4. Is this idea good for the boss?

If the answers are yes, proceed. If the answers are no, find ways to turn them into yes or find a way to structure your argument to address the shortcomings. Perhaps you are pushing for a process improvement that will shrink headcount. It is good for the bottom line, but perhaps bad for the boss's ego. Point out how the reduction will make your boss look more statesmanlike, ready to tackle greater challenges, and eventually manage more people.

After you have taken stock of your idea, stand back and look at the organization as a whole. It is your responsibility to present the idea in a compelling manner; it is not the leader's responsibility to buy it. Frame your arguments in a way that focuses on improvements to the whole organization, not just to your department or your bottom line.

Action Steps

Here are some action steps you can take to become a more effective salesperson and upward coach.

1. Identify the Outcome

Know to what end you are working. This may sound obvious, but it is common for people to have little understanding of how their roles affect the big picture or the organization as a whole. It is up to the project leader to communicate the objectives of the project or program and how it will affect the organization. Definition of outcome begins with strategic intent, and the project leader must iterate it in documents and in formal and informal conversations with the team and others in the organization. We see good examples of this with successful professional sports teams, such as the New York Yankees, the Los Angeles Lakers, and the Detroit Red Wings. Winning games is not the goal; winning the championship is the goal. Veteran players reinforce the organizational mantra and guide new players in winning the ring.

2. Enlist the Support of Senior Leaders

In almost every organization, support from the top is essential to launching any project. After all, it is the senior leaders who are responsible for allocating resources, such as monetary expenditures, equipment, and employee time. Permission, however, is different from support. Permission is the OK; support implies participation. The team behind Toyota's new brand, Scion, a line of vehicles targeted at the Millennial Generation, went straight to the top with its pitch. Rather than charts and graphs, the pitch to chairman Hiroshi Okuda was a music video. While Okuda did not pretend to understand the music, he did know that the idea was sound: you market vehicles to kids differently than to septuagenarians, and he gave the go-ahead.[3]

When a senior leader, often referred to as a "champion," believes in a project, she will actively campaign for it. She will enlist the support of senior colleagues as well as communicate the project's virtues throughout the organization. The champion's active participation gives the project an importance that it would otherwise not receive and, as a result, gains needed support.

3. Identify the Nay-Sayers

It is important to know who may be out to kill your idea. Machiavelli warned his readers centuries ago about those in the shadows who could sabotage another's fortune. Despite our progress in science and technology since Renaissance Florence, we have not progressed much in human terms; every good manager must realize that there are some above and below him in rank who will reject any of his good ideas. The reasons for this are as complex as the human condition: jealousy, greed, avarice, or simple disagreements. The point is not to dwell on the human psyche, but to understand that opposition exists and to prepare to overcome it. Project leaders need to know who may oppose them and why. A plan that is well communicated and supported by senior management can negate nay-sayers, but it is still important to find ways to work with the opposition. One way is to enlist their support. If that fails, keep them away from the project, especially if they have any say about funding for it.

4. Build a Support Group of Peers

Ultimately, a project succeeds because of the efforts of those who work for the project leader. Their commitment is essential, which is why it is crucial that the leader build support for the ideas behind the project. Communication is essential in setting expectations, delegating assignments, offering recognition, and fostering two-way bonding. If the project leader allows team members to contribute ideas, it ceases to be "my project" and morphs into "our project," in which all team members have a stake. A sterling example of this is the implementation of the process-based quality initiative Six Sigma.

The foundation of the initiative relies on implementation by the organization's employees. This grassroots support drives the Six Sigma initiative and ensures that it is adopted within every level of the organization.

5. Tear Down the Barricades

For all the talk about the horizontal flattening of organizational hierarchies, there remain many silos wherein functions do not speak to functions. Project leaders need to scale those walls in person. It is not enough to send a memo. Sometimes a meeting will do, but often you will need to be creative. Invite people to come to your energy room, the cavern of ideas, where they can see and experience for themselves what you and the team are trying to do. If you are really daring, you might even get together after work for a beer or pizza, or even go bowling together. Nothing breaks down barriers better than bowling a few frames, especially if no one is good at it. Soon laughter will ensue, and conversation about the project can occur, and meeting times will be established.

6. Create Excitement About What You're Trying to Do

Bringing excitement to an idea helps to create allies and generates the momentum that will sway fence-sitters. One way to generate excitement is to create a communications vehicle for reporting results, such as a website; a series of emails; or an announcement bulletin posted in heavy traffic areas such as lobbies, copy rooms, and lunchrooms. For really big news, video broadcasts and banners work well. The campaign achieves two things: it recognizes the team's achievements and it lets others in the company partake in the excitement.

We see this kind of excitement generated at technology and software companies. Engineers and marketers alike want to get on board with projects that have the most chances of success. Pretty soon, the enthusiasm for the project gains momentum, and people come forward to contribute ideas and suggestions and even offer help in the form of network assistance. All of us want to be associated with winners, and the more the leader can foster a winning spirit, the more chance the project has to succeed.

Are You Listening?

These action steps are directed upward, but it is also useful to address the role of the leader at the top. In short, listen up! The most successful leaders are those who rely on the ideas of others; they mix and mingle with their people to find out what's going on as well as to listen to other ideas. Consider the example of Howard Schultz of Starbucks; when he tours his stores, he makes it a point to listen to the ideas of the people running the coffee shops. One idea that resulted was Starbuck's branded music, an idea that a store manager suggested. In this regard, Shultz is following the lead of another retailing pioneer, Ray Kroc, who encouraged his McDonald's franchisees to come up with new product ideas. As a leader, not everything you hear will be music or the next Big Mac, but there might be some small germ of an idea that will one day take wings and soar, if you only listen.

As you sell up, it is important that the compromises you make do not come at the expense of integrity. We have seen how corrupt cultures distort people, but the reverse is also true. Few people at WorldCom set out to be corrupt, but when things got sloppy and no one spoke up, eventually one person crossed the line, then another, and finally many more. So speak up for your values as well as the ethics of all.

Moving Forward

Become a great coach for upper management in the same way that you want to become a great coach with your own team. Understand that selling up is ultimately about moving forward. Don't try to fight past battles by trumping an old adversary. Look for ways to collaborate with people. Create win-win propositions that take the organization forward. People at the top of the organization want to stay at the top, so look for ways that your ideas will help them. Coach up in a way that not only benefits them, but also benefits the whole organization. "Leading up is a call to building on the best in everybody's nature," writes Michael Useem. "Leading up requires great courage and determination . . . but we all carry a responsibility to do what we can when it will make a difference."[4]

And finally, remember Jack Smith. He didn't get the committee to buy his ideas the first time, but his career was not over. Smith was a team player. Sometimes you can make important allies if you accept a defeat with dignity. Therefore, if your ideas are not accepted the first time, you may try again or you may move on, but always look for ways to support the team. In the process, you will keep your skills tuned and ready for the next time you're ready to sell an idea.

Selling up through the organization is essential to getting things done. Whether you are arguing for the merits of a new computer system or illustrating the benefits of an organizational transformation, your ability to make your voice heard as well as listened to is vital to organizational health. Rallying others to your cause is how you translate words into action and transform selling into meaningful coaching. And that's how things get done.[5]

Notes

1. Taylor, A. GM gets its act together. Finally. *Fortune*, April 5, 2004.
2. Useem, M. *Leading up: How to lead your boss so you both win.* New York: Crown Business. 2001. pp. 2–3.

3. Warner, F. Smart company: Learning to speak to gen Y. *Fast Company,* July 2003.

4. Useem, M. *Leading up: How to lead your boss so you both win.* New York: Crown Business, 2001, p. 6.

5. The authors would like to acknowledge the work of Joel DeLuca, Ph.D., consultant and author of *Political savvy: Systematic approaches to leadership behind the scenes* (Evergreen, 1999) for his influence in shaping some of the ideas in this article.

◆ ◆ ◆

For **John Baldoni,** leadership is a passion; teaching it to others is his calling. Baldoni is a leadership communications consultant who works with Fortune 500 companies as well as non-profits. He is a frequent speaker on the subjects of communication, motivation, and leadership, and he has spoken to corporate, law enforcement, military, and university audiences. His articles are widely published and have appeared in such publications as the *Harvard Management Communications Letter, Leader to Leader,* and the *Wharton Leadership Digest.* Baldoni is the author of five books on leadership, including *Great Communication Secrets of Great Leaders* and his newest, *Great Motivation Secrets of Great Leaders.* Contact: www.johnbaldoni.com; john@johnbaldoni.com.

Marshall Goldsmith has recently been named by the American Management Association as one of fifty great thinkers and leaders who have impacted the field of management over the past eighty years. He has been described in *The Wall Street Journal* as one of the top ten executive educators; the *Economist* as one of the most credible thought leaders in the new era of business; *Forbes* as one of five most-respected executive coaches; and *Fast Company* as America's preeminent executive coach.

Dr. Goldsmith has a Ph.D. from UCLA and is an adjunct professor at Dartmouth's Tuck School of Management. He has been asked to teach in executive education programs at Michigan, MIT, and the Wharton School. He is one of a select few consultants who have been asked to work with over seventy major CEOs and their management teams.

Dr. Goldsmith is co-editor or author of eighteen books, including *The Leader of the Future* (a *Business Week* best seller), *Global Leadership: The Next Generation,* and *The Art and Practice of Leadership Coaching.* Contact: www.marshallgoldsmith.com/; marshall@marshallgoldsmith.com.

PART THREE

LEADING CHANGE

CHAPTER ELEVEN

COACHING AT THE HEART OF STRATEGY

Laurence S. Lyons

Observing the Coaching Scene

Imagine them, perched at the corner of a highly polished mahogany table in some elegant boardroom. They appear to be business colleagues, come together to clinch a deal. The observer may suppose them to be friends—or perhaps adversaries—working through some evidently complex problem. They take turns at drawing on a whiteboard, one passionately elaborating on a point, the other deep in thought. A fresh pattern of thought sparks insight; highly animated, they evaluate every possible angle, moving toward a considered plan of action.

To the casual observer, the practice of executive coaching may appear to involve little more than holding an animated conversation. But behind the immediate "here-and-now" setting in which such an exchange takes place, many worlds are to be found. One describes the executive's career that stretches beyond today, well into the past and future. Any modern career is set within a world of work in which the ground rules are in a state of flux. Central to this, we find the immediate present, the world of today, populated by colleagues in various teams, managers, direct reports, associates, suppliers, and customers. The specific configuration of relationships can include government, trade unions, banks, shareholders, stock markets, and so forth. Permeating this is the competitive or purposeful world of the organization in which the executive works. And then again, there is a world beyond the boundary—one all too often neglected in management books—desperately needing to be acknowledged, although not explored, during the coaching process. This is the non-business, non-work, social, personal, family world. We must accept that there is life beyond work.

In order to be fully effective, a coaching dialogue must be able to integrate these worlds. Good coaching has the capacity to help an executive or team develop competencies and business effectiveness within any or all of the domains.

To complicate this picture, membership in the work teams to which the executive belongs (for example, project team, task force, or committee) is often fluid; people come and go. Team, personal, and organizational objectives also change over time. In addition, the organization itself is often in a state of reformulating its own identity, mission, and structure.

Yet this apparently simple coaching dialogue does take place. Our research shows that it is consistently successful when performed well. Amazingly, a seemingly simple "coaching conversation" accommodates turbulence and uncertainty, yet repeatedly succeeds in producing outstanding results. For the practitioner who has a limited perception of coaching as simply a collegial conversation, coaching will undoubtedly fail to deliver durable success. But coaching will be successful both in a strategic sense and over time when acted out as a structured dialogue of emerging purpose.

Dialogue

Good coaching is difficult to do. Perhaps the greatest challenge is to engage the executive in a dialogue of emerging purpose. The disarmingly simple question, "What should we talk about?" can be hard to answer well. Thus, the coach often works with the executive as a kind of scout, together selecting an appropriate path. Coaching is potentially both high-impact and high-risk. Dire consequences can result from setting off in the wrong direction—disappointing to both the executive and the business. In contrast, identifying the right path will reap high reward.

Dialogue is at the heart of coaching. In an interview, we find two people. One is typically a senior executive of a large corporation, responsible for a significant part of the business, the other an executive coach—neither an employee of nor a technical consultant to that corporation. The executive has million-dollar spending authority. The coach has no corporate authority whatever. But through dialogue alone, the external coach exercises considerable influence. With neither formal authority nor direct accountability, the coach's greatest ambition is to profoundly affect the way that the executive thinks and behaves.

Rapport is vital to make sure that the dialogue gets off the ground. The "chemistry" of the pair must quickly establish trust and credibility; the executive must have confidence that the coach is not simply wasting time. Good listening skills on the part of the coach, together with the ability to deliver honest feedback, are crucial to keeping the dialogue grounded in reality—not in fabricated supposition or unsupported beliefs. Between them, coach and executive need to agree on how to separate transient, situational factors from those that are innate and require attention. This sifting can often require delicate judgment when the setting is a turbulent corporate environment. Every effort made in teasing out fact from raw data is well rewarded; carefully validated data is a key determinant of the quality of the outcome of the coaching venture.

The directional or strategic power of any coaching dialogue lies primarily in the nature of its questions. Questions may be asked to surface submerged issues or may be asked to help the executive to reconsider some position or proposed course of action. The executive's attitudes or opinions may become either reinforced or challenged; the person's current path will be either confirmed or probed. Even when the dialogue confirms the validity of a person's existing game plan, it adds value—boosting the executive's confidence while keeping business risks in check.

Coaching re-engages with reality when good questioning is followed by inspired analysis, detailed action planning, and follow-through back in the work environment. Working together with the executive, the coach crystallizes their conversation in an action plan. The endpoint of a coaching interview invariably involves the executive planning to try out some new behavior. Most importantly, the full value of any coaching activity can only be realized when a new behavior is actually performed in the real world. At this stage—after the coaching interview has ended—the coach encourages the executive to follow up and execute the plan. In a sense, the coach now acts as both a memory and a conscience. Thus, coaching is best seen as an ongoing process or durable system, not just a single interview event.

A good coach need not be an expert in the executive's job type or industry. A good coach does not even have to possess as wide a range of social skills as the executive. With a sound appreciation of business and interpersonal dynamics, a good coach is simply a process person who can establish rapport; is informed about the executive's immediate environment; is honest and courageous in providing feedback; is a good listener; asks good questions; is visionary and analytical; and is a good planner who seeks follow-up and closure.

The sheer power unleashed in the coaching process must surely obligate the executive and coach to consider several serious questions, such as: What constitutes success in this dialogue? Who, specifically, is my client? How should confidential issues be treated? Which topics fall outside the purview of coaching, and how are those affecting work performance recognized? In the face of these ethical conundrums, the coach must strive to align dialogue in a direction punctuated by validated objectives. The coach must be brave enough to urge the executive to move forward—often by confronting some taboo topic, hitherto deliberately ignored. The dialogue will always help the executive pursue selected objectives—yet not be overly directed by the coach. After all, coaching is concerned with facilitation, not giving advice. Although the necessity remains for the executive to persevere along the most successful route that can currently be identified, there is no promise that the path will be simple to find or easy to travel.

This brings us to two crucial insights into good coaching. First, it is necessary to look behind a dialogue to realize that it will not simply "happen" without background. The most robust coaching relies on broadly informed dialogue. Quite a lot of work may have to be undertaken in the collection, validation, and analysis of information before real coaching can begin. The kind of information that is assimilated includes current facts about the markets, technology, or political environment in which the executive is working. Impressions held by colleagues, associates, and direct reports provide vital indications about the executive's personal interaction. Sometimes the only possible way forward is to begin with an executive's own anecdotal information, but coaching in a vacuum is a dangerous game.

The second insight to be gained takes us far beyond the one-to-one interview. By incorporating the ethos of the organization within the coaching dialogue, it becomes possible to relate an individual's behavior to purposeful organizational change. When the whole organization is engaged, coaching becomes strategic. Moreover, within a modern learning organization, team coaching and the development of strategic thinking may become one and the same thing.

For the coach, strategy need not reside in quarterly profit targets alone. Those committed to strategic coaching will enrich the meaning of strategy to at once embrace individual, team, and corporate actors. Strategic executive coaching is an inclusive, practical approach, incorporating the idea of a dashboard or balanced scorecard, and it is well-adapted to a complex world in which even the ground rules are in a state of change.

Transforming People

For the sponsor, a coaching initiative might be viewed as a self-contained project, rather than as part of an integrated corporate strategy. However, whenever coaching succeeds in aligning the needs of the business with the developmental needs of its people, it cannot help but be strategic in nature.

Many organizations face a situation in which an entire block of talent shifts when issues of succession and development emerge. Typically, this occurs during mergers, downsizing, or block retirement. The creation of a career path to retain top talent and a drive to expand into global markets are also examples of situations demanding a strategic coaching response. Whatever the cause, a gap opens up that has to be filled for the organization to remain strategically healthy. So at one leading automobile manufacturer, fast-track engineers are today being coached to become tomorrow's senior leaders. Elsewhere, a Fortune 500 IT innovator has implemented coaching within a program that has integrated five separate operating countries into a cohesive and highly successful business region.

For the person being coached, the experience is invariably strategic. Coaching offers the executive a golden opportunity to step back and reflect on personal development. By expressly allocating precious work time, the coaching interview momentarily suspends the immediate pressures of the day and encourages the individual to think about "just me." From this viewpoint, the coaching intervention is able to break the pedestrian logic of mere reaction and repetition. For once, the executive has time to look dispassionately and proactively at more broad-brush issues in a far wider context. The individual may well start to consider the interface between work and life. Work is within life; work is a part of life. In order that executives may learn and develop at work, they must first understand where they are in their careers and in their lives. Often, reflection on one's purpose will validate or challenge one's current position. Such consideration may encourage an individual to move forward or to move on to something new. To the extent that coaching sensitizes people to reflect and act in a more purposeful way, it is again strategic in nature, helping to align the organization with the people who are in it.

In times of major organizational change, coaching often provides the necessary impetus for building and motivating teams. Team coaching helps establish and then build a collection of individuals into a fully functioning business network. The resulting team unites people across functions and divisions, often including members outside the formal organization. Time and again, we have seen a team-coaching process motivate people to coalesce. Provided that the group contains that critical mass of people needed for the business to move forward, a nascent transition team starts to emerge. Many team members will have recently taken part in individual coaching sessions, and so will be ready to think strategically at the moment the team starts to form. When a foundation of trust has been established, the conditions for cohesion are in place, and the team spontaneously ignites in a dialogue of business improvement. Such teams are enthusiastic; such teams have solutions that will work; such teams are unstoppable. A well-designed team-coaching process brings together the right people and raises the broadest challenge, in an environment in which failure is not an option.

Coaching also plays a special role at the most senior level in an organization (that is, with the board of directors or senior management team). At this level, issues are often motivational rather than technical. Technically, the coach will play a unique role as interpreter by insisting that jargon be transformed into business concepts that are commonly understood. Motivationally, members may differ significantly in their beliefs about the purpose of the business and may hold conflicting expectations about what success means and how to measure it. Then again, business owners may hold wildly different views about asset valuation and a preferred exit or merger strategy. Located at an intermediate level in large companies, divisional and regional boards often grapple with a particularly perplexing question: How can we find ways to add value from our unique vantage point in the overall structure? In all these cases, coaching offers yet another framework for dialogue. Coaching provides a climate within which vital, although seemingly intransigent, issues may be brought to the surface, confronted, and then dealt with. Coaching offers the senior team a practical tool to break any logjams that are in the way of progress.

In all of these cases—for individuals, teams, and boards—coaching offers a structured dialogue of emerging purpose, directed toward success. As Figure 11.1 shows, with the right conditions in place, coaching is organizational transformation; coaching is team development; coaching is strategy in motion.

FIGURE 11.1. THE STRATEGIC COACHING MODEL.

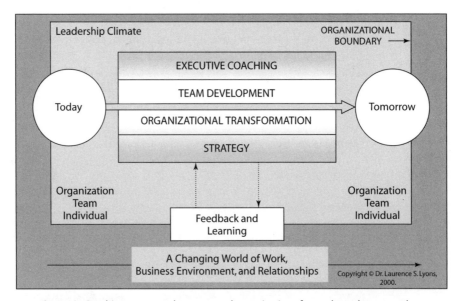

Strategic Coaching gets people, teams, and organizations from where they are today to where they want to be tomorrow. The leader is committed to ensuring the existence and maintenance of the coaching process and its alignment with business results.

Leadership

In an era in which leadership is replacing management and learning is replacing instruction, coaching is surfacing as the accessible face of strategy. Business strategy no longer commands an exclusive domain secreted within the impersonal body of an abstract "organization." Today, as demands on everyone's time intensify, strategy is manifest in the flesh and blood of each executive. Coaching is not simply a passing fad; it offers a pragmatic supporting context in which modern strategy flourishes. In today's turbulent world, strategy has developed into something that emerges, always tracking a moving target. And the preferred vehicle—responsive enough to reduce the risk in successfully traveling toward that ever-changing destination—is to be found in the dialogue of coaching.

Any dialogue that brings an executive closer to goal achievement in the real world truly succeeds at a strategic level. Achievement-oriented dialogue reaches outside the immediate interview to make real things happen. Coaching has the power to let strategy come alive and, therefore, to work in practice. Executive coaching has become current simply because it has become relevant. Coaching facilitates success and is congruent with the way we want to work and the way we have to work. It is relevant to the modern world of business because it is holistic and adaptive. Coaching is also a method that respects people as individuals, not merely as cogs in the business machine. Rooted in conversation, coaching is evolving as a natural vehicle of leadership.

A Radically Different World of Work

As knowledge work relentlessly replaces manual work, we are witness to the dawn of perhaps the most meritocratic workplace environment in history. Management is no longer perceived in terms of maintaining the business machine, but is seen as the motivator and leader of men and women. Our understanding of the essence of management is reeling from radical change.

The management metaphor has, until now, been extremely useful in helping executives become more systematic and better organized in order to plan, motivate, and control. But the word "management" has come to represent an attitudinal straitjacket that can stifle, and often excuse the need for, that kind of truly innovative thinking that has become a prerequisite for success. As markets become more efficient and intensively competitive, ideas of coercion and control—together with a reliance on rigid rules—hinder, rather than help, businesses succeed.

Noticeably, the adjectives used to describe management work have already started to change. Terms once borrowed from engineering and finance are being replaced with descriptions from the social and humanist vocabulary. Thus, the "efficient company" has become a "learning organization." Language is not the only thing changing. The perspective is shifting steadily and surely from labor to knowledge; from management to leadership; from product to consumers and service; from routine operation to inspired creativity; and from task repetition to marketing innovation. As technology and automation shift the boredom of work from people to machines, the human world of work that remains challenges our intellects, not our muscles.

Fast-paced competition means that businesses can no longer afford to reward the routine repetition embedded in the all-too-rigid "management" model. A new culture, one that prizes sensible action and appropriate adaptability, is challenging as well as complementing written strategic plans. These vast tomes were invariably out-of-date on the day they were published and contained too many untested or generalized as-sumptions to be workable in practice. Long delays in the planning cycle allowed the organization to meander aimlessly while waiting for the control loop to close. It is not easy to enter into dialogue with a written plan. These days, competitive advantage is not to be found in written plans alone. Corporate success is now intimately related to the ways in which individual executives think, act, and interact on a daily basis. To win and receive reward, executives must now do the right thing, not simply the written thing. It is not enough to take problems to others and await a response. The competition simply will not stand back and wait. Today's successful executives do not "need the meetings," instead they "meet the needs."

The change in the nature of work is not only radical, it is also deeply pervasive, as leaders continue to shift operations into the global arena. Worldwide, a realization that a key source of competitive advantage is to be found rooted in the social fabric of the company is opening up new vistas of opportunity. Whereas the technical business process was only recently seen as the dominant lever of change, we have come to rec-ognize the human "etiquette" of the organization as a potent value driver. If we get the formula right, the currently emerging leadership culture offers leaders a genuine opportunity to make the world a better place.

Coaching offers us a unique response to help address that challenge at every level.

The Learning Executive

A complete overhaul is taking place in the way we see the relationship between edu-cation and work. In the traditional model, predicated on executing a single profes-sional function over an entire lifetime, learning was confined to a single burst of training followed by years of practice. This sequence has now become less relevant for many. Today, "Education for Life" is rapidly replacing "A Job for Life" as the domi-nant career model. No longer does a specific job last for a lifetime; several jobs frag-ment a career, while learning has become continuous, rather than a one-time affair.

Executive skills must match the situation. Modern business is too dynamic to allow executives to succeed with the old rigid and simplistic assumptions. On a personal level, all executives face a recurring challenge in pragmatically responding to revolutionary trends and pressures in the world of work. A fresh dexterity is now demanded. Simply "painting by the numbers" no longer works in a world that demands so much more than a single prescribed answer. So today's successful executives must embrace self-development and learning. At a time when organizations can no longer guarantee work for life, individuals have taken on "Learning for Life" as the paradigm model.

Fortunately, such an approach also helps to meet pressing organizational needs. Everywhere we find cycles becoming shorter, with businesses in a never-ending race to find a quicker way to reach a globally expanding market. The trend is also for work to make increasing demands on employees' time. In such a frenetic climate, executives cannot undertake learning as a separate activity. To keep technical knowledge up-to-date, an executive may have no alternative but to spend time off-site, but leadership skills are best learned in the workplace and on the job. Learning must be applied immediately, responding to issues of the moment. This "just-in-time" teaching of skills is another form of executive coaching.

Executives need knowledge and skills to cope with situations as they come up. Often the circumstances are ambiguous. An executive may need to deal with a troublesome colleague; start a new assignment; present a difficult business argument; become more "visible"; or communicate more effectively with direct reports. The coach fits into the new learning model perfectly by allowing the executive to learn, modify, and apply a suitable approach in a particular business situation. Coaching allows executives to learn while at work, while keeping up the pace.

Striving for Success

Executives are invariably concerned with issues of corporate, team, and individual success. Because they face new rules of competition and new definitions of success, modern executives must find ways to align and balance these components. They must choose activities that truly add value over efforts that merely appear effective. This may seem little more than common sense, yet it reflects a genuine attitudinal shift in the workplace. It is another important area in which a coach can challenge and validate the client's perspective. This can also engender a sense of empowerment in that the executive wants to "do the right thing."

Within the broad category of "knowledge work," mundane and passive stewardship continues to lose ground to creativity and innovation. In addition, the basis of reward is shifting from an emphasis on effort to a focus on results. Arriving at the office well before the official start time and regularly working late into the night and on weekends are no longer automatically seen as characteristics of an effective executive.

Technology has allowed working styles to be more open and flexible while, at the same time, allowing work and life to impinge on each other, making both more stressful. Coaches can help executives to negotiate this delicate interface without being intrusive. Once again, the coach needs an ethical position and rules of engagement or terms of reference within which to operate. As we embrace information technology, giving ourselves more freedom in choice of lifestyle, we usually prefer—and even insist—that the value of our work contribution be measured in terms of outcomes or results. For knowledge workers in particular, the time of day or the geographic location of their efforts has become irrelevant. Outcome, not input, now attracts reward.

In yesterday's business world, the "numbers" and the routine mechanics of operations lulled organizations and their executives into believing that they were fulfilling a purpose simply by repeating traditional formulas. Certainly, repetition worked well in the factory model, but repetition is no longer a guarantee for success in a service and knowledge economy. A new style of leadership is called for. This shift from management to leadership is primarily one of outlook and attitude. Leadership moves us from rigidity to flexibility; leadership allows us to adapt in a more uncertain environment; leadership urges people to take responsibility, to take the initiative, to do the right thing, and thereby to excel.

It is not surprising to find that dynamic leadership is overthrowing the familiar and traditional "social norms" established in the era of stable hierarchical management. The successful executive today must follow this trend in order to achieve desired outcomes in a business world that is becoming more volatile.

Leadership has become crucial in creating value and achieving competitive advantage in the modern work organization. Leadership is not exclusive to a few "top executives"; it is class-free and pervasive. A leader treats people as responsible adults and encourages all to act in the interest of mutual success. A leader promotes a sense of individual worth and community and diligently directs activity toward the business ambitions of the organization. The "culture" and leadership style of an organization are not a consequence of doing work in a certain way. Instead, they are a healthy context within which excellent work is done. Managers motivate, whereas leaders inspire. Inspired companies are winners. Corporations need far fewer managers and far more leaders, and coaching offers a direct and practical way to instill this new culture into corporate life.

Coaching provides a route to leadership. Coaching can unlock the latent leadership potential in managers and reinforce leadership where it already exists. A culture of coaching can nurture leadership. And when coaching aligns the development of the individual, the team, and the organization toward a mutual definition of success, then coaching becomes leadership. Leadership through coaching offers a strategic and practical direction for all.

Coaching in Practice

It can be as lonely at the periphery of a modern networked organization as it is at the top of a traditional pyramid. Problems can come from talking too freely inside an organization, however flat or virtual it may be. Work colleagues become tomorrow's interested parties. Truly innovative concepts can sound like crazy ideas in the early stages, and few executives want to take the risk of appearing foolish. Even private discussions can contain political topics that, when touched on, even tentatively, can establish a position from which it is difficult to reverse. Leaders need a safe and supportive theater or laboratory in which to rehearse and refine their ideas. Coaching meets this need.

Coaches present executives with an opportunity to engage in a dialogue of development. Where there is no coach, the chance for this reflective dialogue may be missed. When executives have no one to talk to, there is no tested or evolved dialogue, there is no attitude formation, and so an important part of executive thinking—thinking through—is missing. In all these ways, coaching is supportive of executive and organizational learning. Coaching provides a platform for practical action directed toward intelligent and strategic intent.

Every organization is different; each has its unique definition of success. In whatever way the dimensions of success are articulated by each board, team, or individual executive, coaches are charged with finding a developmental path to progress. In striving for success, leaders must find ways to advance the business, while respecting core organizational values and fundamental beliefs. These must be understood by coaches at a visceral level. To deliver quality, a coach must see far beyond the superficial level, at which all corporate value statements look similar, and discover in detail the actual values in play. Then again, as the world progresses to continuously repaint an ever-emerging strategic organizational context, these values are destined to develop and change over time.

External and Internal Agents

Most leaders acknowledge that, in order to remain healthy, an organization must reach out to its stakeholders and into the environment. Indeed, a modern organization will actively extend its social fabric through dialogue with coaches, consultants, and others. Yet, it is a source of astonishment to many that an organization's maintenance functions require any interaction from outside.

The traditional or legal definition of a corporation can fool us into believing that it will remain forever self-sufficient. The need for external nurturing agents may seem to fly in the face of this belief. However, the "outside" or external aspect of the organization has been long recognized in "systems theory" as extremely important. In today's organizations, interaction with the environment is being rediscovered as a vital activity required to reduce business risk. Here again, the coaching opportunity supports another crucial facet of leadership: the need to be in touch with the reality beyond the formal boundary of the organization.

Yet, an organization that regards executive coaching as a service provided entirely by external suppliers can never attain a true climate of leadership. Modern corporations must be capable of maintaining cohesion in the newly evolving, flatter, and networked workplaces. Today's leaders do not seek to set themselves apart, but instead are determined to replicate their best leadership behaviors in those around them. They are also open to absorbing, as well as propagating, such exemplary behaviors. Thus, internal coaching—or internalized coaching—is vital to working in the modern, cross-functional network in which all participants find it natural to coach.

However flat an organization may be, executives will always need to interact with their direct reports. Here again, coaching provides the executive with a foundation for dialogue that is well-suited to leading "free agents," who are less likely to respect positional power as a legitimate motivator.

The term "mentoring" is widely used to describe an activity closely related to coaching. A mentor is likely to have had a successful personal track record in a role similar to that of the client. Thus, the nature of this relationship may tend to contain relatively more content than process. Reputation and trust toward the mentor are powerful determinants in making the chemistry work. A senior mentor can be a great asset who is likely to be able to tap into an otherwise inaccessible range of useful business contacts.

When working in the same organization, a mentor requires no learning curve to absorb culture. Steps should be taken—and periodic checks should be made—to ensure that the internal mentor does not inadvertently become a compromised interested party in the day-to-day operations of the person being mentored. There is only one other essential qualification: a good mentor simply needs to be a good coach.

The coaching approach is also spilling into all kinds of work relationships. For example, some organizations have instituted an informal "buddy" system, which can be little more than sharing contact information at training events. Some larger divisions of Fortune 500 companies are now putting coaches on the payroll as full-time employees. It is not uncommon for senior executives to take their coaches with them when switching companies. This becomes part of the hiring negotiation process, along with share options and other benefits. The sheer pervasiveness of the coaching relationship in organizations today—whether inside, outside, or between organizations—confirms that coaching is seen as an effective style of working with the blurring boundaries in and around organizations.

A Blueprint for Success

Coaching has been able to draw practitioners from many established fields, including consultancy and counseling. An important challenge facing them all is to link personal development of individual clients to attainment of solid business results. Only when this can be achieved consistently can a coaching program hope to fully justify the investment that it demands.

The formula for success in achieving this will display a number of characteristics. Coaches must address issues that are individual, team, and organization-wide; they must act in a way congruent with the organization's style of leadership; they must promote and facilitate positive organizational development; they must be practical; and they must help in the achievement of business results.

In combining these elements, the Strategic Coaching Model (see Figure 11.1) provides a modern blueprint for business success. Couched in a culture of modern leadership and based on the powerful dynamics of human interaction, the model simply asserts that coaching is at its best when located at the heart of strategy.

◆ ◆ ◆

Laurence S. Lyons (www.lslyons.com) is an accomplished coach, consultant, public speaker, and author. A former technical director at Digital Equipment Corporation, he has been described as a "leading authority on business transformation" by Henley Management College, where he is a member of the associate faculty and Founding Research Director of the Future Work Forum.

Dr. Lyons is regarded as a pioneer in the field of executive coaching; he has coached hundreds of senior and high-potential executives in organizations in the United States and across Europe. Many of his personal coaching clients are to be found in *Who's Who.*

Dr. Lyons holds a Ph.D. and MSc from Brunel University and the CIM (Diploma in Marketing). He is an invited member of the Leader to Leader Institute Thought Leaders Forum (formerly the Drucker Foundation). Contact him at lslyons@lslyons.com.

CHAPTER TWELVE

CROSSING OVER

Making the Transition from Executive to Executive Coach

Brian Tracy

What is the highest paid work in America? *Thinking*!

The value and importance of any decision can be measured by the likely *consequences* of that decision. The highest paid work in America is thinking because of the enormous possible consequences of thinking well or thinking poorly. Your ability to think effectively, and to help other people think effectively about their lives and work, are more important than any other contribution you can make.

The market demand for personal coaches at all levels, and in all areas of activity, is growing rapidly today. The reason for this is simple: *coaching works!*

We know that, in sports, all top athletes have coaches, sometimes several. In many cases, average players become stars as the result of the right coaching, from the right person, at the right time, with the right focus. This should be your goal as well.

Creating a Second Career

The official retirement age in America today is about sixty-five. Set in Germany by Otto Von Bismarck in 1870, this age was picked up in the Social Security debates of 1934-1935 by Franklin D. Roosevelt and Congress. Today, however, it has no relationship to reality.

The average white-collar worker or executive at the age of sixty-five is as sharp and as alert as a fifty-year-old in 1950. Today, we find a direct relationship between how busy and active you keep yourself, how involved you are in the lives and work of other people, and the quality of your life. The busier and more active you are, the healthier you will be, the more energy you will have, the stronger will be your immune system, and the longer you will live.

What this means is that the true retirement age today is really closer to seventy-five than to sixty-five. So if you make the transition into executive coaching, you can create a second career for yourself that will keep you *in the game* and performing at your best for many years.

Start with Yourself

The market for coaching has increased by 500 percent in the past few years. Thousands of people have hung out their shingles as "Personal Coaches" or "Executive Coaches." Virtually anyone can get into coaching at some level. All that is really required is desire, experience, and ability, which everyone claims to have.

For you personally to make the transition to executive coaching, you should obey one of Murphy's Laws: *Whatever you want to do, you have to do something else first.*

The first thing is to ask yourself the question, "Why?" *Why* do you want to be an executive coach? What is your aim? What is your mission? What is your purpose? What are your goals? Why would you choose to be an executive coach rather than to do something else with your time and your life?

Probably the best answer to this question is that you want to help *other* people realize their full potential by learning and practicing some of the things that have helped you to realize more of *your* potential throughout your career. Coaching is very much a "helping profession." Only those individuals who genuinely care about helping other people are capable of becoming excellent coaches.

Prepare for Competition

The first thing you will discover when you decide to become a coach is that there is an enormous amount of *competition* out there. Many people think that coaching is both highly paid and fairly easy. This conclusion is both true and false. Some coaches do an extraordinary job with their clients and charge substantial fees, but the 80/20 rule applies. Fully 80 percent of coaches struggle to make ends meet.

For you to truly excel in coaching, which is your goal, you must approach this new occupation as if you were starting a new business. The more time you spend in *thinking* about the how, when, where, and why of coaching before you begin, the more effective you will be in the long run.

Imagine No Limitations

Start with your ideal vision of your career as a professional executive coach. Imagine waving a magic wand and creating the perfect job for yourself. What would it look like?

During this visioning exercise, imagine that you have *no limitations* on what you could be, have, or do as a coach. Imagine that you can learn everything you need to learn, overcome every obstacle that will appear in your way, and achieve any goal that you set for yourself. Imagine that you have unlimited potential.

The greater *clarity* you have with regard to your ideal future vision as a coach, the easier it will be for you to plan, prepare, and implement your plans. Remember the Six P Formula for Success: *Proper Prior Planning Prevents Poor Performance.*

Decide on Your Mission, Purpose, and Goals

Once you have a clear vision of your ideal future as a coach, you can define your *mission*. Your mission is what you want to accomplish for your individual clients. It can be as simple as, *"My mission is to help my clients to achieve the very most of health, happiness, and high income in their lives and careers."*

Once you have determined your vision and your mission, you must determine your *purpose*, the "reasons why" you want to be a coach. For instance, "My purpose is to utilize my talents, skills, and experiences to help other people to be more effective than they ever could be without my help."

Finally, once you have established your vision, purpose, and mission, you must set clear, specific, written *goals* for your coaching business. You must determine how much you want to earn, how many hours you want to work, how many clients you will serve at a single time, and how you will measure success in each area.

Identify Your Special Talents and Skills

Begin with yourself. Identify the most important things that you have learned in your career that would be helpful to other people. You must be absolutely clear about what you are going to bring to your coaching clients based on your own knowledge and experience.

Even more important, you must be sure that coaching is the right choice of occupation for your future career. Have you been a coach or mentor to other people in the past? Do you have a successful track record of guiding and influencing others to be more effective in their work and personal lives? Most of all, do you enjoy the process of working with executives on a one-to-one basis to help them improve the quality of their lives and work? Last, are you good at it? This is very important.

Market Yourself Strategically

There are four key principles in strategic marketing that will apply in creating your new coaching career. The more accurately you think through each of these principles, the more effective you will be and the faster you will get the results you desire.

1. Specialize in a Particular Area. Principle number one is *specialization*. This is the starting point of your success. You must decide where and how you are going to specialize in bringing your unique talents and abilities to the coaching market.

You can specialize by the level of executive that you are most qualified to coach, at least at the beginning. Some coaches work with individual salespeople. Others work with sales managers. Some coaches work with mid-level executives; others work only with "C" level executives in Fortune 1000 corporations.

You may decide to specialize in a particular industry in which you have considerable experience. This is always a good idea, because you will have both confidence and credentials in this industry, which will make it easier for you to get started and to get results.

You may decide to specialize in a geographical area. You may decide to specialize with a particular level of manager or executive who has a particular problem or need that you feel you are uniquely qualified to satisfy.

Practice *idealization* when you think about specializing. Imagine your ideal coaching client, the client you would most enjoy coaching and who would most benefit from your special talents. If you could write out a description of your perfect coaching client, what would he or she look like?

2. Set Yourself Apart. The second part of strategic marketing is *differentiation*. This is your area of "competitive advantage," and it is perhaps the most important factor in determining how successful you will be as a coach.

In what way can you differentiate yourself from any other coach who is also interested in working with your ideal client? What is your personal "area of excellence"? What is it that you have done in the past that makes you *superior* in your ability to coach the kind of people you want to coach?

Especially, what is your "unique selling proposition?" If a decision maker were to ask you why he or she should retain your services rather than the services of someone else, what would your answer be, in fewer than fifteen words?

The development of competitive advantage, differentiating yourself from your competitors so that you are seen to be the superior choice, is the very essence of successful marketing. The greater clarity you have in this area, the easier it will be for you to select the ideal coaching situations for yourself.

3. Find Your Market Niche. The third key to strategic marketing is *segmentation*. Once you have determined your areas of specialization and differentiation, you then ask: "Who and where are the prospective coaching clients who can most benefit, the soonest, from the special qualities and abilities that I bring to the coaching relationship?"

Imagine that you were going to write an advertisement for your services. Instead of talking about yourself and your background, your advertisement would be like a "help wanted" ad, in which you describe the ideal coaching client you would like to attract. How would you describe him or her, in terms of age, occupation, income, work situation, location, and size of business? When you write an advertisement describing your *perfect customer*, you will be defining the exact market segment on which you should concentrate.

4. Focus Your Efforts. The fourth marketing principle is that of *concentration*. In this final phase, you concentrate all your time, resources, and energies on seeking out and persuading exactly those prospective clients you can help the most with what you bring to the table. You can even develop a quick *checklist* of qualifications that you review with a prospective client. If the prospective client does not fulfill the description of the person that you are most ideally suited to help, you will be able to determine that this person may not be the right client for you.

The Marketing Mix

In addition to the four keys to marketing strategy, there are five "Ps" that you must define clearly on paper before you launch your coaching career. These are your *product, price, promotion, place,* and *positioning.*

1. Determine Your Value Offering. Your *product* is a clear description of your coaching *process*. You lay out a map or blueprint that describes how you will work with a particular client over a specific period of time. This map will explain what you will do in your initial meetings, how you will establish goals for the coaching process, how you will create benchmarks and systems of accountability for your client, and the clear, specific results that your coaching process will achieve over time.

The number one reason that people do not hire coaches is because they are vague or unclear about exactly the process that will take place once they do. Your clarity with regard to the exact product and the process you offer will help you tremendously in this regard.

2. Decide How Much to Charge. The second aspect of marketing is your *pricing* structure. A good rule of thumb is for you to set your annual income goal at about *double* what you are currently earning. This is because 50 percent of your revenues will be consumed in support activities and expenses that are currently being paid by your company. In other words, to realize your current income, you will have to charge twice as much as you are currently earning, at least in the beginning.

Once you have determined how much you want to earn, you must then determine how much you can charge per hour as an executive coach. This will depend on your current level in your industry, the industry norms for coaching in the areas in which you wish to specialize, and your competition. This number is a moving target. You must be prepared to adjust your hourly rate up or down depending on external circumstances.

If you only wish to work part-time, you must decide how many hours per week, per month, and per year you intend to invest in coaching, and then decide how much you will have to charge per hour in order to achieve your financial goals. Some coaches charge $25 per hour; some charge $250 per hour. Top coaches charge $2,500 per hour and are fully booked. Your pricing strategy is a fundamental and essential part of your business planning.

3. Determine How to Market Your Services. The third part of marketing is your *promotional* activities. Exactly how are you going to market and sell your services against competition? You will require business cards, brochures, letterhead, envelopes, and other sales materials that tell what you do.

How will you make yourself known to your prospective clients? Will you be able to promote yourself via word-of-mouth, the very best and least expensive method? Or will you have to advertise and promote your services in a variety of other ways?

The very best way to promote yourself is to piggyback on your existing contacts, both within your company and within your industry. Go from the known to the unknown. Start where you are already comfortable and familiar with the environment. Your ability to *sell your services* is going to be the determining factor of how many of your services you actually sell.

4. Decide Where You Are Going to Work. The fourth P refers to *place*. Where are you going to work? Will you conduct your consulting services in the offices and places of business of your clients? Will you consult by telephone? Will you use email or other forms of correspondence? What geographical area will you work in? Do you want to conduct live coaching within driving distance of your home, or are you prepared to travel to work with clients farther away?

5. Determine the Words That Describe You. The fifth P stands for *positioning*. Your positioning in the hearts and minds of your clients and prospective clients can be as important as anything else you do. Here is the rule: *Everything counts!* Everything that you do either helps or hurts. Everything adds up or takes away. Everything about your appearance, sales, marketing, promotional materials, and reputation contributes to the words that people use to describe you when you are not there.

The best companies are those that give a lot of thought to how their activities affect the impressions that their customers have of them. The very best coaches do the same.

Again, imagine that you have a magic wand and that you could wave it to create any impression or reputation that you want about yourself. If you could write down a description of how you want other people to think about you and talk about you, what *words* would you use? Whatever answers you come up with, you must then be sure that everything you do helps to create this *positioning statement* among your clients and would-be clients.

Three Key Areas of Coaching Expertise

As an executive coach, there are three key areas in which you must excel in your work with your clients. They are *goal setting* in the three key areas of life, *setting priorities* in every area, and *personality development* issues. It is to improve in each of these areas that a person hires a coach in the first place. The better you are in these areas, the more effective you will be, and the more clients you will attract.

1. Goal Setting. The three key areas of goal setting are *career goals, family goals,* and *personal goals.*

Career Goals. In helping your clients set career goals, you help them develop *clarity* five and ten years into the future. You help them think through and define how much they want to earn and what skills they will have to acquire or develop to achieve that level of income. You help them develop strategies to become better known in their industries and to develop contacts who can help them. Your central focus in working on career goals revolves around income improvement and promotion.

Family Goals. In helping a client deal with family goals, clarity is essential. You help your clients define their ideal lifestyles. If they had no limitations, what improvements would they like to make in their relationships with their spouses or children and the ways that they spend leisure time, both together and alone? In this area, the critical concept is that of *balance* between career and family.

Personal Goals. The third area of goal setting has to do with personal goals, especially with regard to health, fitness, longevity, and retirement. Your clients need to develop clarity regarding their financial goals. How much do they want to earn? How much do they want to save? What kind of an estate do they want to accumulate over time?

Other areas of personal goal setting have to do with learning and personal development. They may include involvement with church activities or political parties.

They may include creative goals and personal fulfillment goals. The more you can help a client in this area, the better will be his or her overall quality of life.

2. Setting Priorities. The second area of coaching has to do with setting priorities. Once you have helped the client develop clarity with regard to career, family, and personal goals, you help him or her to set priorities in every area of life.

There are many books and articles on the subjects of time and personal management, and you should be thoroughly familiar with the various strategies and techniques that a person can use to take control of his or her time and life.

3. Personality Development. The third area of coaching that is most in demand has to do with personality issues. Many people are being held back because they lack certain personal skills that render them less effective than they could be. They may sometimes come across as abrupt, arrogant, impatient, rude, and demanding. Your job is to help them identify the areas in which they feel improvement could help them and then give them guidance and encouragement to modify their behaviors in these areas. Sometimes this form of coaching can be the most helpful of all.

Physician, Heal Thyself!

If a person wishes to become a psychiatrist or psychotherapist, the first thing he or she is required to do, after completing training, is to go through a process of psychotherapy. It is only by experiencing the process of counseling as a patient that a psychotherapist can understand what is necessary to genuinely help someone else.

In the same sense, one of the best ways for you to become an *excellent* executive coach is to think through and write out your answers to the various questions and concerns presented in this article. By thinking through these questions and issues for yourself, you will become vastly more competent in helping your clients to think through these issues for themselves.

By taking the time to determine your areas of specialization, differentiation, segmentation, and concentration, you will be able to advise your clients how to best use these thinking tools to be more effective in their work.

By thinking through the issues of product, price, promotion, place, and positioning, you can help your clients to be vastly more effective in their work, to be paid more, and to be promoted faster.

Perhaps most important of all, by thinking through the key issues in this article, you can decide whether executive coaching is the right field for you and, if so, determine how you can become a great executive coach.

◆ ◆ ◆

Brian Tracy is one of the foremost authorities on personal effectiveness in the United States and throughout the world. He works intensively each year with entrepreneurs and executives in large and small companies, showing them how to identify clear priorities in every area of their lives. His clients learn practical strategies and techniques to double and triple their key results while gaining more time for their families and personal lives.

Tracy is the author of thirty-six books, including *TurboCoach* and *Turbostrategy*, and more than three hundred audiovideo learning programs, many of which have been published in twenty-two languages.

His Focal Point Advanced Coaching & Mentoring Program, which he gives personally in San Diego four times each year, is perhaps the finest personal coaching program in the world. Contact: www.briantracy.com; briantracy@briantracy.com.

CHAPTER THIRTEEN

SURVIVING THE TRANSITION FROM LINE MANAGER TO EXECUTIVE COACH

David Noer

Wally's Wake-Up Call

Wally was an outstanding general manager who bombed as an executive coach. As a line manager, he was focused, decisive, disciplined, and able to give direction and purpose to a large, complex organization. As a coach, he was judgmental, controlling, and more concerned with his needs than with those of his client. Unfortunately, I saw it coming and wasn't able to stop it. When Wally, a former client, retired early and decided to become a coach, he asked to buy me lunch and "pick my brain." He didn't really want to hear what I had to say, so his brain-pickings were slim, and despite the good food, I left with a bad taste in my mouth. A year later we had lunch again. This time I picked up the tab, and Wally was much more receptive to the outcomes of his cerebral mining. It had been a difficult year, in which he had learned the difference between what had made him successful as a line manager and what is necessary to be an effective coach.

Wally's wake-up call was not unique. With the increasing acceptance and use of executive coaching, there are many former line managers struggling to become coaches. Understanding the differences between the skills of management and coaching is a key success factor for those managers who have decided to become executive coaches. For those who agree that the acquisition pain is worth the gain, here are some practical tips to facilitate that transition and to avoid the big three derailment factors for executive coaches: confusion, collusion, and lack of clarity as to who is the client; solutions looking for problems; and the creation of a dependency relationship—all of which are discussed later in this article and in more detail in the article "The Three Derailment Factors," published in *Coaching for Leadership*.[1]

Differences Between Line Management and Coaching Skills

For many, the transition from line management to coaching is a painful experience. Some managers have become very effective coaches, while others move into other endeavors. The following perspectives contrast managerial and coaching skills and summarize developmental challenges.

- *The approach is opposite.* Successful line managers get things done using the traditional skills of controlling, evaluating, directing, and planning. These traditional "ings" have their roots in turn-of-the-century scientific management and are found in the curriculum of most of today's business schools. Managers using these skills are task driven. To succeed, managers often take personal responsibility to make things happen. On the other hand, successful coaches engage in helping relationships. Helping relationships are the opposite of controlling relationships. The core helping skills are empowering, listening, facilitating, and supporting. The payoff is enabling *the person being coached* to take action. The very skills that make line managers successful—controlling, evaluating, and directing, although effective in the managerial world, are trouble when applied to a coaching relationship because they will make the person being coached defensive and angry. See Figure 13.1. for a summary of the differences.
- *Helping skills are not the currency of the realm in the managerial world.* In today's lean, mean, downsized environment, managers are rewarded for doing more with less, doing things quickly, and, in many cases, viewing people as costs to be minimized as opposed to assets to be developed. Coaching requires patience, time, process skills, and person-centered relationships. As a result of this mismatch,

FIGURE 13.1. CHANGING LINE MANAGEMENT "INGS" TO COACHING "INGS."

From	To
Controlling	Helping
Evaluating	Empowering
Directing	Supporting
Planning	Listening

effective coaching skills are often negatively reinforced in organizational environments.

- *Developing authentic, relevant coaching skills requires both courage and hard work.* Most line managers already have good business and system skills. The two skill sets that typically require development are intra-personal insight and interpersonal competence. Intra-personal insight requires self-awareness and an understanding of the effects our drives and motivations have on others. For example, many managers have high control needs. In order to be effective coaches, these managers must be self-aware and manage themselves to ensure that their own control needs do not get in the way of a client-centered coaching relationship. Intra-personal insight requires the courage to look in the mirror, see ourselves, and adjust our behavior to help our clients, not ourselves. Interpersonal competence involves listening, attending, and communication skills centered on others. Developing intra-personal insight and interpersonal competence is a *good news* and *bad news* proposition. The good news is that most successful managers are smart enough to learn these skills. The bad news is that it is an against-the-grain experience, that is, it is as much an emotional journey as it is a cognitive one.

Ten Tips for Line Managers When Engaging in a Coaching Relationship

The following tips are the result of my experiences with a number of people who made the transition from line management to executive coaching. They offer a practical checklist of some of the major *do's* and *don'ts* in a coaching relationship.

1. Start with the person being coached. Gain a solid understanding of where he or she is emotionally. Avoid the following:
   - Assuming he or she is feeling the way you want him or her to feel.
   - Making speeches.
   - Starting with logic, policy, or data.
   - Moving the focus from the person being coached to "the organization," or "strategy," or "the market," or your own ideas, perspective, or feelings.
2. Use feeling probes, such as the following:
   - "There is a lot of change going on. How are you feeling about things?"
   - "I'm wondering how you're handling all this change on a personal level. How is it affecting you?"
   - Tip 1: Don't be reluctant to begin with some disclosure of your own, such as, "I don't know about you, but I'm a bit confused."
   - Tip 2: Don't worry about coming off as clumsy or intrusive; the people you are coaching are *dying* to externalize their feelings. They will be flattered!

3. Demonstrate understanding and active listening by naming the feeling or paraphrasing:
   - "Sounds like you are anxious about your job."
   - "Let me see if I understand. You're OK with the decision, but are upset with the timing and anxious about the increased workload."
   - "You're feeling uncertain about where you'd fit in."
   - "What I'm hearing is that you aren't sure you'd want to relocate even if there were a good job at the other end."

4. Avoid prescribing. The name of the game is helping the people you coach externalize their feelings and not assuming responsibility for "fixing" their problems. Don't say the following:
   - "What you need to do is. . . ."
   - "You shouldn't feel that way. It's better to feel. . . ."
   - "Unless you change your attitude, you're not going to get anywhere. Here is the first thing you should work on. . . ."
   - "OK, you've given me a lot to do. Let me work on some of those issues and I'll get back to you."

5. Help frame the issues, but leave the person you are coaching in control. Here are some examples:
   - "Sounds like you've got to decide whether to stick around and see what happens or look outside."
   - "It appears that you're stuck between your anger at the organization and your excitement over your new job. You need to find a way to get through that."
   - "You've really got to make a choice of holding on to the past or letting go and moving on."

6. Help is defined by the helpee, not the helper. This is a major issue for line managers conditioned to direct and problem solve. Don't let your need to solve the person you are coaching's problem eclipse the problem.

7. Monitor the airtime. The person being coached should talk more than the coach.

8. Silence is awkward, but it often leads to a deeper level of interaction. Don't be afraid of it. Many managers are compelled to initiate structure and talk. Effective coaches are able to harness the power of silence.

9. Don't wallow in feelings. When the time is right, move from the heart to the head:
   - "The context for this discussion is the merger. Here are the milestones your division agreed to meet."
   - "This might help give you some perspective. The organizational game plan is. . . ."

10. Helping involves multiple body parts: the heart (feelings), the head (concepts and thoughts), and the feet (action). Effective coaches use all three.
    - Most managers have been conditioned into a head-and-foot orientation. Working with feelings is usually an against-the-grain activity.
    - Heart work is very powerful, particularly if the person you are coaching is going through a major transition. Many line managers are uncomfortable dealing with feelings and emotions and thus miss the opportunity to authentically connect with the person being coached.

Beware the Big Three

The big three derailment factors in executive coaching are alive and well. During the past few years, I have noticed that managers making the transition to coaching are particularly susceptible. What follows is a brief description of each factor and some suggestions for line managers.

Factor One: Confusion, Collusion, and Lack of Clarity as to Who Is the Client

When the client is anyone other than the person receiving the coaching, there is danger of derailment. This is particularly true when the boss wants you to "fix" someone or the management committee wants you to "help" a top executive. Coaching is a very personal relationship and it needs to be completely confidential and totally voluntary. As former line managers network in order to build their coaching practices, they are frequently hired by their friends to help someone else. Although these contacts can serve to open doors, contracting should be done directly with the person receiving the coaching, and that person should be given free choice with regard to proceeding. Extra efforts should be made to assure the client of confidentiality, and the board or the client's boss should never be given any information without the client's explicit permission. However, even with the best of intentions, there is always the possibility that the client will retain a coach who is referred by an executive in order to please the boss or because he or she is afraid to say no. This is definitely not a good way to begin an authentic coaching relationship.

Factor Two: Solutions Looking for Problems—Coaches Enamored of a Single Model or Approach

All coaching clients are not the same. They often have very different needs, and a cookie-cutter approach will not work. Two of my recent clients will serve as examples. The first is a high-potential executive with a very real chance of becoming the CEO of a regional financial services company. He is great technically, but has a blind spot in regard to his people skills. Unless he makes some changes, he won't get the top job. We are currently working on increasing his awareness of the impact he has on others and skill building. The second client was hired into a senior position from outside her company. She is having a very difficult time accepting and adjusting to the organizational culture. We are working on value clarification, behavioral rehearsal, and testing the limits of her ability to make changes.

The way I work with these two clients is driven by their needs, not a single model, diagnostic approach, or assessment process. Many new coaches have a tendency to look for a universal tool that they can apply to all clients. Once they find one—an instrument, an analytical process, or a structured intervention—they try to force fit it to all situations. Former line managers tend to apply processes and techniques that worked within the culture of their past organization, regardless of whether they fit the client's organizational environment. New coaches need to develop a wide repertoire of approaches, treat each situation as unique, and above all, listen to and respect the perspectives and ideas of their clients.

Factor Three: Creation of a Dependency Relationship

When done well, coaching is very powerful. It is, however, a temporary and artificial process. Coaches are not employees or bosses and they lose their value if they behave as such. The goal of coaches should be to empower clients to solo, to take action without them. Too often, clients and coaches collude to create a mutual dependency relationship; coaches need the revenue or the illusion of control, and clients need a crutch. This kind of dependency relationship perverts the coaching role, diminishes both the coach and the client, and trivializes the coaching process. Former line managers with histories of long-term employment relationships in bureaucratic organizations have a tendency to prolong coaching relationships. This is particularly true if they are perceived by the clients as strong and take a paternalistic approach. It is very important that the coach and the client agree on an exit strategy at the beginning of the coaching relationship. It is even more important that they adhere to it.

A Powerful Gift

For those line managers willing to make the necessary adjustments to their skills and orientation, coaching is a wonderful career capstone. Helping people grow and develop is affirming and gratifying. When managers combine their business experience with a coaching orientation, they bring a best-of-both-worlds skill set to the coaching relationship. This equips them to offer a powerful gift to their clients and themselves.

Note

1. Noer, D. The three derailment factors. In M. Goldsmith, L. Lyons, & A. Freas, *Coaching for leadership.* San Francisco: Jossey-Bass, 2000.

◆ ◆ ◆

David Noer is an author, researcher, consultant, and educator. He has written six books and numerous academic and popular articles on the application of human spirit to leadership. Noer is the Frank Holt, Jr., Professor of Business Leadership at Elon University and heads his own consulting firm in Greensboro, North Carolina. His consulting practice involves executive coaching; team development; dealing with the human aspects of mergers, acquisitions, and downsizing; mission, vision, and value development; as well as strategic planning. The common thread of his work involves helping organizations and people through transitions by harnessing the power of applied human spirit. Contact: www.noerconsulting.com; david@noerconsulting.com.

CHAPTER FOURTEEN

COACHING BUSINESS LEADERS

Richard Gauthier and David Giber

In our work we are sometimes asked to comment on the difference between coaching senior-level leaders and coaching individuals at other levels. In answering, we find ourselves talking about impact and consequence, both of which seem more far-reaching when coaching leaders. Simply put, the stakes are often higher. In *Leadership Is an Art*, Max DePree writes, "The first responsibility of a leader is to define reality. The last is to say thank you." In between the first and last responsibilities, DePree describes the leader as "steward of relationships, of assets and legacy, of momentum and effectiveness, of civility and values."[1] The process of effective leadership is complex and the consequences, both good and bad, affect many people inside and outside the organization. Coaching senior-level leaders, especially those in business, also has far-reaching consequences, especially when it involves developing or refining the skills and competencies required to deliver on the stewardship responsibilities of leadership.

Leadership matters. It follows then that the practice of coaching leaders matters too, and we should make every effort to maximize our opportunities for success. For us, the keys to ensuring a successful development challenge lie in the set up, the preparation, and the preliminary work that set the foundation for success. Granted, it's not the glitzy part of the coaching engagement, but attending to the fundamentals is essential for a substantive developmental experience that will make a difference. Beyond the basics, as business coaches, we need to be concerned about aligning the development plan for the leader with measurable objectives based on the goals of the organization. Our goal is to help participants develop a full understanding of where they are currently (in terms of competence, behavior, effectiveness, support from their stakeholders, and approach) versus where they need to be to hit the goals. Often, we find that their stated priorities and "agenda" are out of synch with how they actually spend their time and attention, which limits their effectiveness. The development plan is based not only on behavioral feedback but also on a synthesis of information on what the participants need to accomplish strategically—where and how they will move their organization forward into the future.

Mary Beth O'Neil points out that "the essence of coaching is helping leaders get unstuck from their dilemmas and assisting them in transferring their learning into results for the organization."[2] In the coaching process we practice and teach, we sometimes find that novice coaches see their role as helping leaders find solutions to the shortcomings they exhibit or the issues they confront. In our teaching, we emphasize that "the solution" is the easy part; the coaching challenge is to help leaders understand what the problem is and how it is impacting their organization and to develop the capacity to move toward a solution and the capability to encourage and coach other leaders to do the same. We've found that effective coaching creates leaders who often turn out to be effective coaches.

The Coaching Process

The coaching process we use is fairly standard. It generally consists of five phases: contracting, assessment, goal setting, development planning, and evaluation. Although all five steps are important, we try to guard against moving too quickly through the "set-up," the preliminary assessment and planning phase that identifies the issues and sets the foundation for the success or failure of the engagement. In fact, the set-up may occupy the first two to three months of meetings. The questioning abilities (along with the patience) of the coach are key. The success or failure of the entire engagement is often dependent on the coach's willingness to gather the pieces of an emerging puzzle, help assemble a clear picture of the goals and challenges at hand, and partner with the client to lay a firm foundation for success. We'd like to share the process and tools we use with senior-level business leaders to assemble those pieces (the data), put them together (the goal), and build that foundation (the development plan) for success.

Our preparation begins before we contract with the client. We have indicators that help us determine whether or not the engagement has a chance for success. We won't, for example, coach someone whose manager we are already coaching. If two people we are coaching within an organization have a reporting or interdependent relationship, too often what should be an act of coaching becomes an act of mediation. Besides, coaching is about advocacy, and a coach should never have to choose between two client positions on an issue.

We also won't coach clients who are reluctant to be coached but begrudgingly agree because their leader wants them "fixed." If a client doesn't recognize the issue, acknowledge the problem, and bring a sense of urgency to change, things are not really going to change. Coaching is often a little about repair and a lot about development. Fixing the leader's reluctant employee is almost always about temporary repair, seldom about meaningful development, and the improvement is generally not sustained. Under the "fix my employee" category, we're more interested in coaching the frustrated manager than the employee.

Finally, if the client to be coached has already been written off by determined key powerbrokers in the organization or is targeted for termination, we aren't inclined to contribute. If, however, we receive a request to coach a leader, and all indicators point to developmental possibilities, we have an engagement and create a contract.

The Coaching Assessment

With senior leaders, we use a multi-part approach to assessment that allows us to develop a full sense of the person, the job challenge, and how he or she is perceived in the organization. The approach includes 360-degree feedback and/or interviews, a personality assessment, and having the client prepare an autobiography and a leadership assessment.

We first gather available data. Most helpful would be a 360-degree feedback document. If one is not available, we set one up. It is important to gain up-front commitment to the follow through on the 360-degree process, that is, some level of sharing data with those who have provided feedback. We often spend a full session understanding and interpreting the 360-degree results with our clients, sometimes connecting them to a personality assessment.

Among the best-validated personality assessments, the Hogan Personality Inventory is a favorite of ours because it tends to reveal the clients' self-perceptions while giving us insight into who they are and what they care about and value. One of our clients, for example, scored very, very low on the "sociability" part of the assessment and wanted to address the issue of his painful shyness. The impulse fix would be to develop "win friends and influence people" strategies that had him extend himself by walking around, reaching out to his people, glad-handing, small talking, and being as personable as possible. But the Hogan indicated that he didn't have it in him. We concluded that the lack of authenticity in the glad-handing approach would label him a phony beyond repair and that the developmental effort would fail. Instead, we and the client created a strategy that accounted for who he genuinely was (painfully shy) and, although it took longer, we built a support structure for him consisting of a few trusted, influential colleagues who cleared the way and helped establish his credentials. With that support, he hesitantly moved out of his comfort zone, extended himself as far as he could, was finally accepted, and ultimately proved to be an effective leader of his division.

Other instruments, of course, are available (Myers-Briggs, NEO PI-R, and others), and if our clients have recent samples, we include them in the initial assessment. We have found that the ideal situation is to combine a 360-degree evaluation with a personality assessment that covers the core aspects of personality that have impact on interpersonal and work effectiveness.

Next, we commit to interviewing managers, senior executives, direct reports, peers, and anyone else designated by the client. We prefer to conduct up-front interviews with the participant's direct manager, that person's manager, and often, the HR partner to validate the critical goals and strategies the person is responsible for. Meanwhile, the client commits to returning to some of those who offered 360-degree feedback and follows up with conversations designed to gain useful, specific information behind the numerical data. (See Marshall Goldsmith's article in this book, Chapter Four, "Coaching for Behavioral Change," for details on how to make the most of this follow-up process). Now, before turning our clients loose on those who provided feedback through the 360-degree assessment, we role play the follow-up interviews to prepare the client to listen carefully, probe in a positive way, and gather specific, actionable information, all while being open and avoiding any sign of defensiveness. We offer a precaution here. One-on-one role playing with a senior-level leader can be awkward, and we're often tempted to avoid it. No matter how sophisticated the client, those kinds of interviews can be difficult. They require non-defensive, open listening, asking open and closed questions, knowing the difference and when to use which, probing for specifics and examples, and using a body language and tone of voice that are reassuring and non-threatening. And, of course, practicing the hardest task of all: learning, in the face of criticism, to just say, "Thank you." All of this takes practice, and the client should not be practicing during those important information-gathering sessions. Coach and role play the client through the process before he or she goes out. Awkward as the role play is, the coach, the client, and those being interviewed will appreciate the effort.

Between sessions, we ask our clients to write and send us a one- to two-page autobiography. We offer no guidance beyond those stark requirements because we are interested in the choices the clients make when they have to sum up their lives in a few pages. The sorting process they go through, the incidents they cite, the people they reference, and the situations they describe are all very telling and helpful in understanding their value bases and shaping influences. It is also sometimes striking who or what they leave out of their narratives.

In our next session, we explain how we interpret what we read in the autobiography, and we reveal the insights we've gained and the assumptions we've made as we read the text and the subtext. This usually leads to a rich discussion and better understanding between the coach and the client. One manager's memorable autobiography began with a story of when he woke up on the ground outside his childhood home after one of his brothers had pushed him out of the second-story window and knocked him out. The more revealing parts of the story were not only that the client then proceeded to go back in the house and resume fighting with his brother but that their parents did not react with major consequences. Not surprisingly, as a manager, this client would often "test how much people could take." His tolerance for conflict led him into arguments that could be emotionally damaging to others, but for him were simply "good debates." For a person such as this, who was motivated to change his impact on others, the first step is to help him clarify the origins of his style as a leader and its powerful connection to his life experience. The second is to work with him to share with others his desire to change and his willingness to have them signal him if he is too persistent in an argument or not listening. Third is the need to anchor this change in two reinforcing systems: personal and business. In this case, the client's ability to deal with conflict was directly tied to whether the organization would promote him to a higher, more visible level of responsibility. We also urged to him to share his feedback and coaching commitments with his family, which became a further source of positive reinforcement as he changed.

At this session clients also share what they learned during the follow-up discussions with those who offered 360-degree feedback. Together we listen for and identify emerging themes. We then share the information gleaned from our interviews with the client's manager, direct reports, peers, and others. We seldom present this information in a written report. The temptation to review the text with an eye toward identifying the person interviewed is near irresistible. The client is encouraged to jot down themes as we read our notes. We stop at the end of each interview and ask the client what he or she heard and noted. For us as coaches, it's not enough to simply feed back the information. Rather, it's very important to understand how the client is processing and understanding the information. If the client hears something that we don't, or we pick up on something the client missed, it's up for discussion.

On the table at this point, we will have identified a number of potential developmental opportunities through the 360-degree data, follow-up discussions, personality assessments, biographical perspective, interview information, and theme identification. Now it's time to use the information to determine our focus for the rest of the engagement. We brainstorm a list of developmental possibilities, most of which should come from the client, not the coach. Once the list is complete and every conceivable possibility explored, we set a framework for deciding which one or two (seldom more than two) to concentrate on.

Setting a Development Framework

At this point, as business coaches, we must be concerned with aligning the development plan for the leader with measurable objectives based on the goals of the organization. We often find that our clients are inclined to want to respond primarily to the data and address the issues that surface in the feedback process. We had a client, for example, whose feedback indicated that she should delegate more, provide more timely and incisive feedback, and consider with better foresight the global implications of her decisions. All were worthy developmental opportunities for any emerging leader, but only one was relevant when we considered that her organizational goals were to build a new service organization with inexperienced people, focused primarily on a defined, industry-specific regional customer base. Now, as a leader, the data indicated that delegation and global scope were shortcomings, both interesting and challenging to pursue. Unfortunately, they were not terribly relevant to the capabilities she needed to work on to serve her business goals and, eventually her career aspiration to be senior vice president of new product and service development. We chose to focus on listening better and providing more timely, incisive, and positive corrective feedback and on developing as a directive and developmental leader—leaving improving delegation and global perspective for another time and place.

So in choosing development opportunities, we often suggest to our business leaders that they do more than simply respond to feedback. We encourage them to take a broader perspective consisting of four parts: (1) the feedback they have received on the specific competencies measured in the 360-degree instrument; (2) their personal career objectives; (3) the organization's goals; and (4) the goals they have set for their own groups. We ask, based on the information we have, which of the improvement opportunities identified will address the broadest range of objectives, have the greatest impact on the business, and take the client the furthest in his or her career goals. Clients choose and settle on the work to be done, having discussed their choices with their managers and/or mentors.

This is also a point of reflection for the coach. While the importance of understanding the business context and challenges of the client seem obvious, the specifics of how this is done are critical to the long-term effectiveness of the coaching and whether the change transfers and takes hold on the job. The effective business coach should have a grounded understanding of these mastery challenges for developing leaders and the key dilemmas that leaders must respond to with increasing versatility, depth, and impact. The coach must decide and be honest with himself or herself and the client about which of these areas he or she has some level of expertise and experience in and can provide help with. While the general business experience of many coaches may be wide, in order to create lasting change, the coach must understand the specific leadership challenge of the client and have a sense of how the challenge may play out in the culture and organization.

The starting point for the coach who is developing his or her knowledge of organizational dynamics and the business environment is to examine and learn about the key leadership transitions in level and responsibility that most leaders experience. These transitions usually demand new behaviors and approaches where coaching can make a critical difference. It is during such transitions that the application of behaviors that may have worked in the past do not work under the new demands of the organization. At these "stepping up" points, where leaders are most prone to fail, they can also be most open to learn. Fundamentally, many of these transitions involve major changes in the person's understanding of what the job is and what is required to succeed. Using the process we have outlined to help the clients reexamine their perspectives on how their jobs may be changing is critical. As coaches, our job is to continually challenge and expand the leader's definition of his or her role and help rethink it.

Once the client settles on one or two developmental opportunities and we've decided we can coach and contribute, we test the client's choice against an adapted cost/benefit analysis. We ask, "What's it going to cost you, your people, and the organization if you don't develop in this area?" After that list is generated, we ask: "How will your getting better at this competency benefit you, your people, and the organization?" This simple cost/benefit inquiry tends to validate the choice and motivate the client. We are now ready for the final phase of preparation: goal setting.

Setting Change Goals

We use a tool called a "Blueprint for Development" that describes the developmental opportunity, the current state, the future state, and the plan for action. The key here is to capture the plan simply enough so that the client can review the action plan daily in a thirty-second review. We have our clients start by describing the issue in a phrase: "Need to provide more incisive and timely feedback" or "Need to be more authentic and comfortable when interacting with top-level senior executives in the organization." The client then briefly describes the current state: "When I provide feedback, I tend to hedge and ramble for fear that. . . ." The next step is to describe the future state, what it would look like when the client is offering incisive, timely, positive feedback to his or her reports, manager, and peers. "I shall be perceived as forthright, insightful, and substantive when I offer. . . ." The current and future states frame the action plan, which the development blueprint and the coaching support.

The specific action plan is an outline of commitments, activities, learnings, resources, timelines, and measures that form the blueprint for the remainder of the coaching engagement. We usually dedicate an entire meeting to developing the action plan and, before that meeting, we encourage our clients to once more hold brief discussions with trusted colleagues. In those discussions they share their developmental objectives, ask for suggestions and ideas to include in the action plan, request ongoing feedback during the development period, and invite themselves back in three months for more feedback. The action plan must be aligned with the leadership agenda of the client, that is, the short- and long-term plan that drives their priorities, attention, and use of time. We urge leaders to review how they spend their time and whether it needs be shifted if they are to accomplish their developmental plans and increase their impact in the business. In most organizations, the client's manager should clearly understand the action plan. The reason is simple: not connecting to the boss and the organization may put the coaching process at risk of not gaining needed resources and support.

The client is also encouraged to use the Internet to read timely articles and identify other resources to gather ideas for the action plan. Meanwhile, we, too, draw on our resources, networks, experiences, and colleagues to prepare for the meeting. In our work as business coaches, we are often specific and intentional about the use of assignments and tools. The style of coaching may at times be more directive or consultative as we prepare clients to try new approaches to critical conversations, meetings, decision making, or problem solving that will fuel their thinking and accelerate their behavioral change.

The action plan starts with the following question: "*What* am I going to do to close the gap between my current state and my future state?" We brainstorm as many "*What's*" as we can and then prioritize by criteria, favoring those that will move us furthest and fastest toward the desired future state. We focus on the top three "*What's*" and ask the next question: "*How* we are going to accomplish each '*What?*'" Here is an illustration:

Let us picture a leader who is moving to a more complex, strategic, senior-level role. Her feedback indicates that she is viewed as a focused and an outstanding role model but does not spend enough time coaching her staff and is not delegating effectively. An analysis of how she spends time reveals that she spends too much time diving into the details of the work and not enough on the larger strategy. We now have three "*what's.*" A critical *how* will be deciding on actions that will change her approach to increased delegation.

The "*How*" section of the action plan is where you and the client will succeed or fail. The "*What's*" are easy; it's the "*How*" to do the "*What's*" that not only defines the real work to be done but determines whether or not the plan will succeed. We need two or three specific "*How's*" for every "*What*" in the plan. In this example, how will the leader share a new approach to mutually determining roles and responsibilities with her staff? Or how will she spend less time on project tasks and more time analyzing customers and competition, which will force her to delegate? Then we need to discuss the "*Who.*"

Who needs to know the plan? Whose support is required to accomplish the "*How's*"? What do we need from them and how will we get it? Once all of that is established, we must consider by "*when*" this all has to happen. After identifying *what, how,* and *who,* we focus on setting up a time line with milestones to mark our progress, thus solidifying a deadline for each action item.

The final item in the action plan is a measuring and/or monitoring process. We discuss various measures we could use to monitor our progress and determine whether or not we're on track and moving toward our goal. This is a critical piece that completes the cycle back to the business context that we established during the preparation phase. What are the measurable impacts of the behavioral changes the client is attempting? How will the team and organization benefit? How will the client's boss, direct reports, peers, or others in his or her support network be kept informed and stay invested in the client's progress?

The fact is that people do what the organization measures, and if the client and the organization value this effort, our leader's progress must be systemically measured and, if successful, acknowledged and rewarded. Whenever possible, the development plan must be tied to the organization's evaluation process. It should be part of the cycle of expectation and goal setting and have a direct impact on compensation, bonuses, and promotion.

Now, with the set-up complete, let the coaching/client journey begin. With solid data, follow-up feedback information, personality assessments, internal support, focused and purposeful developmental objectives, a cost/benefit justification, a gap analysis, and a detailed action plan—complete with milestones, measures, and rewards—chances are in six months to a year we're going to arrive at the desired future state.

And that's really what coaching is all about: helping transport someone from where he or she is to where he or she needs to be. The verb "coach" derives from the old English noun describing the vehicle for transporting royalty, moving from one place to another via the coach. When we consider our business royalty, the esteemed business leader with the keys to the kingdom and stewardship in his or her hands, we realize that, when it comes to coaching, the truth of the phrase "the more things change the more they remain the same." And as with most successful journeys, the key is careful, detailed preparation—having the patience and taking the time to build the foundation and chart the course that will assure the client a successful journey.

Notes

1. DePree, M. Leadership is an art. New York: Dell, 1998, p. 11.
2. O'Neill, M. B. Executive coaching with backbone and heart. San Francisco: Jossey-Bass, 2000, p. xiii.

◆ ◆ ◆

Richard Gauthier is a highly skilled and respected consultant and executive coach with more than twenty-five years of experience in organizational development, leadership, marketing, and communications. Currently a Principal Consultant at Linkage, Inc., Gauthier addresses a wide spectrum of customer challenges in leadership, customer satisfaction and retention, change management, management development, alignment, and total quality. His extensive experience and versatility enables him to apply his coaching expertise to senior- and middle-level leaders and teams across many different functions and industries. Gauthier is also on the faculty of Linkage's Master Level Executive Coaching Certification Program.

Prior to joining Linkage, he worked at ODI as a vice president and worldwide leader of ODI's Voice of the Customer practice. As practice leader for customer focus, he worked with clients to develop customer-focus strategies and standards, achieve breakthroughs in customer service, and enhance profitability through customer loyalty and retention. Gauthier has also held senior positions in corporate communications and public relations at Digital Equipment Corporation, the Gillette Company, and Wang Laboratories. He has published articles in a variety of publications and has been a guest speaker at Boston College, Boston University, and MIT's Sloan School of Management. Contact: rgauthier@Linkage-inc.com.

David Giber is a senior vice president in charge of leadership development, new programs, and research at Linkage, Inc., with more than twenty years of experience in organizational development, human resource management, leadership development, and executive coaching. Nationally known as a leader in his field, Giber has helped create award-winning leadership development systems for top organizations in many industries. He has consulted with leaders from a wide variety of international corporations, universities, and other organizations on such issues as succession planning, management development, action learning, executive coaching, workforce assessment, and developing performance and selection systems. He helps leaders achieve professional and personal success by focusing on the "hard" business skills they need as well as on personal development and leadership qualities. Giber synthesized the components of the coaching system described in this article into Linkage's unique, high-impact approach.

He has served in director-level positions in human resource management and leadership development for leading companies in the high-tech, financial services, and travel industries. He is an industrial/organizational psychologist and is an editor of two top-selling books in the field, *The Leadership Development Handbook* and *Best Practices in Organization and Human Resources Handbook* and the forthcoming *Best Practices in Global Workforce Management*. Contact: DGiber@linkageinc.com.

CHAPTER FIFTEEN

COACHING AND CULTURE

Toward the Global Coach

Michel Moral and Pamela Warnock

An absolute change in the business environment is upon us. In the bright new world of "GloCos," a term coined by Goldman Sachs in 2003 to describe the world's Top 25 Global Companies,[1] the needs of both organizations and management have changed irrevocably. The *global manager* is now a standard by which most executives will be measured. The corresponding term *global coach* comes to mind immediately, once it is clear that *cultural competency* will be a prerequisite for managers in the future. Companies and management in this new global workplace also will increasingly use innovative technology and new business structures, such as *virtual teams*, to accomplish in minutes work that was previously done over many weeks and many frequent flyer miles.

Consequently, coaches and the coaching industry must rise to the challenge. In order to provide continued excellence in coaching, we must integrate real knowledge of cultural differences and corresponding innovative organizational structures as they influence both the global workplace and managers in a multicultural work environment. Awareness of cultural differences can be the key that leads to success or failure in the multicultural business context, and mastering culturally relevant coaching skills may be an essential component to executive coaching in the future.

A New Playing Field

Natalija, a bright Czechoslovakian global manager, has identified a promising employee on her Chinese team in the Hong Kong office. She contacts the employee directly and offers him a managerial position on her staff. The employee's shocked silence is palpable to Natalija over the phone. She has made him uncomfortable but she doesn't know why.

Natalija was not aware that, even though she is an upper-level executive, in a Chinese context, she may not be seen as having the right to pull this employee out of his team and promote him. For the Chinese, a *collectivistic*[2] culture, group affiliation is considered much more important than individual recognition, as opposed to a more *individualistically*-oriented cultural background typical of most Northern European and North American business people.

Natalija is also having some difficulties with her team in Tokyo. She eventually comes to the conclusion that the German coach who had been very helpful in a team-building exercise in the Johannesburg office of her multinational might be just the person to help one of the key specialists on the Japanese team. A few weeks later, she receives a call from the upper manager of the Japanese team, who appears to be quite offended. The German coach has refused to disclose what was being said during the coaching sessions. Natalija soon learns that the concept of "confidentiality" is interpreted quite differently in Japan.

Natalija also is very uncomfortable with a team she cannot drive and control like a "squad." She feels that mainly providing business direction is not "real" management. Natalija comes from a culture in which a high rank implies full power over lower-level employees and where instructions have to be followed—no questions asked.

Business has changed. With innovation in telecommunications, corporate teams are now dispersed on a global scale and will be increasingly so in the future. *On-site teams*, for which a face-to-face direct relationship on a daily basis is possible between managers and subordinates, are increasingly being replaced by *remote teams*, of which employees work from home, from locations close to their residences, or from another country.

The widening variety of geographical locations for employees in global companies has led to increased contact between individuals of diverse backgrounds and cultural beliefs. These cultural differences introduce an additional level of complexity in the arena of management in the global marketplace. Issues related to the use of power, the importance of hierarchy, performance and outcome evaluations, gender and ethnicity, and even such seemingly innocuous issues as the use of humor in the workplace, may present significant challenges.

In addition, the new crop of international executives coming from emerging markets, such as Central Europe and China, will soon add their belief systems and practices to the "mix" of global business. Currently, the typical international manager's behavior is based on a North American model, and he or she is seen as an assertive person who thinks *inductively*,[3] communicates and deals with conflict *directly*, and works hard toward attaining short-term objectives and keeping timeframes. With the arrival of Asian colleagues, for example, the executive marketplace may be obliged to expand its array of desirable behaviors to include such things as long-term vision, discretion, subtlety, and respect for historical resources.

New Business Environment

Helen, a U.S. citizen, is a large-accounts executive for an American telephone company. Among her clients is a national bank that has just merged with a huge European financial institution. Consequently, Helen is now responsible for managing sales teams in France, Germany, Italy, and the UK. However, she is not comfortable dealing with her European colleagues, who have what seem to Helen to be endless business lunches, during which wine and beer are consumed. Her customer is also now considering a relocation of back-office support services to a location in Bombay. After an initial visit to discuss bidding with local telecommunication companies, Helen is somewhat shocked to discover that quite different negotiation practices are commonplace in India. Helen's personal coach back in New York is also at a loss as to how to support and empower her. The coach is embarrassed and feels inadequate.

In addition to experiencing *culture shock*,[4] Helen is discovering the effects of global business transformation. This transformation involves fundamental changes in the way business is done on a global scale and is being driven by leading corporations aiming for dominant worldwide status.

For example, GloCos are moving vigorously toward new "vertical" organizational layouts, which are far from the classical pyramid shaped "by country" management system of the past. This shift prioritizes the *functional* needs of the company over geography. Additionally, trends toward *externalization* and *delocalization* in global business have created a breakthrough toward improving *expense to revenue ratios (ERR)*. Other multinational companies will now be forced to follow the above-mentioned GloCos and their modified business practices in the new global marketplace, if they are to survive.

The *matrix* management model, as defined by Frederick Taylor in 1911, was a landmark concept, but impossible to implement until powerful information technology systems became available to handle increased volumes and complexity of data. Viewed in terms of a multidimensional matrix model, the relative importance of product categories, marketing channels, customer segments, and geography can now be reexamined and prioritized in terms of the company's priorities worldwide. Gone are the days when a multinational company had local management deciding on local branch strategies. Even distribution channels are most often designated within the larger matrix organization and are no longer country specific. Lines of communication are based on need and expediency, as opposed to an imposed hierarchy. This organizational model can be immediately reactive and extremely efficient.

Lowering product costs via manufacturing, marketing, and distribution savings, together with a shift toward minimizing infrastructure expenses, have been areas of business concern in recent decades as well. Executives now focus on the *expense to revenue ratio (ERR),* which indicates how they compare to their competitors in terms of *efficiency.* A low ERR demonstrates that superfluous expenditures have been eliminated, usually through a combination of improved technologies together with reorganization strategies, such as *vertical structures, delocalization,* and *externalization.*

Vertical structures lead to savings by eliminating layers of management and hierarchy and by centralizing administrative and financial tasks that were previously replicated in each country where the global company has branches. Vertical structures also allow for the implementation of *standard operating procedures,* resulting in tighter overall control in international business. Change and unexpected events at any of the global company's locations can subsequently be addressed quickly by *virtual teams.*

Delocalization and externalization became popular in the 1980s, when business focus was on *production cost hunting.* Large plants were often relocated to areas of the world where labor costs were significantly lower than in economically prosperous countries. In increasing efforts to cut *infrastructure expenses,* all back office activities are now exposed to possible relocation to countries where high skills are available at lower cost or to being outsourced. It is important to understand that delocalization of back office services has become possible only because of the implementation of *vertical structures*—itself a consequence of improved information management.

Thus, we see clear trends of global companies moving toward a model of lean, adaptive, and efficient international operations in which *business* and *functional unit* executives are increasingly required to manage diverse and semi-autonomous teams from afar.

The Global Executive

In tandem with the need to integrate organizational change in order to remain viable in the global marketplace, businesses now need a new kind of manager. This new breed of executive will be someone who is able to master an innovative array of business concerns and methods, such as virtual teams, remote operations, complex changing environments, decision process uncertainties, and, of course, cultural differences. Consultants and publications have already identified these people as *global managers* or *global executives* and have defined their skills, qualities, and strengths as well as possible weaknesses. An interesting characteristic of current *global managers* is that they usually employ the "manager as coach" model themselves and are therefore familiar with coaching techniques. Today's global managers are accustomed to leadership in its myriad forms worldwide and most often bring practical personal experience to their own management repertoires.

In the new business environment, efficiency prevails, and the ability to react quickly to change is the top criteria of global companies. Of course, such innovations are oriented toward streamlining tasks rather than managing people. Ongoing needs for flexibility and human interaction, however, can be addressed by the use of equally innovative organizational tools such as *virtual teams,* which in turn imply profound changes in management. For example, reportees are far away and dispersed, and it is not possible to exert as much control as if everyone were housed together in the same building. Consequently, when using virtual teams, it becomes helpful, even necessary, to empower intermediate levels of management and to strongly encourage initiative. By taking the initiative, however, employees are encouraged to take more risk. It is crucial, therefore, to establish an environment in which employees are allowed to make mistakes and to reinforce an overall *blame-free* atmosphere of corporate culture.

Classic management techniques, such as *directing* or *delegating,* will not work particularly well, and *facilitation* is preferable when working with teams and individual employees in this model. The paradox is that, despite a strong task orientation, new global organizations need to focus much more attention on their people, whose subsequent involvement, dedication, and commitment to the team will bring about the most positive business outcome. The new global executive has to be not only a business specialist but also a human specialist.

Cultural Competency

Olivier is an experienced Swiss manager who works for a petroleum company. He receives a new assignment: reorganizing operations in Southern Africa. In Botswana, the general manager of the subsidiary just retired, and he must promote one of the existing intermediate managers. Olivier favors a competent Korean expatriate, but a local person argues that he deserves the job, being the son of a tribal king. Olivier is now faced with managing a difference in cultural beliefs where *ascription*[5]—promotion according to status—is valued, as opposed to achievement. As with Helen, Olivier experiences culture shock.

Skill at dealing with cultural differences cannot be underestimated. It can be crucial to success or failure for the global manager. Some hierarchically oriented cultures, who may be accustomed to a more *autocratic* management style, would be especially uncomfortable working in the changing workplace described in the previous section.

French executives, for example, may particularly dislike the idea of interdependence and the sharing of management prerogatives. *Hierarchically* oriented cultures, such as France and many Asian countries, prefer a social structure that includes stratification and the existence of "respected superiors," while *egalitarian* cultures, such as the United States and most Northern European countries, favor social differentiation based on professional achievement.[6]

For the global executive, there are three types of relationships in the workplace that are likely to be affected by cultural differences: the executive (1) as a member of a multicultural management team; (2) as the leader of a multicultural team; and (3) as an individual relating with others—peers, upper management, or customers.

Regarding teams, cohesion in multicultural teams can often be very high and provides its own source of satisfaction and motivation for team members.[7] However, it appears that either team cohesion is almost immediate, and trust is evident right from the start, or it will not happen at all. Therefore, global managers need to be aware and well-versed at encouraging the *swift trust* phenomena, or risk failure. This apparent paradox may be due to the fact that team members are encouraged to contribute as individuals and think for themselves. Also, cultural differences may afford some protection against the pressures of autocratic or normative management.

Issues related to individual relationships in the global workplace stem from the varying perspectives regarding ways of being, thinking, and behaving. An *inductive* American will not easily accept the deductive approach of a French person, considering this as a lack of *pragmatism.*[8] A very *particularistic*[9] African, whose culture easily tolerates exceptions to rules, will be hurt by the *universalism* of a Swiss, who most likely prefers the same standards and procedures applied to everybody. A German person will always start and end a meeting on time, and this may possibly upset the *polychronic* employee who expects that the company bus will leave only when it is full.[10] Ultimately, an experience in expatriation that goes poorly may result in the previously mentioned *culture shock*, which can be understood as a transitory form of depression.[11] Interestingly, ending an expatriation and returning to one's country of origin often induces the same effect and has been called *reverse culture shock*.

New Challenges for Executive Coaches

Werner is currently coaching the general manager of an airline company operating in the Middle East and Eastern Europe. The manager is an Egyptian citizen who has lived in California and Malaysia in the past, but who is currently based in Stuttgart. Werner sometimes has difficulties understanding his client, who can be very factual and rational, but may suddenly switch to long digressions on the political dynamics of the airline industry.

The question for executive coaches is the following: How shall we adapt to the changing environment? Do we, for example, continue using our current coaching rules and tools, possibly adapting some of them, or do we need to invent new concepts to cope with cultural differences and the new global marketplace? Are the precepts behind much of coaching theory culturally neutral or even applicable in a multicultural environment? How do I coach someone whose background is very different from my own?

While cultural differences in business have been addressed by such authors as Hofstede,[12] Trompenaars,[13] Lewis,[14] Marx,[15] and Brake, Walker, and Walker,[16] the domain of intercultural coaching remains largely unexplored.[17] There are two reasons for this. First, most multinational companies, until very recently, have continued on in the "country-specific" mode of operations. They have been slow to incorporate the lessons learned by the GloCos and are now scrambling to catch up. Second, although the number of managers capable of dealing with multiple cultures is increasing, the coaches actually able to provide quality services oriented to the multicultural business environment are still very uncommon. This is not because of a lack of coaching expertise, but due to the fact that relatively few professional coaches have had concrete experience themselves in international operations. It is only now, with the arrival on the coaching scene of a certain number of former global executives who acquired international experience by having worked themselves in differing multicultural settings for years, that this need will start to be addressed.

In regard to coaching techniques, we can identify a number of challenges. First, tools developed and appropriate for one culture, especially psychometric tests, might need to be reconsidered for another culture. For instance, an *introverted* Italian employee, as measured using the Myers-Briggs Type Indicator, might end up actually appearing more *extraverted* "in person" than an *extraverted* Finn or Japanese person. Additionally, a significant number of the tools currently used in coaching were developed based on management techniques that are dated or inappropriate and therefore unhelpful in a multicultural environment.

Second, if we assume the coachee is in an executive position in a modern global corporation, the notion of hierarchy may be significantly changed. The global executive now relates to a cloud of superiors, subordinates, peers, customers, and service providers, some of whom may not even be employees of the same company. Written procedures may exist, and everyone's role may be described in a job definition, but a significant part of decision-making processes relies on individual relationships and mutual trust. The new companies are made up of a fine-tuned camaraderie, where everyone has an area of expertise but serves a common vision. *Cohesion* is more important than discipline, and *action* is the primary source of job satisfaction.

Expectations are also key in the interactions between the coach and the coachee. In addition to the emotions generated by the interaction between two personalities in coaching, there is another emotional interaction that is caused by the coming together of two cultures. Most coaches have a good understanding of the psychological theories that attempt to explain human behavior, but relatively few coaches are aware that the meeting of two cultures triggers something else, which we can describe as an encounter between two different visions of life. Our response to these differences is not normally one of which we are conscious; it is not at the level of emotions, but rather is expressed through cognitive processes, such as *prototyping, categorizing,* and ultimately *idealizing* or *pejorating.*[18]

Toward a Global Coach

The average modern global executive is usually more familiar with cultural differences than today's average coach, he or she spends his or her whole life in international meetings and has no problem flying on the same day from Kuwait to Bolivia to mediate a business squall. Traveling is easier for the international manager than for the coach, and conference calls with peers, subordinates, and bosses who are physically located in different countries have become the accepted method of communication in the international workplace. Dealing with cultural differences becomes a normal aspect of day-to-day business interactions.

However, although most coaches have a limited familiarity with cultural differences at this time, many may have a better understanding soon. Becoming well-versed in cultural differences via training and self-education is quite possible, and it is analogous to the therapist who has no personal experience of divorce, but is trained well enough to help the patient who is recently separated. In addition to her knowledge of human nature, acquired training, and personal self-exploration, today's coach should consider cross-cultural training. A special responsibility also rests with coaching supervisors who may misinterpret the actions of a *global coach,* based on limited knowledge about cross-cultural differences and a lack of experience in multicultural business settings.

As mentioned above, cultural differences have been studied in depth for many decades now. A vast array of multicultural learning tools and resources has subsequently been developed and can lead the interested coach from a general awareness of culture to the acquisition of a deeply integrated knowledge of cultural differences. It is now clear that a combination of didactic and experiential training methods provides the best path toward understanding and eventual *cultural competency.*[19]

Training on virtual teaming is less common. Current management classes usually focus on *directing a team* or *facilitating projects.* The problems of business at a distance are just now coming to the forefront, together with other concerns regarding the use of modern technology. Specialists agree that maintaining human relationships has become increasingly important, not less so, with the use of technology. Despite breakthroughs in terms of usability and reliability, technology cannot replace the need for person-to-person contact and that most subtle and rich information source, nonverbal communication, which is lost over a long-distance phone line.

"If you don't know where you're going, it is difficult to say if you are lost." This ancient Chinese proverb tells us that what we do should be tied to a deeper understanding of what we intend to accomplish. It does not mean that there is only one understanding or one truth, but rather like having a good map in hand when we arrive in a new city; it helps to know which way to turn next. The *global coach* has to understand that interactions between people are also interactions between cultures.

Notes

1. Who will produce the next GloCo? *Goldman Sachs—Global Economics Weekly,* 10 December 2003; and *Getting globalization right,* Goldman Sachs, 2003.
2. Hofstede, G. *Culture's consequences* (2nd ed.). Thousand Oaks, CA: Sage, 2001.
3. Inductive modes of thinking start with facts—some examples being the United States and Switzerland—while deductive cultures, such as France, favor reasoning stemming from theoretical bases.
4. Ward, C., Bochner, S., & Furnham, A. *The psychology of culture shock.* London: Routledge, 2001.
5. Trompenaars, F., & Hampden-Turner, C. *Riding the waves of culture: Understanding diversity in global business.* New York: McGraw-Hill, 1998.
6. Hofstede, G. *Culture's consequences* (2nd ed.). Thousand Oaks, CA: Sage, 2001.
7. Leigh, A., & Maynard, M. Virtual teams. In *Leading your team: How to involve and inspire teams.* London: Brealey, 1995.
8. Hall, E. T., & Hall, M. R. *Understanding cultural differences: Germans, French and Americans.* Yarmouth, ME: Intercultural Press, 1990.
9. Trompenaars, F., & Hampden-Turner, C. *Riding the waves of culture: Understanding diversity in global business.* New York: McGraw-Hill, 1998.
10. In monochronic cultures, people concentrate on one activity or relationship at a time and are usually always on time. In polychronic cultures, people may deal with multiple tasks or relationships simultaneously and may have a more flexible concept of time management, as noted in Hall, E. T., *The dance of life: The other dimension of time.* New York: Anchor Books/Doubleday, 1981.
11. Ward, C., Bochner, S., & Furnham, A. *The psychology of culture shock.* London: Routledge, 2001.
12. Hofstede, G. *Software of the mind: Intercultural cooperation and its importance for survival.* New York: McGraw-Hill, 1991.
13. Trompenaars, F., & Hampden-Turner, C. *Riding the waves of culture: Understanding diversity in global business.* New York: McGraw-Hill, 1998.
14. Lewis, R. *When cultures collide: Managing successfully across cultures.* Yarmouth, ME: Intercultural Press, 1999.
15. Marx, E. *Breaking through the culture shock.* London: Brealey, 2001.
16. Brake, T., Walker, D., & Walker, T. *Doing business internationally: The guide to cross-cultural success.* New York: McGraw-Hill, 1995.
17. The only solid reference currently available is the text *Coaching Across Cultures* by Philippe Rosinski (2003).

18. Ward, C., Bochner, S., & Furnham, A. *The psychology of culture shock.* London: Routledge, 2001.
19. A comprehensive starting point is Fowler S., & Mumford M., *Intercultural sourcebook: Cross-cultural training methods.* Yarmouth, ME: Intercultural Press, 1995.

◆ ◆ ◆

Michel Moral has spent most of his career in international settings. After several years in sales at IBM France, he joined IBM Euro Coordination. Involved in many of IBM's business units, he was program manager for large systems and operations manager in networking systems. He was involved in the telecommunications and media industries as well as the government industries. Within IBM, Moral supervised business units that had, on average, $2 to 4 billion annual revenues; participated in the establishment of the IBM Emerging Markets Organization, which covered Asia, the Middle East, and Africa; and led the information technology team.

In 2003 Moral founded a coaching and consulting practice. Subsequently, he has worked with many senior-level executives and department managers, as well as other coaches. Currently, Moral teaches coaching and intercultural management at several universities and business schools in the Paris area. Contact: mmoral@attglobal.net.

Pamela Warnock is a psychologist, systemic therapist, and CTI trained coach currently specializing in multicultural issues in the workplace. Warnock has lived and worked in North and South America, the Middle East, and Europe and is currently employed with an international organization headquartered in the Paris area, which consists of employees from thirty member countries as well as numerous affiliated non-member nations. There she provides conflict resolution, management consultation and coaching, cross-cultural training, and adjustment and psychological support services to employees and their families. Within the multi-cultural workplace, Warnock's areas of special interest are mediation and conflict resolution; harassment; gender and diversity issues; best practices in management; and mental and physical health issues as they relate to expatriation.

CHAPTER SIXTEEN

WHEN LEADERS ARE COACHES

James M. Kouzes and Barry Z. Posner

Leadership is a relationship. Sometimes the relationship is one-to-many, and some-times it is one-to-one. Regardless of whether the relationship is with one or with one thousand, leadership is a relationship between those who aspire to lead and those who choose to follow. Success in leadership, success in business, and success in life have been, are now, and will always be functions of how well we work and play together. Leaders are wholly dependent on their capacity to build and sustain relationships.

Evidence abounds for this point of view. For instance, in examining the critical variables for success in the top three jobs in large organizations, Jodi Taylor and her colleagues at the Center for Creative Leadership (CCL) found that the number one success factor is "relationships with subordinates."[1] Claudio Fernandez-Aráoz, a part-ner and a member of global search firm Egon Zehnder International's Executive Committee, is very direct about the importance of relationship skills. After studying success and failure in the executive ranks around the world, he concludes that "Serious weaknesses in the domain of emotional intelligence predict failure at se-nior levels with amazing accuracy."[2] We were intrigued to find that even in this nanosecond world of e-everything, personal opinion is consistent with the facts. In an online survey, respondents were asked to indicate, among other things, "Which is more essential to business success five years from now—skills in using the Internet or social skills?"[3] Seventy-two percent selected social skills compared to 28 percent for Internet skills. Internet literati completing a poll online realize that it's not the web of technology that matters the most, it's the web of people.

Similar results were found in a study by Public Allies, a non-profit group dedicated to creating young leaders who can strengthen their communities. Public Allies sought the opinions of eighteen- to thirty-year-olds on the subject of leadership.[4] Among the items was a question about the qualities that were important in a good leader. Topping the eighteen-to-thirty-year-olds' list was: "Being able to see a situation from someone else's point of view." In second place was: "Getting along well with other people."

These days we're constantly being asked to learn new skills, take more risks, try out unfamiliar behaviors, and, like all humans, we fail a few times before we succeed. These requests can cause us great distress and create extreme discomfort. We're not likely to embrace the challenges unless we trust the person guiding and coaching us. So forever erase from your minds the image of the coach as that stern-faced, chair-throwing, dirt-kicking, ass-chewing tough guy who yells orders to the players. Maybe it makes good sports theater, but it definitely does not produce outstanding business performance. What you'll get instead is a demoralized group of disengaged constituents who'd rather quit than excel.

Success in the one-to-one leadership context is dependent on the ability of the leader to build a lasting relationship in which the talent sees the coach as a partner and a role model. In other words, you can't order others to perform at their best or improve what they do because of a position you hold. You can only get extraordinary things done because you have a heart.

Yes, heart. It turns out that the best leaders are caring leaders. We discovered this while researching for our book, *Encouraging the Heart,* and we'd like to apply some of those lessons to the role of leader as coach. Here are three essentials that contribute greatly to establishing and sustaining a successful coaching relationship:[5]

1. Set clear standards;
2. Expect the best; and
3. Set the example.

Set Clear Standards

Tony Codianni of Toshiba America explains it this way: "I have a need to be personal with my folks. To me there's no difference between work and personal life. Encouraging comes from the heart. It's heart-to-heart, not brain-to-heart. It has to be genuine."

Codianni is one of those people who loves people. He loves buying them presents; he loves inviting them out on his boat; he loves to cook for them. Codianni has nineteen first cousins, and he's taken them all to Italy. Ask anyone who works with him, and they'll all tell you they love to be around him. He makes them feel good.

But don't ever mistake Codianni's love of people for a willingness to forget about standards. Exemplary leadership is soft and demanding, caring and conscientious. As Codianni puts it, "I always tell trainers in my group that they have to master the program first, and then they're free to change it." To Codianni, having a clear set of expectations about what people will achieve is part and parcel of being caring.

The first prerequisite for encouraging the hearts of our talent is to set clear standards. By standards we mean both goals and values, because they both have to do with what's expected of us. Values serve as the enduring principles that enable us to maintain our bearings wherever we are throughout our lives. Goals are those shorter-term ambitions that provide us with the metrics for measuring progress.

Human beings just don't put their hearts into something if they don't believe in it. We won't commit with energy and intensity to something that's not a fit for us personally. It's like wearing a pair of slacks that are too tight. It's uncomfortable, we look awkward, we feel embarrassed, and we can't move around easily.

We know from the research we've been doing since the late 1970s that values make a difference in the way people behave inside organizations and how they feel about themselves, their colleagues, and their leaders. But when we take an even deeper look at the congruence between personal and organizational values, we find something quite provocative.[6] We find that it's the clarity of *personal* values that drives an individual's commitment to an organization. Shared values do make a difference, but it's personal values that determine the fit between an individual and organization.

Exemplary leader-coaches also make sure that work is not pointless ambling, but purposeful action. Goal setting affirms the person, and, whether we realize it or not, contributes to what people think about themselves. As University of Chicago Professor Mihaly Csikszentmihalyi points out: "It is the goals that we pursue that will shape and determine the kind of self that we are to become. Without a consistent set of goals, it is difficult to develop a coherent self. . . . The goals one endorses also determine one's self-esteem."[7]

People need to know whether they're making progress or marking time. Goals help to serve that function, but goals are not enough. It's not enough to know that we want to make it to the summit. We also need to know whether we're still climbing or whether we're sliding downhill. Therefore, effective leader-coaches also provide constructive, timely, and accurate feedback. Encouragement is a form of feedback. It is positive information that tells us that we're making progress, that we're on the right track, and that we're living up to the standards.

The wonderful thing about encouragement is that it's more personal than other forms of feedback. Encouragement requires us to get close to other people, to show that we care about other people, and to demonstrate that we're really interested in other people. When leaders provide a clear set of standards and provide positive feedback on how we're meeting those standards, they encourage people to reach inside and put forth even more effort to get extraordinary things done.

Expect the Best

Successful leaders have high expectations, both of themselves and of their constituents. The belief that "I know you can do it" is a potent performance enhancer. It definitely is not some tasty pabulum that leaders dispense to help us keep a positive outlook on life. When someone else believes in us, we're much more likely to believe in ourselves. While high and low expectations influence other people's performance, only high expectations have a positive impact on both another's actions and feelings . And, most significantly, only high expectations can improve performance.

Nancy Tivol, executive director of Sunnyvale Community Services (SCS) in California, is a wonderful example of this principle in action. She believes strongly in her own ability and in those of every staff member and volunteer. When Tivol first arrived at SCS, volunteers were, in her opinion, underused. Many board members and paid staff felt that volunteers didn't have the skills to handle interactions with clients, donors, and corporate contacts. Tivol believed they did. Today, SCS has volunteers doing things previously done only by staff members. Indeed, more than seven hundred volunteers run the front office, the agency's three food programs, the Community Christmas Center, the agency's computer operations, and the Volunteer Language Bank—all under one director of volunteers. Most of the lead volunteers are over sixty-five years of age, and volunteer hours have increased from 6,000 to 20,000 annually, which enabled paid staff to be reduced through attrition from twelve to eight full-time equivalents.

Not only that, but SCS became the country's only emergency assistance agency that has not turned eligible clients away because available funds have been depleted. Under Tivol's leadership, SCS has increased its funding for the emergency assistance program for low-income families during a recession and a period in which many agencies experienced significant funding cutbacks!

Previous administrators, as well as paid staff, had made certain assumptions about volunteers. They assumed volunteers would be neither motivated enough nor skilled or experienced enough to take on the responsibility that the agency would require. As a result, volunteers were mostly employed at jobs that demanded little of them and they were given only minimal responsibilities. The bottom line was that they weren't given the opportunity to explore or demonstrate their own capacities beyond the performance of the most menial tasks. Their beliefs held the volunteers back; Tivol's beliefs encouraged the same group of people to excel. She placed volunteers in responsible positions, gave them the training and direction they required, and encouraged them to do their best. And they did just that!

What was the motivation that drove the volunteers? Why did the SCS picture change so radically under Tivol? The key was her high expectations of the volunteers, and her expectations literally breathed new life into the people around her. She prophesied their success.

This demonstration of belief in another's abilities comes not only in organizational settings. It can show up anywhere. A moving and powerful instance came to us from Idaho businessman Don Bennett. Bennett was the first amputee to climb to the summit of Mt. Rainier. That's 14,410 feet on one leg and two crutches!

During a difficult portion of the climb, Bennett and his team had to cross an ice field. To get across the ice, the climbers had to put crampons on their boots to prevent slipping and to dig into the ice for leverage and stability. Unfortunately, with two crutches, and only one boot with a crampon, Bennett got stuck in the ice. He determined that the only way to get across the ice field was to fall face forward onto the ice, pull himself as far forward as he could, stand up, and then fall forward again. He was going to get across the ice field by falling down.

On that particular climb, his teenage daughter, Kathy, was with him, and she saw what was happening to her dad. While the team leader cut holes in the ice so Bennett could hop onto clear snow and traverse the ice field, Bennett's daughter stayed by his side through the entire four-hour struggle. As Bennett hopped, she shouted in his ear: "You can do it, Dad. You're the best dad in the world. You can do it, Dad!"

After Bennett told us this story, he added: "There was no way that I was not going to make it across that ice field with my daughter shouting that in my ear. You want to know what leadership is? What she did is leadership." Kathy's belief in her father and her verbal encouragement touched a place deep within Bennett, strengthening his resolve and commitment.

It's no wonder, then, that when people tell us about leaders who really make a difference in their lives, they frequently tell us about people who have believed in them and encouraged them to reach beyond their own self-doubts, to more fully realize their own greatest strengths. They talk about leaders who treat them in ways that buoy their self-confidence, making it possible for them to achieve more than they themselves initially believe is possible.

The thoughts and beliefs we hold in our minds are intangible. They can't be weighed and measured like raw materials or finished products. But seen or not, measurable or not, they have an enormous impact on the people around us. Exemplary leaders know this and know how to purposefully hold in their minds high expectations for themselves and for other people.

Set the Example

In research with Christy Tonge, we found that the factor most related to coaching effectiveness is "investing in the relationship." (There's that leadership-is-a-relationship finding again!) And, of all the items used to measure coaching behavior, the one most linked to success was "this person embodies character qualities and values that I admire."

In our continuing research on the qualities that people look for and admire in their leaders, time and time again we find that, more than anything else, people want leaders who are credible. Credibility is the foundation of leadership.[8]

People want to believe in their leaders. They want to believe that their leaders' words can be trusted and that their leaders will do what they say. Personal leadership credibility, we've found, makes a huge difference in performance and in commitment to organizations. A group's loyalty, commitment, energy, profitability, and productivity, among other outcomes, are directly linked to the credibility of the leader. Our findings are so consistent over such a long period of time that we've come to refer to this as the first law of leadership: *if you don't believe in the messenger, you won't believe the message.*

So exactly what is credibility? What is it behaviorally? How do you know it when you see it? When we ask people these questions, their most frequent response is: "They do what they say they will do."[9]

When it comes to deciding whether a leader is believable, people first listen to the words and then watch the actions. They listen to the talk and watch the walk. Then they measure the congruence. A judgment of "credible" is handed down when the two are consistent. If people don't see consistency, they conclude that the leader is, at best, not really serious about the words and, at worst, is an outright hypocrite. Constituents are moved by deeds. Actions are the evidence of a leader's credibility. This observation leads to a straightforward prescription for sustaining credibility over time: DWYSYWD—Do What You Say You Will Do.

Over and over again, it's the same story. Wherever you find a strong culture built around strong values—whether the values are about superior quality, innovation, customer service, distinctiveness in design, respect for others, or just plain fun—you'll also find endless examples of leaders who personally live the values.

Personal involvement is what setting the example is all about. Terri Sarhatt, customer services manager of the Applied Biosystems Division of Perkin-Elmer, learned how important that is even in situations in which the rewards are tangible. Sarhatt was looking for a way to increase the amount of supportive communication she had with employees at the company, and as luck would have it, her decision to become more personally involved coincided with the annual distribution of stock options. At Applied Biosystems, as in many high-tech companies, people often receive stock options when they've had a good year, and because Applied Biosystems has been growing at around 20 percent for the last few years, it's been a regular occurrence.

In years past, Sarhatt would receive the options from her manager. She would then present options to her direct supervisors and request they do the same with their direct reports. In 1998, she decided to use a different tactic. She wanted to thank folks directly, so she asked her direct supervisors if they'd mind her meeting with each of their employees who were going to receive stock options. Her direct reports thought it was a terrific idea.

"I personally thanked them for the specific projects and the work they had done," said Sarhatt. "The employees were surprised that I would actually take the time out of my busy schedule to sit down with each of them separately, have a cup of coffee, and discuss their accomplishments. One of my supervisors informed me later that her employee appreciated the time I spent with her more than she appreciated the actual stock options!" As we have found so often in our research, the gift of personal time mattered most.

Sarhatt also told us that it's "the 'little' things that make such a BIG difference!" And that's the point. It doesn't take a grand plan to begin to set the example for encouraging the hearts of others. It doesn't take a huge budget, it doesn't take psychotherapy, and it doesn't take the boss's permission. What's most critical in all these examples is that the leaders took the initiative. Being a good role model is no exception. It has to become a conscious priority.

It's About Caring

Along the journey to developing yourself as an exemplary leader-coach, there is a fundamental question that you must confront: How much do you really care about the people you lead?

Now our hunch is that you care a lot. You probably wouldn't be reading this book and this chapter if you didn't. But this question must be confronted daily, because when you care deeply, the methods that we've described will present themselves as genuine expressions of your caring. When you care little, they'll be perceived as nothing more than gimmicks, and you'll be thought of as a phony.

One of the oldest observations about human behavior is that we tend to mirror those around us. If we're around someone who's sad, for example, we pick it up. Even if we enter the room full of vim and vigor, we find that our energy starts to leak out when we're in the presence of negative emotions. Put yourself in the position of a person being coached. Imagine spending your days with a down-in-the-mouth, negative, and pessimistic leader. What a depressing thought.

But what happens to you when you enter a room full of upbeat, supportive, appreciative, and enthusiastic people? You tend to be uplifted yourself, don't you? We much prefer to be around positive people. And, by the way, researchers have also found that positive, hopeful, and optimistic people get more done in their lives and feel both personally and professionally more successful than do their more negative counterparts.

As the leader, you set the tone. When it comes to your role as leader-coach, the talent in your organization will grow and thrive only when you establish a clear set of high standards, display a strong belief that those standards can be achieved, and then demonstrate by your own actions that you practice what you preach.

When you integrate these three essentials into your daily practice, you will loudly and clearly communicate the message that "I care about you. I care about your future. I care about your growth. I'm here to create a climate in which you blossom and flourish." Not only will others find great joy and success in this caring climate, so, too, will you.

Notes

1. Taylor, J. Telephone interview with Jodi Taylor, Ph.D., on Center for Creative Leadership, April 1998. Taylor is now with Summit Leadership Solutions.
2. Aråoz, C. F., personal interview. Also, The challenge of hiring senior executives. In C. Cherniss & D. Goleman (Eds.), *The emotionally intelligent workplace: How to select for, measure, and improve emotional intelligence in individuals, groups, and organizations.* San Francisco: Jossey-Bass, 2001.
3. *Fast Company,* "Where Are We on the Web?" October 1999, p. 306.
4. Public Allies. *New leadership for a new century.* Washington, DC: Public Allies, 1998.
5. Kouzes, J. M., & Posner, B. Z. *Encouraging the heart: A leader's guide to rewarding and recognizing others.* San Francisco: Jossey-Bass, 2003.
6. Kouzes, J. M., & Posner, B. Z. *Credibility: How leaders gain and lose it, why people demand it* (rev. ed.). San Francisco: Jossey-Bass, 2003.
   Posner, B. Z., & Schmidt, W. H. Values congruence and differences between the interplay of personal and organizational value systems. *Journal of Business Ethics,* 1993, *12,* 171–177.
7. Csikszentmihalyi, M. *Finding flow: The psychology of engagement with everyday life.* New York: Basic Books, 1997, p. 23.
8. Kouzes, J. M., & Posner, B. Z. *The leadership challenge* (3rd ed.). San Francisco: Jossey-Bass, 2002.
   Kouzes, J. M., & Posner, B. Z. *Credibility: How leaders gain and lose it, why people demand it* (rev. ed.). San Francisco: Jossey-Bass, 2003.
9. Kouzes, J. M., & Posner, B. Z. *Credibility: How leaders gain and lose it, why people demand it* (rev. ed.). San Francisco: Jossey-Bass, 2003.

◆ ◆ ◆

James M. Kouzes and **Barry Z. Posner** are the authors of the award-winning and best-selling book, *The Leadership Challenge,* with over one million copies in print. They've co-authored six other leadership books, including *Credibility: How Leaders Gain It and Lose It, Why People Demand It; Encouraging the Heart;* and *The Leadership Challenge Workbook.* Kouzes and Posner also developed the highly acclaimed *Leadership Practices Inventory* (LPI), a 360-degree questionnaire assessing leadership behavior.

They were named by the International Management Council as the 2001 recipients of the prestigious Wilbur M. McFeely Award. This honor puts them in the company of previous recipients Ken Blanchard, Stephen Covey, Peter Drucker, Edward Deming, Francis Hesselbein, Lee Iacocca, Rosabeth Moss Kanter, Norman Vincent Peale, and Tom Peters. Kouzes and Posner are frequent conference speakers, and each has conducted leadership development programs for hundreds of organizations around the world.

James M. Kouzes is an Executive Fellow at the Center for Innovation and Entrepreneurship at the Leavey School of Business, Santa Clara University. Not only is he a highly regarded leadership scholar and an experienced executive, but the *Wall Street Journal* has cited him as one of the twelve most requested non-university executive education providers to U.S. companies. A popular seminar and conference speaker, Kouzes shares his insights about the leadership practices that contribute to high performance in individuals and organizations. Contact: www.leadershipchallenge.com; jim@kouzesposner.com.

Barry Z. Posner, Ph.D., is dean of the Leavey School of Business, Santa Clara University, and a professor of leadership. He served previously as managing partner of the Executive Development Center and has also served as associate dean with responsibility for leading the school's MBA and undergraduate programs. He has received the Dean's Award for Exemplary Service, the President's Distinguished Faculty Award, and several outstanding teaching and leadership honors. An internationally renowned scholar and educator, Posner is the author or co-author of more than one hundred research and practitioner-focused articles. Contact: www.theleadershipchallenge.com; bposner@scu.edu.

CHAPTER SEVENTEEN

COACHING THE COACHES

David Ulrich

The word "coach" is both a noun and a verb. As a noun it stipulates a person who instructs or informs others; as a verb it means the act of teaching or training someone to do something. Coaches (the people) in sports, drama, and music coach (the action) participants to greater performance by defining what should be done, observing what is done, and offering feedback on what will be done. In business settings, coaches play similar roles. They help aspiring managers learn what should be done by offering pointers, learn what is done by observation, and improve what will be done by providing feedback. Management coaching may occur at many levels of a company, from CEO to line supervisor. Each coach has a unique style and approach, but coaches may learn and adapt techniques that help them be better at what they do. This chapter presents elements of a coaching philosophy and steps in a coaching process that have been used in multiple settings to help aspiring managers manage better.

Philosophy

Coaching does not mean doing for others, but means helping others to get things done. Coaches help athletes play the game better, even if they do not personally play the game. Player coaches generally do not perform as well as sideline coaches. Management coaches may not be the best managers, but they must be observers of good management and motivators for good communication. In an early coaching assignment, I observed a leader in team meetings. I paid attention to a few things, such as how did he interact with people before the meeting? Was his style formal or informal? Did people approach him or not? How did he manage the meeting? Did he follow an agenda? How did he make decisions? How did he treat others during the meeting? How did he follow up after the meeting? Did he follow up on actions taken with regard to decisions made during the meeting? The ability to make these subtle observations comes from having "your head on a swivel" and examining the nuances of behaviors and their consequences. With this data, I then engaged him in a conversation on what he did and what he could do to reach his goals.

Coaches earn their credibility by having a history of success. Coaching is both a learned art from experience and a disciplined science from education. Becoming a legitimate coach is a Catch-22: those you coach must have confidence in you, yet you don't earn confidence until you have coached others. Early coaching experiences may begin with friends and allies who trust you and whom you can help and counsel. Like sports coaches who learn from being assistant coaches at high school or college levels before becoming head coaches in the pros, management coaches master their craft from working in the managerial trenches. My early coaching was often with those whom I had known in other settings. For instance, I might have met and developed a relationship with an executive in a development course. Over time, as I matured as a coach from successes and failures, I was more likely to be invited to coach those whom I did not know beforehand.

Coaching is ultimately a relationship. Sometimes the smartest and most technically proficient people are not the best coaches. Coaching requires sharing information and ideas in ways that change the behavior of others. Coaches are not measured by what they know, but how what they know changes what others know and do. Transfer of knowledge flows from relationships of trust. Coaches must be credible and trusted by those whom they coach. In most of my coaching relationships, we start by getting to know each other. This requires listening and learning to like the person I am coaching and sharing with him or her some of who I am. Building a personal bond and professional affection founds the coaching process. Many of my coaching assignments begin with a conversation about personal issues, such as hobbies, families, and personal goals. Once the manager knows I care about him or her personally, we can commence the more rigorous process of managerial coaching. Until a relationship of trust is forged, coaching is more rhetoric than results.

Coaches may be from inside or outside the company, each with pros and cons. Those from inside know the subtleties of the company, the network of relationships within the company, and the likely impact of their counsel. Those from outside the company often have credibility based on external validity, bring innovative ideas to the coaching experience, and may be candid when insiders might temper their remarks. For internal coaches to be credible, they must develop an independent streak; for external coaches to succeed, they must discern organizational nuances. Most of my coaching has been from the outside as an external consultant. However, in many cases, I have partnered with an internal coach, such as an HR professional. The HR person's role is to help the business leader in more day-to-day routine transactions, while I do episodic coaching around events or in predictable timeframes, typically every six to twelve weeks.

Giving honest feedback, both positive and negative, can be personally risky at times. As the givers of feedback, coaches may not always be popular with their coachees, who have often deluded themselves into thinking that there are no behaviors they need to change.

Constructive feedback concentrates on the behaviors, not the person; it focuses on the future more than on the past; and it helps the person self-discover. I recall having collected 360-degree feedback results from a leader whose data indicated significant concerns. I set the stage for sharing this data by reminding him that without struggles, we do not make progress and that honest looks in the mirror lead to improvements. Then we examined the data together and non-defensively worked to figure out why it was given as it was, what it meant in terms of his behaviors, and how he could productively respond. In reviewing feedback, the saying, "We judge ourselves by our intent and others judge us by our behavior" has come in useful. The philosophy of this quote has helped me coach a manager to see that her intent may be to clarify and focus attention, but her abrupt and direct questioning of employees may communicate a lack of sensitivity and concern. Coaches must bring unfavorable views to the surface and deal with negative data in helpful ways.

Coaches ask questions that require self-reflection, because learning is more powerful when the learner learns by choice rather than by edict. Coaches who pose insightful and timely questions help managers see the impact of their behavior on others and help managers improve their behavior. Some of my favorite questions are: "What do you want?" which helps clients focus on goals and purposes; "What are the options?" which generates out-of-the-box alternatives; "What are the first steps?" which turns ideas into practices; "How would you know?" which defines measurable outcomes; and "What decision can you make now to move forward?" which focuses attention. These questions help the coach engage the client in reflection, so that the client owns the result and the process of achieving the result, and these maxims form a coaching philosophy that enables a coach to be the person who helps a manager make positive changes in both attitudes and behavior.

Coaching Process

A process for coaching may take many forms, which define the actions of being a coach. In my coaching, I have adapted the following steps, depending on the situation, but these steps offer a template for thinking about how to engage the client in changing behavior. I also like pictures or images that capture the message I am trying to communicate. Figure 17.1 is the summary of this coaching process. At first blush, this is a complex figure, but each step enables me to draw and build this figure and coach a client through a self-improvement process.

Step 1: Clarify Your Business or Organization Strategy

Every manager works for an organization. Organizations exist to accomplish goals through strategies they craft and deploy. Coaching in the context of strategy assures that the manager has a clear sense of what he or she is trying to accomplish and sets the criteria for being a successful manager. A strategy is a succinct statement of what

FIGURE 17.1. A COACHING PLAYBOOK.

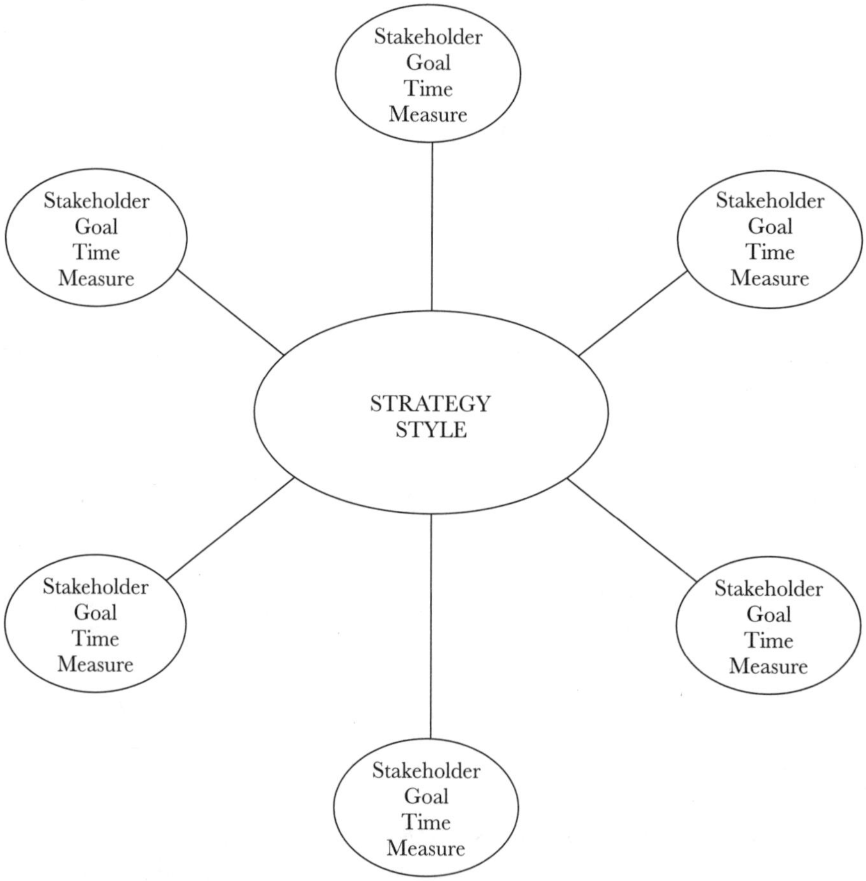

the manager hopes to accomplish and how resources will be applied to that purpose. Questions to clarify strategy include the following:

- What is your business trying to accomplish?
- Who are your primary customers? Why do they buy from you versus a competitor?
- What are your top two or three priorities right now?

Step 2: Describe Your Personal Style

Every manager has a style or way of getting things done. This style is based on dozens of choices about how the manager makes decisions, processes information, treats people, and prefers working. The combination of these decisions forms an identity for the manager that can often be captured in the image others have of the manager. Sometimes these images are crafted and positive; at other times, they are created by a sequence of actions. Sometimes these images help accomplish business goals; sometimes they do not. Each style has its positives and its negatives and may be modified by identifying and changing behaviors that led to the style. Questions to address managerial style include the following:

- What is your managerial identity? How are your known by others? How would you like to be known by others?
- What are you managerial strengths and weaknesses?
- How do you generally treat others, make decisions, handle conflict, manage information?

In the middle circle of Figure 17.1, you can write the strategy and style for the manager. This is at the heart of the coaching process.

Step 3: Define Stakeholders

Every manager gets work done through, with, and by others. These others may be considered stakeholders for the manager. The stakeholders often include those who might be above the manager (such as the boss, the boss's boss, and the board of directors), those peers of the manager (such as managers in other units who participate in the manager's success), subordinates of the manager (including employees or those who report directly or indirectly to the manager), and those outside the boundaries of the company (for instance, customers, suppliers, and investors). These stakeholders may be identified by asking the manager whom he or she must interact with to accomplish the work. The list may be stable over time or vary depending on assignment. Questions to help define stakeholders include the following:

- Who must you interact with to reach your strategy?
- Who is affected by the work that you do?
- Who would you turn to in order to define your managerial style?

The stakeholders may be identified in each of the satellite circles in Figure 17.1.

Step 4: Specify Goals for Each Stakeholder

Stakeholders have an interest in and impact on a manager's success. To reach a business strategy, each stakeholder must provide something. For example, direct reports must become a cohesive team and employees overall must demonstrate commitment. For managers to deliver on their strategies, they should discuss and clarify with each stakeholder his or her goals. Questions to specify stakeholder goals include the following:

- In the next period of time (three, six, twelve, or twenty-four months), what do you want to accomplish with each stakeholder?
- What does each stakeholder contribute to your reaching your strategy?

These goals for the stakeholders may be included in the satellite circles in Figure 17.1.

Step 5: Prioritize Each Stakeholder and Goal

Not all things worth doing are worth doing well. Some things are more important than others, and some stakeholders and their goals are more central to managerial success than others. Managers who try to relate equally all the time to all stakeholders end up serving none. Managers must prioritize stakeholders based on how central they are to achieving the business strategy. Strategies are time-bound, and the key stakeholders for the next three months may be different than the stakeholders for the succeeding three months. For example, in an organizational transformation, it might be critical in the next three months to get your direct reports on board with your agenda before going to the broader employee population in the subsequent three months. Questions to prioritize stakeholders and goals include the following:

- How important is each stakeholder for reaching your goal?
- Rate each stakeholder from 0 to 10 for the next period of time.
- Divide 100 points across the stakeholders to prioritize their impact on your strategies.
- Rank the stakeholders (from high to low) in terms of impact on your strategies.

These ratings may be placed on each satellite circle in Figure 17.1.

Step 6: Allocate Time

Managers' most valuable asset is their time. Where managers spend time communicates what matters most and sends signals to others about what they should do. Coaches can help leaders focus their managers on what they can and should do with each stakeholder. When leaders are aware of how they have spent their time and thoughtful about where they should spend time, they make informed decisions. Involving other organization leaders in this coaching process can be helpful. In one case, a leader prioritized engaging employees in his vision for the next six months (about one hundred work days). He concluded that he should spend about fifteen days on this agenda. We invited the head of human resources into the meeting and told him that the leader could invest fifteen days on communicating his vision in the next six months. We invited the human resources professional to conceive how to spend this resource in the most effective way. I have done similar work with heads of marketing and sales when the leader wanted to spend time with customer; with heads of finance when the leader wanted to connect better with the investment community; and so forth. Spending time thoughtfully turns ideas into actions. Questions to help leaders allocate time include the following:

- How much time in days do you think you should spend with each stakeholder, given the priorities you have set?
- What specific behaviors and actions can you take with each stakeholder to accomplish your goals?
- How would these actions show up in your calendar? Remember that your calendar should probably be 30 to 40 percent unscheduled, as events arise that merit attention, but the other 60 to 70 percent can be structured to ensure that you accomplish what matters most.
- How will you track your return on time invested?

In Figure 17.1, you can begin to put time in days for each satellite circle.

Step 7: Determine Success

Strategies and goals turn into success when they are measured. These measures may be outcomes (what results) or behaviors (how things happen), but what they are should be specified. Coaches help determine measures of success that managers can track on their own. Questions to help determine successful measures include the following:

- How will you know you have succeeded in your overall strategy and in your goals with each stakeholder?
- How will you monitor your progress?

Conclusion

To coach means to have a philosophy that is based on the maxims and beliefs of being a coach. It means to help managers turn their aspirations into action by engaging them in a disciplined process of change. Being a master coach means developing both a philosophy and a process that is uniquely tailored to you as a coach and to the person you are coaching. This is the coach to coachee relationship.

◆ ◆ ◆

David Ulrich is currently president of the Canada Montreal Mission for the Church of Jesus Christ of Latter-day Saints, where he works with missionaries and members throughout Quebec and Ottawa to establish the church. He will do this assignment while on a three-year sabbatical (until July 2005) as a professor of business from the University of Michigan. Professionally, he studies how organizations build capabilities of speed, learning, collaboration, accountability, talent, and leadership through leveraging human resources. He has helped generate multiple award-winning databases that assess alignment between strategies, human resource practices, and HR competencies.

Ulrich has published more than one hundred articles and book chapters and twelve books, including *Human Resources Business Process Outsourcing* and *100 Things You Need to Know to Manage People Effectively and to Design Better People Practices*. Contact: www.rbl.net; dou@umich.edu.

CHAPTER EIGHTEEN

WHY COACHING CLIENTS GIVE UP AND HOW EFFECTIVE GOAL SETTING CAN MAKE A POSITIVE DIFFERENCE

Marshall Goldsmith and Kelly Goldsmith

A review of research on goal setting has helped us better understand two key areas of concern for leadership coaches: (1) why people give up on goals and (2) how effective goal setting can help ensure long-term goal achievement. An understanding of the dynamics of goal setting and goal achievement may help coaches understand why their clients sometimes lose motivation and how they, as advisors in goal setting, can increase the odds that their clients will "stick with the plan" and reach desired targets.

Why do people so frequently give up in their quests for personal improvement? Most of us understand that "New Year's resolutions" seldom last through January—much less for the entire year! What goes wrong?

Six of the most important reasons that people give up on goals are listed below. Following each reason is a discussion of implications for leadership coaches and ideas for "preventative medicine" in planning—so that clients will ultimately be more likely to achieve their change objectives.

Ownership[1]

I wasn't sure that this coaching idea would work in the first place. I tried it out—it didn't do that much good. As I guessed, this was kind of a waste of time!

One of the biggest mistakes in all of leadership development is the rollout of programs and initiatives with the promise that "*this* will make *you* better." A classic example is the performance appraisal process. Many companies change their performance appraisal forms on a regular basis. How much good does this usually do? None! These appraisal form changes just confuse leaders and are seen as annual exercises in futility. What companies don't want to face is the real problem—it is seldom the form—the real problem is the managers who lack either the courage or the discipline to make the appraisal process work. The problem with the "this will make you better" approach is that the emphasis is on the "this" and not the "you." Coaching clients need to understand that ultimately only *you* can make you better.

Successful people tend to have a high need for self-determination. In other words, the more that leaders commit to coaching and behavior change because *they* believe in the process, the more the process is likely to work. The more they feel that the process is being imposed on them or that they are just casually "trying it out"—the less likely the coaching process is to work.

Coaches and companies that have the greatest success in helping leaders achieve long-term change have learned a great lesson—don't work with leaders who don't "buy in" to the process.[2] As coaches, we need to have the courage to test our clients' commitment to change. If clients are just "playing a game" with no clear commitment, we need to be willing to stop the process—for the good of the company and for the good of the coaching profession.

In goal setting, coaches need to ensure that the change objectives come from "inside" the person being coached and are not just externally imposed with no clear internal commitment. Coaches need to let clients know that they are ultimately responsible for their own lives. As coaches, we need to make it clear that we are there to help our clients do the work—not to do the work for our clients.

Time

I had no idea that this process would take so long. I am not sure that it is worth it!

Goal setters have a natural tendency to underestimate the time needed to reach targets. Everything seems to take longer than we think that it should! When the time elapsed in working toward our goal starts exceeding expectations, we are tempted to just give up on the goal. Busy, impatient leaders can be even more time-sensitive than the general population.

While the "optimism bias" about time is true of goal setters in general, it may be even more of a factor for leaders who are trying to change the perceptions of co-workers. In general, our *behavior* changes long before the *perception* of this change by our co-workers.[3] We all tend to see people in a manner that is consistent with our previous stereotypes and we "look" for behavior that proves our stereotypes are correct. Co-workers are no different from anyone else. Recent research shows that the *long-term* follow-up and involvement of co-workers tends to be highly correlated with changed perceptions of leaders.[4] This is not something that is accomplished overnight. Harried executives often want to "check the box" and assume that once they understand what to do—and communicate this understanding to others—their problems are solved. If only the real world were that simple.

In setting goals with leaders, it is important to be realistic about the time needed for them to produce a positive, long-term change in behavior. Habits that have taken forty-eight years to develop will not go away in a week. Let them know that others' perceptions may seem "unfair" and that as they change behavior, others may not fully recognize this change for months. In this way, when they face time challenges, they will not feel that there is something "wrong" with them or with their co-workers. They will realize that this is a normal part of the change process. Ultimately, as the research shows, perceptions will begin to change, and co-workers will begin to appreciate changed behavior.

Difficulty

This is a lot harder than I thought it would be. It sounded so simple when we were starting out!

The optimism bias of goal setters applies to difficulty as well as time. Not only does everything take longer than we think it will, but it requires more hard work! Leaders often confuse two terms that appear to be synonymous—but are actually quite different—*simple* and *easy*. We want to believe that once we understand a simple concept, it will be easy to execute a plan and achieve results. If this were true, everyone who understood that they should eat a healthy diet and exercise regularly would be in shape. Diet books are almost always at the top of the bestseller lists. Our challenge for getting in shape—as it is for changing leadership behavior—is not *understanding*, it is *doing!*

Long-term change in leadership effectiveness requires real effort. For example, it can be challenging for busy, opinionated leaders to have the discipline to stop, breathe, and listen patiently while others say things that they may not want to hear. While the leader may understand the need to change—and even have a great desire to change—it is still hard to have the discipline to change.

In setting goals, it is important that leaders realize that real change will take real work. Making clients feel good in the short-term with statements like "This will be easy" and "This will be no problem for you" can backfire in the long-term when they realize that change is not easy and that they will invariably face some problems in their journeys toward improvement. Letting leaders clearly understand the price for success in the beginning of the change process will help prevent disappointment that can occur when challenges arise later in the change process.

Distractions

I would really like to work toward my goal, but my company is facing a unique challenge right now. It might be better if I just stopped and did this at a time when things aren't so crazy.

Goal setters have a tendency to underestimate the distractions and competing goals that will invariably appear throughout the year. One good counsel that a coach can give an executive is, "I am not sure what crisis will appear, but I am almost positive that some crisis will appear!"

In some cases, the distraction or crisis may result from a problem; in other cases, it may result from an opportunity. For example, mad cow disease was an unexpected problem that produced a crisis for executives in the meat packing industry. It is hard to focus on long-term leadership development when the company is going through an immediate financial crisis! On the positive side, "Cabbage Patch Kids®" became a craze and started selling far more than anyone imagined. It is hard to focus on long-term leadership development when your toy company has a "once-in-lifetime" short-term profit opportunity!

In planning for the future, coaches need to help executives assume that unexpected distractions and competing goals will occur. Build in time in change projections to "expect the unexpected." By planning for distractions in advance, leaders can set realistic expectations for change and be less likely to give up on the change process when either special problems or special opportunities emerge.

Rewards

Why am I working so hard at becoming a more effective leader? After all of my effort, we still didn't make any more money this year!

Goal setters tend to become disappointed when the achievement of one goal doesn't immediately translate into the achievement of other goals. For example, a dieter who loses weight may give up on his weight loss effort when women don't immediately begin to notice him.

Hewitt Associates has done some fascinating research that documents the positive, long-term relationship between investment in leadership development and long-term financial success.[5] Its research shows that companies that invest in developing leaders tend to have greater long-term profits. There is no research that shows investment in developing leaders produces greater short-term profits.

Increasing leadership effectiveness is only one factor in an organization's overall success. For example, a company may have the wrong strategy or be selling the wrong product. If someone is going down the wrong road, increasing people management skills will only help him or her get there faster!

Leaders need to personally "buy in" to the value of a long-term investment in their own development. If coaching clients think that improving leadership skills will always lead to short-term profits, promotions, or recognition, they may be disappointed and may give up when these benefits don't immediately happen. If coaching clients see the change process as a long-term investment in their own development—and something that will help them become more effective in the long run—they will be much more likely to "pay the price" needed to achieve success.

Maintenance

I think that I did actually get better when I had a coach, but I have let it slide since then. What am I supposed to do—work on this stuff the rest of my life?

Once a goal setter has put in all of the effort needed to achieve a goal, it can be tough to face the reality of maintaining changed behavior. One of the first reactions of many dieters upon reaching their weight goal is to think, "This is great! Now I can start eating again. Let's celebrate with some pizza and beer!" Of course, this mind-set leads to future weight gain and the "yo-yo" effect that is unfortunately so common for dieters.

Coaching clients need to clearly understand that leadership is a *process*—not a *state*. Leaders can never "get there." Leaders are always "getting there." The only way that exercising helps people stay in shape is when they face the reality that "I have to work on this stuff for the rest of my life!" Leaders need to accept that leadership development is an ongoing process that never stops. Leadership involves relationships—and relationships change and people change. Maintaining any positive relationship requires ongoing effort over a long period of time. It doesn't occur because someone "got better" and stayed in this state of "betterness" forever.

In Summary

Coaches can either help leaders set goals that increase their probability of long-term change or help leaders set goals that may feel good in the short-term but lead to disillusionment and "giving up" in the long-term.

The typical advertisement or "infomercial" designed to help people "get in shape" provides a great example of what not to do in goal setting. The message is almost always the same: "For an 'incredibly small' amount of money, you can buy a 'revolutionary' product that is 'unbelievably easy' and 'fun to use.' This product will produce 'amazing results' 'in almost no time' and you will 'have the body that you always wanted.'" Most infomercials imply that you will not have to continue exercising and dieting for years, that you will continue to look young, and that you will have frequent, wonderful sex for the rest of your life.

In reality there is no "easy answer"—real change requires real effort. The "quick fix" is seldom a "meaningful fix." Distractions and competing responses are going to happen, and the higher level the executive, the more likely that they will happen. Improving leadership skills—like getting in shape—won't solve all of life's problems. And finally, great leadership is something that leaders need to commit to for the rest of their careers—at least if they really want to be great!

All of these messages may sound "tough," but at least they are real. Successful people are not afraid of challenging goals. In fact, clear, specific goals that produce a lot of challenge tend to produce the best results!

Coaches who have the courage to tell the truth "up front" and challenge leaders in goal setting can go beyond being "highly paid friends." Honest, challenging coaches can help leaders make a real difference—both in their organizations and in the lives of the people they lead.

Notes

1. For a greater elaboration on this theme, read "It's Not About the Coach" by M. Goldsmith in *Fast Company*, October 2004.
2. For an excellent example, read "Leveraging HR: How to Develop Leaders in 'Real Time'" by Linda Sharkey (of GE Financial Services). In M. Effron, R. Gandossy, & M. Goldsmith (Eds.), *Human Resources in the 21st Century*. New York: John Wiley & Sons, 2003.
3. For a dialogue on this, see "Behave Yourself: A Conversation with Executive Coach Marshall Goldsmith" in the *Harvard Business Review*, October 1, 2002.
4. "Leadership Is a Contact Sport" by M. Goldsmith & H. Morgan. *strategy+business*, Fall 2004.
5. This research is summarized in *Leading the Way*, by R. Gandossy and M. Effron. New York: John Wiley & Sons, 2003.

◆ ◆ ◆

Marshall Goldsmith has recently been named by the American Management Association as one of fifty great thinkers and leaders who have impacted the field of management over the past eighty years. He has been described in *The Wall Street Journal* as one of the top ten executive educators; the *Economist* as one of the most credible thought leaders in the new era of business; *Forbes* as one of five most-respected executive coaches; and *Fast Company* as America's preeminent executive coach.

Dr. Goldsmith has a Ph.D. from UCLA and is an adjunct professor at Dartmouth's Tuck School of Management. He has been asked to teach in executive education programs at Michigan, MIT, and the Wharton School. He is one of a select few consultants who have been asked to work with over seventy major CEOs and their management teams.

Dr. Goldsmith is co-editor or author of eighteen books, including *The Leader of the Future* (a *Business Week* best seller), *Global Leadership: The Next Generation,* and *The Art and Practice of Leadership Coaching.* Contact: www.marshallgoldsmith.com/; marshall@ marshallgoldsmith.com.

Kelly Goldsmith is currently a Ph.D. candidate in behavioral marketing at the Yale University School of Management. She is also conducting research for Yale's Center for Consumer Insights. Kelly is an honors graduate from Duke University, where she majored in sociology, with a certificate in markets and management. While at Duke, Kelly designed and taught a course in "Gender and the Media" and was a market research analyst for an international cosmetics company. After being graduated from Duke, Ms. Goldsmith was a contestant on the nationally televised "Survivor Africa." She then worked for the creators of "Survivor," Mark Burnett Productions and was a casting associate for "Survivor" and "Amazing Race." Contact: Kelly.goldsmith@yale.edu.

PART FOUR

APPLICATIONS

CHAPTER NINETEEN

CASE STUDY

Coaching for Change at Aventis

Laurence S. Lyons

Executive coaching has emerged as the modern way of revitalizing people in organizations around the world. This new and pervasive activity is frequently regarded as a tool to assist personal development. In fact, it has far more to offer in terms of business impact. This chapter illustrates how executive coaching may be incorporated as the central component in a change management program, to dramatic effect. Two global programs based on this design approach within the pharmaceutical giant Aventis exemplify best practice.

Executive Coaching

In its basic form, executive coaching involves a series of development conversations between two people, a coach and a client. The coach will assume that the client is vocationally competent. Executive coaching is certainly not training; its techniques cannot help a bad accountant become better at accounting. With its focus fixed firmly on behavioral development, executive coaching is, in essence, a modern form of process consulting, acted out in the workplace.

Today's external coaching practitioners are drawn from a rainbow of specialist disciplines. We can find the behavioral psychologist, career counselor, and business consultant all freshly re-branded as executive coach. Looking outside the management arena, popular comparisons with the more familiar *sports coach* abound, and carry varying degrees of validity. Then again, a new breed of *life coach* has emerged to further blur the broader definition.

Better Business People

Variety in both style and approach is a healthy sign in any personal development interaction, as the world is full of people with differing needs. While each facet of coaching practice may indeed have something useful to offer, there is only one type sure to gain approval in the boardroom. Quite clearly, in the organizational setting executive coaching exists solely to produce better business people. The ultimate value of executive coaching lies in its ability to help better business people go on to produce better business results.

One individual will become a better business person by expanding his repertoire of interpersonal skills. Another will sharpen her strategic thinking. Yet others will want to learn how to become better team players or hone political savvy. Executive coaching offers individuals a custom-built learning mechanism to grow their own healthy business behavior in whatever way is meaningful to them within their organization.

Headlines of an action plan, agreed between a coach and a client, will call out specific areas for personal change. A global or local change management agenda can be immensely helpful when building such a plan. This remains true even when the coach uses a purely *non-directive* approach, always insisting that the decision to select personal development areas remains squarely with the client.

Business people strive to get good value. Coaching offers most value when its dialogue is "leading somewhere," provided that the destination represents a good place to be and the journey is worth the effort. When coach and client together contract to prioritize development areas—in the light of an organizational change agenda—then coaching will extend its impact to become a powerful tool of strategic intervention.

The Management of Change

Change management initiatives emerge from an organizational will or ambition to become something different. Post-merger integration, product improvement, channel innovation, industry change, or new customer demands are typical events that will have set the stage for these major change initiatives. Their large-scale delivery programs require careful design, and are best orchestrated as the co-development of the organization together with its populace.

Change involves risk. Risk is simply the probability of program failure. It is important to remember that any vision of a future "changed" organization must be founded on certain beliefs, so we are always dealing with a transformation that must necessarily contain untested assumptions. Risk ideally vanishes once a change program has achieved total success; in the meantime it is practically safe to assume that change management *is* risk management. Management of risk is the key to success in any change program. Risk will be well-managed when the program properly engages both the process and social dimensions within the organization.

One ever-present assumption is that the organization itself has the skill and capacity for transformation, especially if it is to continue "business as normal" while doing so. Of course, corporate visionaries can never be fully informed by the personal reality of those who are to experience the change: this is because their new experience has yet to happen. To be effective, change architects must find ways to continually keep a two-way dialogue flowing between vision in the boardroom and reality as experienced by individuals on the ground. The efficiency of this conduit is a good proxy for measuring execution *risk* in any change program.

Achilles' Heel

Those involved in the design and implementation of change programs have long felt that something important is missing in the management toolbox—an effective method for putting strategy into practice.

The crucial moment comes at the point of implementation. Once corporate direction has been established and *hearts and minds* won over, a well-designed change program will call into play dedicated components for anchoring the vision and remodeling behavior throughout the organization. So, at least, goes the theory. In practice, however, this critical stage of change management, where personal drive needs to pick up the baton from corporate intellect, has long been recognized as the weakest link in the whole change management chain. Until now.

A Marriage Made in Heaven

When combined, change management and executive coaching offer the organizational designer a marriage made in heaven. The "top-down" voice of the organization from the former system provides broad direction to the latter. In return, we have at our disposal a behavioral mechanism for locally validating and instilling change in each team, group, and individual. The difference that can be made in the attitudes of those individuals who are being asked to change can be remarkable once this connection is made. Change is no longer perceived only as an externally imposed command. An integrated approach allows for a "win-win" combination in which individuals can graft their personal development onto the corporate agenda. The new connection makes change relevant and desirable to all.

Integrated change management and executive coaching designs can provide the foundations of a cascading values-based change system, as depicted in Figure 19.1. This integrated model has now been used successfully in several organizations. Exhibit 19.1 briefly describes one recent intervention in Aventis that is based on this design philosophy.

Proper application of tools taken from the newly enhanced leadership toolbox makes it possible to construct a system of symbiotic organizational and personal change. Executive coaching can make the designer's dream come true: practical interventions now continuously link corporate intent all the way through to individual behavioral change, effectively, rapidly, and with much reduced execution risk.

Risky Business

This is not to say good program design will always eliminate risk in a change program. Instead, an integrated system shifts the locus of risk from local execution back toward original corporate intent and the environment. This has to be good news. In the extreme, if a change program has to fail, it is better it should do so because the corporate ambition was unattainable, rather than that the execution was inadequate.

Our over-pinning guidelines for program success are clear, if all too infrequently stated. We want good initiatives to materialize. We want locally unworkable issues to surface quickly and signal we have found a problem that needs to be addressed. We are prepared to learn and adjust while in transition. The world may not turn out as we expected. Our failure to sensibly orchestrate our own resources is the outcome to avoid at all costs. Environmental risk may be unavoidable; business risk may be countenanced; execution risk is unacceptable.

The benefits of an integrated system can be summarized by simple rules of risk reduction. *Integrated design reduces execution risk; feedback dialogue reduces business risk.* Programs that consciously set out to satisfy these rules by flexibly linking the necessary social building blocks are poised to succeed.

Agent of Change

Organizations engage outside suppliers for their ability to do essential things that otherwise would not be possible. From their wide experience in other organizations, external consultants may bring with them knowledge of tried and tested techniques. Often an organization is perfectly capable with its own resources to perform certain tasks, yet brings in external suppliers purely to reduce or help manage risk.

In change management work, the general skill the coach-consultant must bring to the table is an ability to orchestrate feedback. Such orchestration ensures that feedback surfaces in whatever forum needs its particular message. This is a very wide requirement, as recipients of feedback may include individual executives, a local sponsor, or the main board.

In order to orchestrate feedback, new communications channels may need to be opened up within the organization. This can be a sensitive activity. It is an area demanding strong role clarity whenever external agents are engaged in a change program, and is best carried out in partnership with the design team or sponsor.

The desired endpoint is not simply to deliver feedback, as this is but one step in a broader process of fostering a wider dialogue. The goal is to create a process through which people in organizations can find pathways for change.

Where this dialogue may lead is purely a matter for the client organization to determine. It is always the client who knows his or her business. It is the client who must own any business decisions. The main job for the agent of change is to ensure that channels are open so that meaningful dialogues can take place.

Feedback

Coaching is founded in feedback. The collective experience of managers, direct reports, peers, and customers all provide raw feedback that must first be validated in a personal coaching session before incorporating into each client's action plan.

Validation takes on special meaning when used in a coaching context. It is a process through which raw data gets transformed into the self-insight on which a personal action plan will rest. There are many ways in which feedback might be inadequate, contaminated, or biased. The need to validate arises because feedback is a product of many factors, which include the general organizational climate; specific local, team, or personal issues that were prevalent when the feedback was collected; the time that the client has been in post; and events that may have occurred after feedback was collected.

As an example, many senior executives today take on a number of roles, so it is not uncommon for their teams to report feelings of alienation. In this case, the executive is less likely to be a poor communicator than a person who has insufficient hours in a day. Validation has to tease out the underlying cause. The validation process allows a client to address genuine skill development areas instead of trying to fix current gripes and merely tinker with apparent symptoms.

While validation tests the feedback, *challenge* tests the client's own beliefs and assumptions. A good coach will always point out to the client those clear instances where overwhelming feedback is at variance with his or her personal view of reality. Without relaxing the pressure to challenge the client, a good coach will ensure that each individual's feedback gets validated at an early stage in their coaching relationship.

Validating, challenging, and selecting personal development areas are part and parcel of the art of coaching.

The popularity of personal feedback in coaching goes hand in hand with our growing awareness of the importance of feedback in organizations. This, too, is a good thing. Feedback is an essential component that change designers tend to forget. Often feedback is the only factor that will make a change design come alive in practice. Seasoned change practitioners notice it is invariably the dotted feedback lines of execution plans that turn out to be most important when sleeves get rolled up at implementation time. In the same way that coaches use feedback to benefit individual executives in developing behaviors, change agents should use feedback to squeeze out risk from organizational change programs. An easy way for consultants to achieve this is to simply treat the collective "organization" as another coaching client.

Providing feedback in an organizational setting, however flat, always involves personal risk when top-level intentions give rise to unforeseen obstacles elsewhere. It may be difficult for an individual to speak up, and for as long as this persists, the organization is really shouldering a hidden risk. Any gap between the sponsor's current expectation of program outcome and what may be believed to be workable locally represents a key source of execution risk. Fortunately, such risk is manageable. Execution risk can be handled through program feedback contained in a dialogue orchestrated by the coach.

Orchestrating Feedback

A fundamental role of an external agent, whether coach or consultant, is to orchestrate dialogue. For this to happen smoothly, rules of best practice have to be in place. Before opening up any new dialogue, the consultant will want to ensure that it is based on validated feedback that has been grounded in reality. In addition to this technical need, social rules of *etiquette* must create a context within which good practice can occur and where people feel comfortable to exchange candid views. Etiquette covers matters such as the treatment of confidential personal information and the use of consolidated data for program feedback.

An individual's action plan may follow one of two basic paths. The normal route is for the corporate values, ambition, and consolidated feedback to become manifest in a plan to develop personal behaviors. Another possible outcome, which is not much discussed in standard coaching texts, occurs when an individual believes the corporate ambition may not be workable.

A coach may observe a recurrent issue is being voiced by several executives in the same program and come to believe that there may indeed be a serious obstacle in the way of the change program objectives. This places the coach in a unique position. The coach is the only person in the system having this collective knowledge. The coach (or coaching team in larger programs) has clear sight of consolidated program feedback, which is also a proxy for the cultural climate in which the program is set. Until

FIGURE 19.1. FROM SPONSOR ENGAGEMENT TO RESULTING BEHAVIORS: KEY PROCESS ELEMENTS IN AN INTEGRATED SYSTEM.

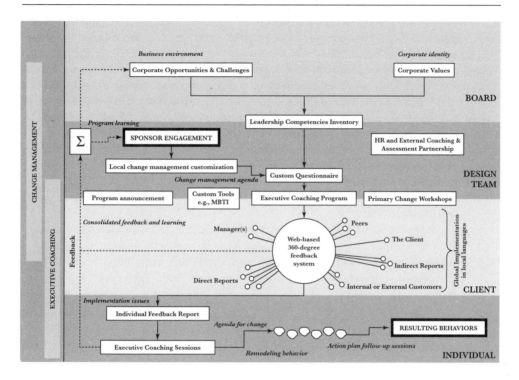

this vital information, presently known only to the coach, finds its way to the design team for validation—and possibly to senior management to trigger a program adjustment—the business is carrying a dangerous risk.

Exhibit 1: Aventis Industrial Operations

Coaching for Change Case Study

Aventis—the major global pharmaceutical company renowned for its prescription drugs and human vaccines—reported core business sales of $17.6 billion in 2002. Industrial Operations is responsible for 50 manufacturing sites around the world, employing some 19,000 people—over a quarter of the company's worldwide workforce. This case study demonstrates how executive coaching can be a driving force within a change management intervention, powerfully stimulating both individual and organizational change.

There are two distinct "clients"—one group and one team. Each is a quite separate global function supported by members of the same human resources organization. Leverage of the excellent relationship enjoyed by HR in each management function was to become extremely valuable in projecting a sense of credibility and program value in the minds of each client, inspiring confidence, commitment, and support.

The Finance Controlling Group holds total responsibility for manufacturing accounting through a group of worldwide site controllers. Those taking part in this program come from across Europe, the USA, Latin America, and Asia Pacific. All site controllers perform broadly similar jobs, each holding a supremely pivotal role in an increasingly empowered and complex organizational structure. Aventis views the leadership development of site controllers as a critical success factor for its business.

Process Development Management Team is responsible for an organization of around 600 employees working in four locations across Germany, France, and the USA. The key role of Process Development is to create robust manufacturing processes taking new chemical formulations from research and development laboratories through to full-scale global production. In a recent reorganization, a top layer of management had effectively been removed, so it became important that the two sub-functions—Chemistry and Biotechnology—work together effectively with minimal top management involvement.

From the outset, HR intended to create more business value than would be achieved from simply providing personal coaching. As these two independent programs ran in parallel, the design team seized every opportunity to cross-fertilize knowledge and best practices in areas of change management and coaching effectiveness. This achieved economy of scale and cost-effective service from the external coaches and consultants.

Working in partnership with the external providers, HR's first action was to assemble a design team that included functional sponsors. The purpose of the first design workshop was to share opportunities and challenges being presented by the business context, and also to assess the full potential of available tools and approaches.

In reality, the ideas of linking coaching to organizational change were developed through this consultation process into a credible implementation plan, which was large scale in scope and change management in nature. As a large-scale endeavor it required comprehensive planning, adequate financial investment, and demonstrable results. As a change intervention, significant importance had to be attached to positioning the programs in the minds of the clients, and in ensuring that the specific business process and contexts were well understood at an early stage of design.

The Aventis board has already signed-off an inventory of company-wide leadership competencies. Much prior work had been done to ensure that the inventory was grounded in agreed corporate values and informed by the strategic challenges facing the company. These competencies are expressed in an Internet-powered 360-degree feedback questionnaire that is being used for coaching senior managers throughout the business. By adding a customized subset to the inventory and using feedback from the questionnaire as the basis of individual coaching dialogues, value-based executive coaching was incorporated as a key change component into both programs. Given the global reach of the intervention, data entry, reporting, and personal coaching were made available in a variety of local languages.

The site controllers' program was based on a new role specification that had been developed in a recent conference. This put significantly more emphasis on strategic support, leadership, and the need to challenge, benchmark, and network. Some nineteen role-specific competencies were compared to those on the standard corporate inventory, which was then extended as necessary.

With its primary focus on interpersonal behavior and the improvement of teamworking, the process development program used a standard competence inventory together with the Myers-Briggs Type Indicator. To consolidate learning and behavior, a team workshop was incorporated at the end of this program.

Design work continued until the team was confident that individual coaching would relate clearly to the business organizational development objectives. Once this point was reached, HR formally made proposals for senior management approval, including the negotiation of costs and the implementation timetable.

The Site Controllers group launched its program as part of a worldwide conference. The process development team utilized a regular management meeting to introduce its program. Customized assessment tools were used in both cases, as were face-to-face and telephone coaching. Importantly, each program incorporated followup coaching and a specifically designed questionnaire to assess results and impact.

Implementation went to plan. One difficulty did occur when some feedback reports were delayed due to late submission. But this was easily resolved through prompt action of the service providers. This demonstrates the importance of service in the supply of assessment tools; we were fortunate to have had a flexible and responsive supplier.

Participant confidentiality was maintained at all times, while the structure of the exercise ensured that valuable aggregated information could be obtained to support the business objectives.

As always with qualitative endeavors, it is hard to measure success. We do know that the programs provided clear evidence of both intent to improve personal performance and the increasing use of personal development plans. At a business level, the process development management team has certainly functioned more effectively. The site controllers are today recognized as providing a new and higher level of support—in line with expectations in their role specification.

Bertrand Cordier, Head of Industrial Operations Controlling reflects, "This program was definitely a vital component in changing the culture, values, focus and behaviors of the Controlling organization."

Describing the program as an "interesting and rewarding experience," Dr. Manfred Worm, Aventis Vice President, Process Development Chemistry, said that the program "provided us with a unique insight into our working preferences and the ways in which others perceive us. It has provided awareness of how we can communicate with others in a manner that they would feel most comfortable."

The HR team and senior management firmly believe in the value of the design team workshops and the investment in the "contracting" stage. Had these been omitted, the personal assessments would probably have gone ahead but with far less enthusiasm on the part of the participants and definitely less impact on the organizational change objectives. Indeed, the full potential of the exercises would never have been achieved if not for the partnership relationship with the coaching consultants and the integrated systems approach.

Summary

At first sight it might seem that executive coaching and large-scale organizational change programs are worlds apart. On closer inspection we find more than a good fit—each has something important to offer the other. By linking organizational development to personal change, integrated programs become increasingly attractive to the very people involved in change. With thoughtful design it becomes easy to create and manage the social paths so vital to the healthy development of an organization and the people within it.

Real-life executive coaching and organization programs are, of course, far more complex than a single chapter could hope to cover. The underlying concept of risk has been introduced in this chapter as a method of unifying some key ideas. The intention has been only to provide a glimpse of what may be achieved with the leadership tools that change architects now have at their disposal. Rather than being worlds apart, we may, indeed, have found opportunities to build a better world.

Acknowledgments

This case study was first published as "Executive Coaching" in *FT Handbook of Management* (3rd ed.), edited by Stuart Crainer & Des Dearlove, ISBN: 0273675842. Publisher: Financial Times Prentice Hall, October 2004.

Thanks to Helen Frost, Aventis HR Programme Support, Frankfurt, for the case study material used in this chapter.

Myers-Briggs Type Indicator and MBTI are registered trademarks of Consulting Psychologists Press, Inc.

◆ ◆ ◆

Laurence S. Lyons (www.lslyons.com) is an accomplished coach, consultant, public speaker, and author. A former technical director at Digital Equipment Corporation, he has been described as a "leading authority on business transformation" by Henley Management College, where he is a member of associate faculty and Founding Research Director of the Future Work Forum.

Lyons is regarded as a pioneer in the field of executive coaching; he has coached hundreds of senior and high-potential executives in organizations in the United States and across Europe. Many of his personal coaching clients are to be found in *Who's Who*.

Dr. Lyons holds a Ph.D. and MSc from Brunel University and the CIM Diploma in Marketing. He is an invited member of the Leader to Leader Institute Thought Leaders Forum (formerly the Drucker Foundation). Contact: lslyons@lslyons.com.

CHAPTER TWENTY

THE EXPERIENCE OF SIEMENS IN SPAIN

Marta H. Williams, Carlos J. Paulet, and Rebeca Arroyo

Siemens has been in Spain for more than one hundred years, officially launched in 1895 when the first Siemens & Halske agency opened in Madrid, responsible for both Spain and Portugal. Currently Siemens concentrates its activities on production, technical services, and the sale of products and systems in the areas of information and communications, transportation, power, medical, lighting, and automation and control. In 1997, Siemens, S.A., brought back a former employee, Eduardo Montes, to become CEO and president of the company. Montes found a company with a strong need to modernize. Siemens in Spain needed to change its culture to match the needs of the 21st century. Many areas needed to be reinforced. Surveys showed that employees were requesting a new type of leadership at every level.

The following case study broadly outlines almost five years of leadership evolution at Siemens led by the CEO, Eduardo Montes, and the director of human resources, Antonio Oliva. Particularly interesting is their innovative use of coaching and 360-degree feedback to relate the HR development program to company strategy. It is another example of the highest form of leadership intervention, which links personal development to corporate goals.

Upon arrival to his new role, CEO Montes was determined to instigate change from within. He did not intend to remove competent executives already in place, many of whom had been in the company for thirty-five years. Instead, Montes' style of approach is and was simple: retain the executives and enhance their leadership abilities.

The company had a long-established leadership culture, although not necessarily one that Montes considered efficient for the pace of the 21st century. The resulting project, which began in 1999 and is still ongoing, includes:

- Building and adaptation of a leadership model linked to corporate headquarters
- Information gathering from past and present leadership definitions and goals
- Creation of a 360-degree feedback instrument in accord with the leadership model
- Multi-round application of the instrument to 418 executives, based on confidentiality and anonymity
- Coaching one-on-one as part of a Leadership Acceleration Program
- Careful alignment of external coaches with the company goals
- Long-term training in coaching skills for executives
- Measurement and analysis at each stage of the process, including:
  - Multiple rounds of feedback
  - Impact studies
  - Evolutionary leadership studies by divisions, levels, and areas
  - Cultural DNA analysis
  - Benchmarking of 360-degree results with the EFQM (European Forum for Quality Management) model
  - Integration of the results of evolutionary leadership with results of employee satisfaction surveys

Description of the Project

Building the 360-Degree Feedback Inventory and the Leadership Model

The human resources implementation team at Siemens decided, before contacting any providers, that it wanted a truly eclectic inventory to measure leadership skills and development. After a year-long search for a consulting firm to accompany the team on the project, members selected The Washington Quality Group (WQG) as partners. WQG began by helping HR collect various survey results, critical success factors, leadership descriptions, information from HR in Germany, and future needs. The collection soon included over three hundred possible items for a 360-degree feedback survey. With the aid of employees at multiple levels, these were reduced and consolidated to sixty-seven. As the process advanced, items were added, changed, or removed, based on the changing goals and priorities of the company each year. In the second round, sixty-one items were used and in the third round forty-six. These were still comparable to items in the first inventory for the great majority. The first-round 360-degree feedback instrument included three questions for verbatim comments, and later rounds also included three questions pertaining to follow-up and the perception of change.

This inventory was organized according to the categories of the Siemens Leadership Model. After consideration, Spain wisely decided to use the Leadership Framework designed in Germany, built around the seven values expounded by Siemens AG. This framework changed and developed over the following years, and the Spanish Inventory continued to follow the lead of the head office in Germany. The Siemens Leadership Framework at the time of writing is shown in Figure 20.1.

The First Round 1998–2001

In the first round, only the top three levels of executives participated in the process. The levels were comprised of the executive committee, the CEO, and the directors of each division that makes up Siemens in Spain; the first-line managers who report directly to the members of the executive committee; and the second-line executives within each division who report to the first line. After some three years, the feedback instrument had been cascaded through three complete management levels to complete the first round. A total of 417 executives received almost 6,000 evaluations from raters, as shown in Figure 20.2.

FIGURE 20.1. SIEMENS LEADERSHIP FRAMEWORK.

WE STRENGTHEN OUR CUSTOMERS - to keep them competitive
Our success depends on the success of our customers. We provide our customers with our comprehensive experience and solutions so they can achieve their objectives fast and effectively.

WE PUSH INNOVATION - to shape the future
Innovation is our lifeblood, around the globe and around the clock. We turn our people's imagination and best practices into successful technologies and products. Creativity and experience keep us at the cutting edge.

WE ENHANCE COMPANY VALUE - to open up new opportunities
We generate profitable growth to ensure sustainable success. We leverage our balanced business portfolio, our business excellence and synergies across all segments and regions. This makes us a premium investment for our shareholders.

WE EMPOWER OUR PEOPLE - to achieve world-class performance
Our employees are the key to our success. We work together as a global network of knowledge and learning. Our corporate culture is defined by diversity, by open dialogue and mutual respect, and by clear goals and decisive leadership.

WE EMBRACE CORPORATE RESPONSIBILITY - to advance society
Our ideas, technologies and activities help create a better world. We are committed to universal values, good corporate citizenship and a healthy environment. Integrity guides our conduct toward our employees, business partners and shareholders.

FIGURE 20.2. FIRST ROUND FEEDBACK RESULTS—PARTICIPANTS, RATERS.

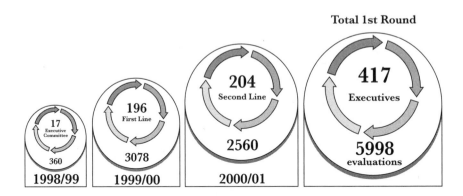

Eduardo Montes was clear from the beginning which leadership qualities he was striving to develop in his executive team. He emphasized that the role of directors had changed greatly in the past few years and identified three key qualities that he was looking for in his leaders:

1. Clear ideas—not necessarily many ideas, but very clear ones;
2. Effective communication skills; and
3. Role model (practice what he/she preaches).

All 417 first-round participants went through a two-day seminar. Montes was present to open each one, which spoke volumes. This was not simply another training program; the CEO was spending his time taking a personal role in its delivery. In his opening remarks, it was clear to all in attendance that Montes considered this program to be vital to the future of the company. In communicating this clear message, and by spending his time with participants, Montes demonstrated the three key leadership qualities his program was promoting.

Participants went through the process in groups of twenty-five, organized by divisions. During the seminar they received information about Situational Leadership and the importance of their credibility as leaders. Participants received their first-round feedback report during a one-on-one session of ninety minutes. This involved analyzing their feedback with a professional coach. As a group, they put together a Group Action Plan, which they presented at the end of the seminar to their division head. On an individual level, during a lengthy session with his or her coach, each person developed his or her personal action plan, concentrating on one or two areas of personal growth. Each individual was expected, on returning to the office, to present his or her action plan to stakeholders: bosses, peers, and direct reports were asked for suggestions on how the program participant could improve his or her leadership. The first round, which began at the end of 1999 and ended at the beginning of 2001, took a year and half to complete. Later rounds took considerably less time, as the seminars were reduced to one day. Also, the feedback process evolved from paper inventories to on-line evaluation tools, greatly reducing the time necessary to receive data and print feedback reports.

First-Round Results

The scale chosen by Siemens was a Likert Scale, 1 to 5, measuring satisfaction, 5 being "Very Satisfied" and 1 being "Very Dissatisfied." The results of the first round were pre-sented as mean averages. The information was viewed "horizontally," or line by line, and also "vertically," or division by division. Base line results horizontally showed a typical "leadership reflection," wherein the line for each group had the same movement as the other lines, or the same "pattern." The executive committee was perceived as having higher leadership skills than the first or second line. In some instances, second-line results were higher than first-line results. This was probably due to the fact that the second line had evaluated the first-line directors almost a year previously. The time span between the measurement of the perception of the executive committee and the second line was almost 1.5 years. Thus, the second-line members were familiar with the system, had rated their own bosses and watched them learn and grow, and were already benefiting from better models of leadership from above, which in itself af-fected their learning curve positively. By the time second-line members were evaluated by their direct reports, they had actually been well into the process for a long time.

The data resulting from the first round gave some interesting food for thought. Considering that the "culture" in Siemens could be that Siemens does in their day-to-day existence, we see that there are stronger areas and weaker areas, and those areas are the same for all the executives, regardless of their levels in the hierarchy. They are all seen as rating higher in customers, corporate responsibility, and company value, and somewhat lower in people and innovation. The four subcategories of peo-ple (drive, focus, impact, and guide) are the areas most needing to be strengthened.

The "pattern" for each executive level is similar in shape, consonant with a "lead-ership reflection" in which leadership behaviors and attitudes trickle down from the top level. In other words, employees tend to follow the lead of their bosses. Their scores are consistently slightly lower than those of their bosses. They are strong in those lead-ership skills in which their bosses are strong; they are rated poorly in those areas in which their bosses are rated poorly; they always have slightly lower ratings.

One clear indicator was emerging: change, if there was to be any, had to come first from the top at Siemens in Spain.

Second-Round Results, 2000–2003

In the second round, once again all participants from the three top levels, in groups of twenty-five, met for a workshop, this time one day, and another lengthy session of coaching. A key aspect of this workshop was to focus on innovation. By now, Eduardo Montes wanted to be sure his directors were innovative enough to carry his plans forward. As a result he requested a study to decipher what innovation "is and is not" in the Siemens culture. The study began on the results of the four items directly mentioning innovation and creativity in the inventory, in an effort to define these concepts more clearly and to see what actions could be taken to accelerate it. The results of this study are presented at the end of this chapter, in a study of how innovation and creativity can be impacted through leadership behaviors and understood more clearly through evolutionary feedback data.

Evolutionary Feedback

The coaches for the second round, Siemens directors, were specially prepared to give "evolutionary feedback," with information from both the first and second rounds. Coaches also put emphasis on understanding and changing the *perceptions* of others, as well as changing *behaviors*. As in the previous round, participants were once again asked to hold post-feedback review meetings with their stakeholder groups to explain their action plans and ask for suggestions.

Second-round data showed improvement for all three executive levels in all five areas of the Siemens leadership model. Nevertheless, while all levels had shown improvement, the *culture pattern* had not changed significantly. Customers, company value, and corporate responsibility were still the stronger areas, while innovation and people continued to be the areas in need of strengthening, especially in impact and guide. (See Figure 20.3.)

Figure 20.4 shows the mean evolution for the aggregate of all executives at the three levels. The mean average has improved from the first to second round. But even more gratifying is the shift to the right of perceptions, indicating a higher degree of satisfaction in the perceptions of the various rater groups. Not surprisingly, the results of the employee satisfaction surveys for these same periods supported the perceived improvement in leadership skills.

To fully comprehend any improvement in leadership skills, it is helpful to look carefully at the perceptions of each rater group (boss, peers, direct reports, and others) to establish from where the perception of improvement is coming.

The dotted line from left to right in Figure 20.4 signifies no change from first round to second round of feedback, shown as 0.00. Positive change is reflected above the dotted line, while negative change falls below the dotted line when contrasting the results from the two rounds of feedback. In this instance, the perceptions of all four rater groups—self, direct reports, peers, and boss—show positive evolution in varying degrees. Peers are the group whose satisfaction has increased the most, while "self" the least. This is quite normal between first and second rounds, as some executives were surprised to find that their self-perceptions were higher than the perceptions of other rater groups evaluating them in the first round. Thus, in the second round they are a bit less "confident" in their self-perceptions.

FIGURE 20.3. EVOLUTION FROM FIRST TO SECOND ROUND.

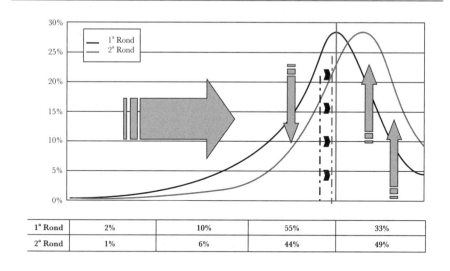

1ª Rond	2%	10%	55%	33%
2ª Rond	1%	6%	44%	49%

FIGURE 20.4. MEAN EVOLUTION OF AGGREGATE OF ALL EXECUTIVES.

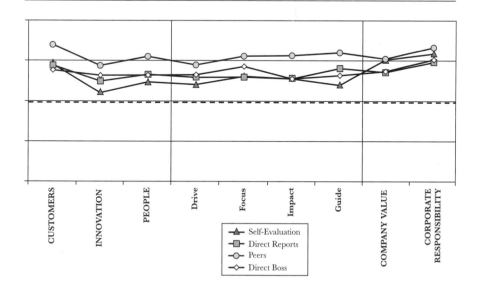

Perceptions

One important objective of 360-degree feedback is to help executives align their self-perceptions more realistically with the perceptions of others. Leadership has to do with the perception of others, and often has little in common with a self-evaluation of leadership skills. The perceptions by rater groups may not be "true" in the strict sense of the word (indeed, sometimes these perceptions vary between groups), but they can be thought to be more "realistic" than the self-perceptions. These perceptions are certainly "true" for the evaluators.

Women Executives

An interesting discovery at this point was to find that the self-perceptions among women executives, on average, was substantially lower than the self-perceptions of male executives. This was borne out in studies in other companies as well. Women executives seem to be more critical in their self-perceptions than men. Yet, at the same time, women are perceived by rater groups as better leaders than men.

Third-Round Results

The third round began with the executive committee in October of 2003, and at this time the first line has just received feedback, while the second line has not yet done so. Thus, there are no final results in hand at the time of writing. The results to date are again positive. The executive committee, once again led by Montes, entered into a phase of face-to-face feedback. (This is recommended only for companies that are well-advanced in this type of program.) Each member gave a short report on his or her strengths, areas for improvement, and action plan to the other members. He or she would then receive helpful suggestions and feedback, always within pre-established limits of respect, generosity, and a true desire to help one another. Each one also studied the evolution of his or her own division and compared it to his or her individual evolution in leadership skills.

It was not surprising to discover that the members of the executive committee who worked hardest on improving their own leadership skills were the leaders of the divisions that had also improved the most. Some of the members are also working with an external coach, with the goal of understanding more profoundly the relationship between individual development and divisional evolution.

A New Style

At the time of this writing, the first line of each division is receiving third-round feedback. In a different style than in rounds one and two, in the third round we are focusing specifically on individual growth and development. There are no seminars or workshops, and instead each individual has a personal coach with whom he or she will be meeting or speaking on a regular basis. The coach's role in the leadership process is to act as a catalyst in order to ensure action planning and, most importantly, follow-up on behaviors to improve.

In six months, there will be an impact study, halfway between round three and round four, so that each executive can have a preview of progress in specific areas of his or her action plan. This will help coach and coachee to adapt the action plan prior to round four. A select group of twenty-three external coaches is working with the first-line directors, using a coaching workbook and manual. There is also an intensive preparation session to understand goals and priorities. The workbook includes specific instruction for the six-month process up to the impact study, as well as recommendations, actions to take, and other valuable resources. A *Siemens Coaching Manual,* organized item by item, with suggestions, articles, and books to read, now resides on the Siemens intranet for use by participants and coaches as a developmental guide.

Corporate Study on Innovation

Innovation was identified as a key area for improvement in first and second feedback rounds. Eduardo Montes had placed heavy emphasis on understanding innovation in Siemens as early as the beginning of the second round. His intention was to help each director build a "framework of reference" in which employees would be more self-motivated and more willing to innovate and take risks.

The study was built around Montes' belief that innovation—at least in Siemens—is not merely casual discovery. It is based on technology, on what the market requires, and on financial feasibility. It is not enough to be creative; creativity must be translated into knowledge, and knowledge into fuel for the GDP (Gross Domestic Product). A study was done on the four items referring to "creativity" and "innovation" in all three rounds of feedback. Results showed that innovation had improved in each round but was still capable of being improved.

In order to further understand the status of innovation in Siemens in Spain, an analysis was needed to see which rater groups felt innovation was improving and which ones did not. The evolution graph on the right in Figure 20.5 shows that peers and direct bosses are of the opinion that innovation is going down, while direct reports and self-perceptions believe that it is improving.

We asked specialists in statistics to perform a series of factorial and correlation analyses on the Siemens data from the first, second, and third rounds, using the four items that speak directly to innovation and creativity. Although there are related behaviors not found in the Siemens inventory, we began to see the behaviors that could be emphasized in coaching sessions that might improve innovation (see Figure 20.6).

A factorial analysis found that three of the four items referring to innovation fell together in one of six factors (Factor 1). When investigating these behaviors, it is possible to extrapolate that in the culture of Siemens Spain, innovation is perceived by employees as achieved through continuous improvement, not by casual discovery. The combination of a constant search for maximizing results added to the careful assigning of responsibilities to employees is what creates innovation "Siemens Style" (see Figure 20.7).

FIGURE 20.5. INNOVATION AND RATER GROUP PERCEPTIONS.

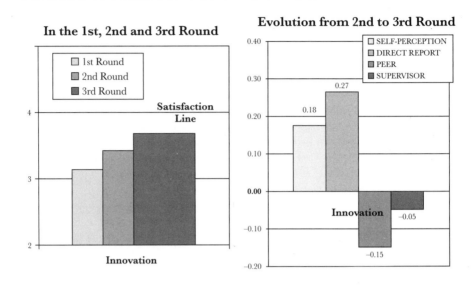

FIGURE 20.6. INNOVATION IN SIEMENS.

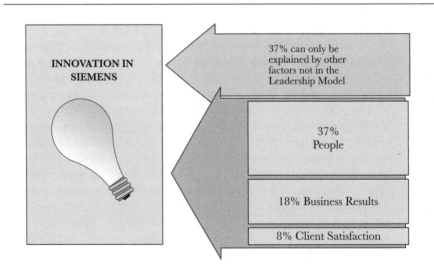

FIGURE 20.7. INNOVATION FACTORS.

	0,746	38. Concentrates on results and steady improvement	Results
	0,672	40. Considers growth a prime objective	Results
	0,667	39. Maximizes productivity and profitability in his/her area	Results
	0,646	8. Sets high standards for him/herself and for others, establishing demanding yet attainable objectives	People
	0,643	42. Questions existing processes in a positive manner and improves upon them	Results
	0,624	**5. Develops and puts into practice ideas to find new alternatives**	I+C
	0,529	10. Prepares for possible changes and is proactive	People
Factor 1	0,528	24. Attracts and develops the best collaborators	People
	0,526	41. Benchmarks with the most successful partners and competitors in the market	Results
	0,504	14. Establishes with collaborators functions, responsibilities and objectives according to the general objectives of the company	People
	0,491	**6. Implements innovations before the competition**	I+C
	0,478	**7. Takes calculated risks and takes responsibility for the results**	I+C
	0,471	26. Takes into consideration the knowledge and skills of each employee before assigning tasks	People
	0,449	11. Makes decisions effectively and takes responsibility for the consequences	People
	0,694	12. Shows flexibility and manages with agility changes in priorities and strategies	People
Factor 6	0,626	**4. Values and stimulates creativity and innovation**	I+C
	0,590	21. Has a positive influence in intercultural environments	People
	0,396	13. Creates and communicates a clear and motivating vision of the future	People

On the other hand, the one item that directly refers to creativity fell in Factor 6, rather than Factor 1. The "companion behaviors" in Factor 6 also come from the people category, but in this case exclusively from people, with no reference to results. Here, for creativity, the emphasis seems to be on flexibility and agility, not on process (see Figure 20.7).

Third-round coaches are placing emphasis on *all* companion behaviors of Siemens style innovation, rather than on the four items that more obviously refer to innovation in general. The belief, or hope, is that it may be easier to leverage innovation in this way. If innovation at Siemens is indeed the result of a constant search for maximizing results by carefully assigning responsibilities to employees, coaches may be able to help by promoting companion behaviors. Round-four results will shed more light on this tactic to "provoke" more innovation in the culture.

ROI—Can It Be Shown in Leadership Development?

Although it is difficult for a leadership acceleration process to full take credit for a clear upward trend in economic results at Siemens in Spain, Montes himself says publicly that leadership development has been a strong contributing force. It is perhaps hard to find a better or more credible testimonial. Figure 20.8 shows the financial growth of Siemens and the number of employees since the project began at the end of 1999.

There are other positive indicators of success. In the past five years, Siemens Spain has twice won an award as the best managed branch of Siemens worldwide. The leadership process pioneered at Siemens in Spain has also been named a "best practice" for Siemens worldwide.

Key Learnings

Managing a project of this magnitude is difficult, if only for the large numbers involved. It is important that client and provider work as partners, learning from each other and developing a relationship built on trust, loyalty, and sharing. Experience has shown that the total confidentiality of the 360-degree feedback and a quality coaching process allow leadership behaviors to be identified and modified.

FIGURE 20.8. FINANCIAL RESULTS AND EMPLOYEES.

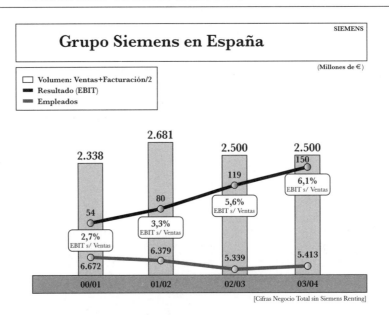

The coaching process must be aligned, coach-by-coach, with the strategic goals and priorities of the company. Siemens HR and WQG spent many hours teaching the WQG coaches what Siemens hoped to gain from the coaching process, using specific behaviors and descriptions of the ideal profile of a Siemens leader. Coaching was carefully monitored, and the twenty-three coaches used a specifically designed workbook in all coaching sessions to assure that the basics were similar in each case. In the continuing spirit of learning, an impact study will be performed after six months.

We have learned that a well-designed 360-degree feedback instrument is incredibly versatile and useful. It does many more things than measure perceptions of behaviors. If it is carefully implemented in the right atmosphere, it can turn into an instrument for the future which can help define and give life to the strategy, objectives and priorities of the company—with maximum speed and efficiency. In this chapter we focused on repeated 360-degree feedback rounds or measurement with a carefully designed instrument. Once we have validated to make sure we are measuring truths and not lies, this instrument can be projected into the future of the company with force. For example, we applied statistical measurements to the data from the first round, and it showed us a series of very useful figures about drivers, factors, and accompanying behaviors that can help to reach goals. When plotted on graphs it gave us very useful information about the company culture—something never measurable until now— and a highway map for training, showing what groups needed help in which areas.

Once we have reached a critical mass of data, if we run a co-relational analysis, we can study the relationship between different items representing behaviors. This in turn allows us to "provoke" certain areas, such as we did with Innovation and Creativity in Siemens, in order to try to maximize the amount of innovation going on in the company now and in the future.

Perhaps the mega driver concept has proven to be the most useful in our coaching work. If we know that by raising certain behaviors, those in turn will raise the perception of other behaviors that are correlated to them, a coach can help his/her coachee to raise the perceptions in respect to multiple behaviors, not just those chosen in their Action Plan, with the same amount of effort. By the study of mega drivers we found that we actually could maximize speed and efficiency of coaching, hence our "leadership accelerator" theory. We feel we can safely assure that working on one or two mega drivers inside the action plan will create a positive impact on the overall perception of an executive as a leader in an efficient way, and in a shorter time span. As a result, we now ask our coaches to include at least one mega driver in all action plans for coachees.

By analyzing fields, such as creativity or teamwork, that need to be more efficient if the company strategy is to be realized, we find that drivers can also be useful. The driver theory is capable, given a large enough mass of data, of indicating what behaviors will hasten executives to "live" the strategy with success, and reach strategic goals in the most efficient way and time. Thus we have the basis of a shortcut to strategic goals, a way to accelerate the right behaviors to provoke the desired end situation.

The most exciting part is that it seems to be working! We now know which executive behaviors will accelerate innovation in Siemens, and our measurements show that the results are on the right track.

The leadership for the process must come from the highest levels of the company and be carefully aligned to strategic results, goals, and priorities. If possible, behaviors must be modeled by the CEO and the executive committee. Too often consultants are told, "Please fix those executives in the second room to the right!" The learning lesson in this case was supported by the CEO, who gave the best reply from the beginning: "Let's start with me!"

◆ ◆ ◆

Marta H. Williams, a native of Washington, D.C., moved to Spain after finishing university studies in the United States. She founded The Washington Quality Group in 1992 with partners John Byrne and Carlos E. Marin, in order to help Spanish executives develop their leadership skills. She founded The Institute of Coaching in 2001, the same year she was given Honourable Mention by the Spanish Federation of Women Entrepreneurs as Business Woman of the Year.

A journalist prior to becoming a consultant, Williams represented ABC News and *U.S. News & World Report* as their Spanish correspondent for many years. She was a member of the founding editorial team of *EL PAÍS,* Spain's most important newspaper. Other interests have long included volunteer work, where she was a founding member of the Mayor's Hotline for Madrid's mayor, the Parents' Association for Children with Congenital Heart Disease, and Parents of Dyslexic Children. She is also a founding member of two women's groups, The Charter 100 of Madrid and the International Woman's Forum of Spain.

Williams is a professor at the executive master level for human resources in San Pablo CEU University and the University of Alcala de Henares. She is often an invited guest on television and radio programs that deal with corporate leadership and executive women in Spain. Contact: www.wqg.es; marta.williams@wqg.es.

Carlos J. Paulet has had an outstanding professional career as an executive development consultant and facilitator. Operating out of Europe since 2000, he is an experienced executive coach, specializing in multi-rater feedback, who has worked with top-level executives in different parts of the world. He is a professor in the master's programs of San Pablo CEU Business School and has received honors for his participation as a guest lecturer at other institutions in Spain and Peru.

Prior to his career in executive development, Paulet was the director of operations and flight service for the American Airlines Latin American Region. With American Airlines he had the opportunity to lead and provide customer service training to a team of 583 professionals distributed throughout Miami, Bogotá, Lima, Montevideo, Sao Paulo, Santiago, and Buenos Aires. Born in Peru and raised in the Dominican Republic, Brazil, and the United States, Paulet is natively proficient in English, Spanish, and Portuguese. Contact: www.wqg.es; cpaulet@wqg.es.

Rebeca Arroyo is director of leadership and development for Siemens in Spain. She studied psychology at the University Comillas of Madrid and has a master's in human resources at the Escuela de Organización Industrial. Since 1999 she has developed and coordinated some of Siemens most important programs. Apart from the leadership process, she has also headed up the Siemens Management Learning program, as well as the High Potentials program in Spain. Contact: www.siemens.es; rebeca.arroyo@siemenss.com.

CHAPTER TWENTY-ONE

THE GENERAL MILLS & PILLSBURY MERGER

Kevin D. Wilde

Mergers and acquisitions are risky business. There are some theories, but sorry few successful models for addressing the daunting post-closing challenges—melding organizations with different operating styles and processes, calming the primal fears of employees, getting through the messiness and disruption of the transition and onto the real business of the new company. A less than fully successful organizational integration carries huge downsides, not the least of which is failure of the deal to generate the promised returns to shareholders.

When General Mills (GM) set out to acquire Pillsbury in 2001, the HR team devoted significant energy and resources to developing a coaching strategy and implementing it throughout the new company. Although there may be bigger business deals than GM acquiring Pillsbury, this merger strategy merits attention, as it has helped GM achieve two important goals. The first is retention. Rather than lose its best people, as is typical of many companies during mergers, GM has held onto the top four hundred value creators throughout the process. The second is high employee satisfaction, especially from employees of the acquired company, Pillsbury.

A Little History

General Mills, the maker of Wheaties and other leading food products, is a one-hundred-year-old company with a long-standing commitment to its employees, the consumers who buy its products, and the communities in which it is located.

In October 2001, General Mills acquired long-time, cross-town rival Pillsbury, a move expected to nearly double its annual revenues to make it one of the largest food companies in the world. The acquisition doubled General Mills' revenues in the high-growth international arena, provided it with an operating platform in twenty more countries (including thirty non-U.S. operating plants), and positioned it for significantly rapid growth through Pillsbury's dough business. With more than one hundred well-known consumer brands and an entrée into nearly every culture on earth, the new company would become a market leader.

The successful integration of an acquisition is one of the rarer corporate phenomena. The issues facing the new General Mills were especially significant, given the dramatic changes in organizational size and composition associated with the acquisition. More than 16,000 Pillsbury employees would augment General Mills' workforce of about 10,500. This included an international workforce that grew from fewer than 1,000 to 7,500 employees, nearly all of them Pillsbury foreign nationals. General Mills' top management knew it had no small challenge on its hands to integrate the two organizations into one productive, highly committed workforce that could deliver on the promise of greater shareholder value.

Six Critical Coaching Spots

GM top management developed a coaching strategy that was focused on how to most effectively build and reinforce a high level of commitment among all the new company's employees. This transition strategy entailed six critical coaching spots:

Early Encounters

Day 1: Strategy and Customer Focus

Structure and Staffing

Performance Management Process (PMP)

Individual Development Plan (IDP)

Climate Tracking

Case Study

Early Encounters

The intention to merge the two companies was announced in July 2000, and due to a prolonged government review, the Early Encounters period was extended from the expected ninety days to seventeen months. Many companies fail because they lose sight of the strategy of the merger and they focus so much on their internal restructuring that they forget about the customer. Realizing this, Pillsbury and General Mills took great pains to coach their leaders to frequently communicate to employees the strategy and purpose of the merger and to stay focused on the overall objective of both companies, to serve customers well.

The goals of Early Encounters were to coach leaders to communicate frequently to employees about the objectives of the acquisition and to address any fundamental concerns or anxieties that the acquisition was bound to create among employees from both organizations.

Leaders were aware that if employees were not supported through these early, anxious stages of the transition and their concerns were not addressed quickly, they would be distracted and less likely to focus on the goals of the new company. Championing the process, the vice chairman formed fourteen standing committees, which blended groups of Pillsbury and General Mills functional and business leaders. In addition, team members met frequently during the seventeen-month period to discuss and plan for Day 1 (the day the merger was finalized), and they shared information gathered from these meetings with their departments. During this time, it was not uncommon for leaders to take their teams out for social functions to get to know each other on a personal level, to talk about where the business was headed, and to discuss how they might support the success of the company. Leaders focused on being visible and available (to ease employee anxiety) and continually restating the acquisition's goals and purpose (to maintain teamwork, clarity, and focus).

During this period, the joint HR function of Pillsbury and General Mills met weekly to guide the planning process leading into Day 1. Although cultural differences were uncovered, for the most part the two companies were quite similar, both in regard to their business models and their customer-centered approaches. HR people took part in both formal training and one-on-one coaching to ensure that they were sensitized to the cultural differences between the companies, that they were respectful of both sides, and that they were focused on retention of employees, especially the four hundred value creators identified as critical to the success of the new company. During this time, HR focused on building relationships between teams and departments across company lines and getting people excited about their futures at the new General Mills.

Day 1: Strategy and Customer Focus

Within a week of Day 1—the day the merger was finalized—ceremonies were held, executives met with their new leadership teams, and announcements were made on the structure and staffing of the new company. All employees were informed which teams they would be on, who their bosses would be, and how their units would run. In essence, everyone knew the answer to the question: *Do I have a job?* For anyone who was not chosen to be part of the ongoing team, there were placement services, and leaders were coached to treat every employee with respect and support. Leaders were also coached on how to conduct business during those first days and weeks.

Structure and Staffing

The bulk of businesses and processes were merged during October and November 2001. During this time, HR and leadership addressed the implementation of the new organizational structure. Challenges during this time were many. These included staffing the new structure with existing talent from both organizations, supporting employees in the transition to new jobs, retaining critical value-added employees, assisting displaced employees, and consolidating human resource management policies and programs.

The Performance Management Process (PMP)

PMP was developed to translate the business objectives of the new organization into clear criteria for individual on-the-job performance, to appraise actual performance relative to expectations, and to link results to salary and incentive rewards.

PMP was seen as an effective mechanism for supporting the achievement of the company's business goals in several ways:

- To synchronize individual efforts with business needs;
- To energize people to perform their best;
- To create a performance culture in which employees are rewarded for achieving results; and
- To develop employees' skills and capabilities and thus grow in their capacity to provide value for the business.

PMP Design. PMP was to be a simple, focused, positive process built on the following principles:

- Individual objectives should be aligned with company and business unit objectives;
- Individuals' performance expectations increase every year along with business demands;
- Performance feedback is a continuous process (not just an annual event);
- The performance appraisal encompasses both *what* is accomplished and *how* the results are achieved;
- An individual's performance during the past year affects that person's base and incentive compensation; and
- Employees and their managers are both accountable for the Performance Management Process.

Before the acquisition, General Mills and Pillsbury had different performance management systems, and the intention was to select the best elements from each system that would support the objectives of the integration. But this intention was also tempered by other realities. Managers and employees alike were already being asked to absorb significant changes. There was also a very limited amount of time to design and implement the new system in the midst of other pressing priorities of the integration. Thus, a pragmatic approach was adopted: Keep it simple, focus on the most critical needs, preserve what is familiar—if it will work—to avoid unnecessary confusion, and save the bells and whistles for later. To further ensure that a pragmatic design would emerge, the human resources function partnered with line managers, who would ultimately implement and maintain the process with their employees.

An integral part of the PMP framework, the Individual Development Plan, would come to be implemented later in the transition. Since so many employees were dealing with a new job, new co-workers, a new supervisor, and new systems, it was critical that supervisors and employees discuss job expectations and work expediency. This transition period was the most vulnerable in terms of a performance dip. If individual efforts were not immediately synchronized, the organizational acceleration needed to recoup the expected post-closing performance slippage and to convert new opportunities and capabilities into performance that exceeded pre-acquisition levels might not have been developed. Because it could quickly focus people on those activities necessary to drive the business forward, PMP was the ideal process, with its direct link to compensation, for addressing the question employees were certain to have: *Can I win at this new job?*

PMP Launch. PMP was launched in January 2002 with several tools and processes, a launch "model" that would prove useful for later transition initiatives as well:

- Line briefings were held to introduce PMP and the benefits it would have for all participants and the new company as whole. Earlier communications with employees had already positioned PMP as one of the key initiatives for the transition.
- HR managers were trained in PMP first; they in turn led the training for all participants, beginning at the top of the organization and then cascading down to lower levels, with managers co-leading the sessions.
- Instructions, guidelines, tips, forms, and supporting materials were provided to managers and employees in a printed workbook and on the company intranet.
- The briefings, training, and materials all reinforced the messages of the acquisition and the role that PMP was to play in creating the kind of organization the new company needed.

Under the shortened initial PMP cycle, managers and employees met to discuss performance objectives and behavioral expectations during January and February of 2002. Managers were encouraged to provide ongoing performance feedback over the next several months. Formal performance appraisals were then conducted during May and June 2002, and the ratings were a key factor in determining merit increases and annual incentive awards in July 2002.

It was our intention to implement the PMP within the international units as well, nearly all of which had been acquired with Pillsbury and were mostly staffed with local nationals. However, the objective of "one company, one culture" had to accommodate very real differences between countries in customs, statutory requirements, social and business cultures, and so forth. Where requested by the local units, Corporate provided translations of PMP materials, but the international units were accorded the latitude to adapt PMP to meet their local requirements and needs.

Interim Results at the End of Fiscal Year 2002

By the summer of 2002, the books were closed on fiscal year 2002 and the first seven months of the transition. On the operational side, plant consolidations were well underway, the headquarters facility expansion was proceeding swiftly, and the integration of key business systems were on target or completed. Organizationally, the key functions had been consolidated—sales, marketing, headquarters supply chain management, client invoicing, and support services—and the U.S. workforce was on a single payroll, compensation structure, and benefits package. The first cycle of PMP, albeit abbreviated, had been completed, and performance ratings had been used to set incentives for 2002 performance. By quickly addressing employee needs, any significant voluntary turnover was avoided, and in fact, overall organizational turnover was running below the 2001 levels of either heritage company. Having met or exceeded most of the objectives set out for the first seven months after closing, the integration process was determined by those involved to be a success.

Unfortunately, the same could not be said for the overall performance of the business. Fiscal year 2002 results were disappointing on several measures: annual growth in unit volume and operating profit were below target; earnings per share had declined significantly; and total shareholder return, although ahead of the S&P 500 index, lagged the average for the S&P Food Products group. While results were respectable, they were not comparable to the levels of performance the pre-acquisition General Mills had been able to achieve. Although we had anticipated a dip in performance immediately following the closing, the actual dip was deeper than we expected.

Nonetheless, top management was convinced that the organization was well positioned to deliver strong performance in fiscal year 2003. The most disruptive part of the transition was over, key organizational and cultural building blocks had been set in place, and the organization was beginning to function smoothly.

Individual Development Plan (IDP)

The IDP process was designed to be fully integrated into the PMP cycle, but rather than implementing it as part of the initial PMP rollout, we delayed it until early in fiscal year 2003, the second cycle of PMP. We positioned it to create additional retention power as employees gained a concrete vision of how they could achieve their professional goals and aspirations within the new company. This delay also made it possible to introduce new processes at a pace the organization could more easily accommodate, allowing managers and employees to focus in 2002 on the objective-setting and performance appraisal elements from the first PMP cycle. It allowed more time to train the workforce in the principles and techniques of IDP and have them put what they learned into practice with one cycle of PMP under their belts.

IDP Design. Prior to the acquisition, each company had a process that planned for employee professional growth and career development. At Pillsbury, this discussion had taken place as part of the annual performance appraisal session, and the development plan was embedded in the appraisal form. At General Mills, the performance appraisal and development discussions were conducted in separate meetings, with separate forms. Because the transition strategy emphasized professional growth and advancement as levers for building employee commitment to the new company, the design team believed it necessary to integrate the development planning process into the overall PMP cycle, but to give it a high profile and keep it separate from the performance appraisal meeting. The appraisal meeting is very evaluative in tone, with clear financial implications for salary and incentive payout, and while it surfaces topics relevant to professional growth, the pressure and "noise" of this meeting can be too distracting for a quality, two-way conversation about career to occur. A meeting devoted exclusively to the development plan would better assure that it received the time and thoughtful effort required to do it well.

Prior to the acquisition, General Mills had made some refinements to its own development planning process for employees; as a result, the modified process had been working effectively and had features that would serve the post-acquisition organization well. Thus, it became the model for the new IDP.

One principle that pervades the new IDP process is that of employee ownership. The employee is expected to proactively direct professional growth toward achieving personal aspirations by taking the following steps:

1. Review the most recent performance appraisal and any other performance feedback from others.
2. Review performance objectives for the coming year and competencies for the job.
3. Draft the development plan.
4. Schedule the IDP meeting with the manager.
5. Set the agenda and conduct the IDP meeting with the manager.
6. Revise the development plan as necessary to reflect the IDP discussion, schedule the agreed-on action steps, and execute the actions with the appropriate assistance from the manager.

The manager is jointly accountable for the outcomes of the IDP by providing the employee with input, feedback, and suggestions during the IDP meeting and by placing the employee's needs and desires in the context of the business's needs and objectives so that development plans are realistic, achievable, and in the best interests of both the individual and the company. The manager is also accountable for facilitating the developmental steps and opportunities identified in the plan, particularly those related to roles, assignments, mentoring relationships, and other steps that might entail additional resources or commitments from the company.

To have the IDP process deliver as much value as possible and yet be simple and straightforward, the design team built the IDP form and meeting around the following areas of employee concern:

- *Professional Goals and Motivations*—What will energize me to grow professionally? What/where do I desire to do/go with my professional life?
- *Talents and Strengths*—What are my abilities and competencies? Where can I bring them to bear on this year's objectives? Are there any that are underutilized and could be better applied?
- *Development Opportunities*—Where do I need to improve to achieve this year's objectives? What will I need to develop in order to be successful in the future?
- *IDP Objectives*—What one strength will I leverage and what one to two development needs will I address this year?
- *Action Steps*—What action steps will I take to achieve these IDP objectives?

The new IDP handbook walks the employee through these four areas and provides guidelines and tips on how to prepare for the session. It also contains specific examples of developmental action steps in three categories—on-the-job assignments, relationships (with bosses, peers, and mentors), and formal learning (courses or self-study)—and guidance on what types of developmental needs these steps may be most suited to address. Likewise, managers are given information about how to fulfill their role in the process and how best to support the employee. Both parties are asked to consider the overall process and the four topics from two perspectives: (1) what is required to improve current performance and (2) what will prepare the employee to achieve personal career aspirations. Both parties are also encouraged to consider actions that not only interest the employee but also deliver the greatest value to the company, as these actions are likely to have the greatest success for all.

IDP Launch. Beginning in June 2002, the IDP process was launched. The process used training and communications strategies and a set of tools similar to those that had made the PMP launch successful. IDP discussions between employees and managers began in August 2002. For this first annual cycle, with the objective to create for the employee a vision of a future with the company, employees were told to place the heaviest emphasis on articulating and documenting their professional goals and aspirations:

- What means most to me in my work and life?
- If I see myself changing roles in the future, what would my new role look like?
- What competencies is General Mills likely to need most?
- How could my own aspirations and goals be best used to deliver results for the company?

Intertwining the employee's aspirations with the company's direction and future needs reinforces identification with the new company and creates a deeper personal investment in its longer-term viability and success. Future cycles of the IDP would address more fully the strengths, development opportunities, objectives, and actions necessary to flesh out the IDP and build on the solid groundwork laid in the early cycles of PMP and IDP.

At the launch, it was announced that specific questions about the IDP process would be added to the climate survey to be conducted in the autumn of 2002 and that the results would be analyzed for each organizational unit. Not only would this help assess the effectiveness of the IDP launch and first-cycle meetings—and identify areas where follow-up efforts, reinforcement, or change might be needed—it would also give managers the extra incentives of top-level scrutiny and comparison with peers to assure that the rollout was thorough and effective in their own part of the organization.

Climate Tracking

Employee perceptions were selected as the key metrics for evaluating the impact of the integration initiatives. The all-employee General Mills Climate Survey, typically conducted every two years, would continue to be used as the main feedback vehicle to assess:

- Perceptions about the new company, its systems, processes, culture, and work environment, and the employees' level of commitment;
- How perceptions had changed from prior General Mills surveys;
- How responses compared with norms for other companies; and
- Perceptions held about specific integration efforts to assess their effectiveness and help identify the need for any additional targeted actions.

In alternate years or at critical junctures during the transition, the company plans to conduct "pulse" surveys with a sample of employees. Those consist of about a dozen questions tailored to specific transition issues and initiatives. The results will enable the transition team to assess the progress of specific initiatives and actions, pinpoint any problem areas, and fine-tune its efforts in the next stage of the transition.

In addition, the team planned to track other relevant organizational metrics, such as overall turnover and the retention of critical value-added employees. The ultimate measure of the success of the integration would be the business performance of the new company.

The 2002 Climate Survey results indicated that the integration had indeed produced a new organization that matched or outpaced the pre-acquisition General Mills on several important dimensions.

Business results had been disappointing for fiscal year 2002, which included the first seven months of the acquisition, with a bigger than expected post-closing drop in key performance metrics. But fiscal year 2003, the first full fiscal year after the acquisition, was a different story, as synergies were realized, the newly merged organization hit its stride, and performance rebounded strongly.

The Lessons Learned and the Challenges Ahead

Looking back over the first two years of the acquisition, the integration strategy was, for the most part, sound. It addressed many areas that were key to building the kind of organization the new company needed. Achieving most of the integration milestones, the company has realized the cost synergies and productivity gains envisioned in the acquisition. The perceptions of the workforce indicate a culture, a performance orientation, and a level of commitment in line with our objectives for the new organization. Most importantly, this has all manifested in strong business performance in fiscal year 2003 that is expected to continue.

The work of the transition has not stopped. There remain many opportunities to leverage the gains made in the first two years of the integration. One major area of effort is to realize the ultimate goal of *a fully committed workforce*. Although nearly two-thirds of the employees (63 percent) indicated in the 2002 Climate Survey that they were highly committed to the company, 11 percent were uncommitted, and another 26 percent were undecided. The survey results have been recast in order to better understand the differences in perceptions between the highly committed employees and the remaining third of the workforce. One early finding is that 65 percent of the variance in perceptions between the two groups lies in three areas: leadership, development, and empowerment. With this deeper understanding of what drives high levels of commitment, General Mills is structuring future initiatives and taking targeted actions to develop higher commitment levels among more employees.

The organization continues to reinforce the Performance Management Process and the Individual Development Plan process. For example, successive cycles of the IDP will place greater emphasis on identifying strengths, development needs, and action steps in order to bring the individual development plans to fruition. In response to formal and informal feedback from managers and employees, we continue to add tools and enhancements that make the new processes even more effective.

A major new initiative that General Mills is currently launching is a leadership development program for all executives and managers, beginning at the top of the organization. The program will reinforce the role of leaders in creating and sustaining the desired culture and performance orientation. General Mills is employing the same communication and launch strategies, tools, and measurement devices that have served the earlier integration initiatives so well.

The experience of the past two years at General Mills has proven that human resources systems can be key drivers of success in the integration of a merger or large acquisition. These are powerful tools for addressing critical employee concerns, creating a cohesive culture, and developing employee commitment—all necessary conditions for imparting momentum and direction to an organization undergoing significant disruption and for building a solid foundation for sustained superior performance.

◆ ◆ ◆

Kevin D. Wilde joined General Mills in 1998 and has led corporate efforts in leadership development, executive assessment, succession planning, and organizational development. He helped to realign the General Mills Institute, which is the company's training and development center, and produced a series of organizational effectiveness initiatives. Before joining General Mills, Wilde spent seventeen years at General Electric in a variety of human resources positions, including manager at Crotonville, GE's management training center in New York. He helped renovate the center's manager development course and helped develop an accelerated Crotonville-in-Europe strategy.

Wilde's earlier assignments at GE spanned a wide range of human resources duties, including recruitment, compensation, labor relations, training, and human resources generalist. He was heavily involved in business globalization efforts, pioneered the use of leadership 360-degree survey feedback, and developed and presented training programs around the world.

CHAPTER TWENTY-TWO

THE AGILENT TECHNOLOGIES STORY

Coaching Across the Enterprise

Brian O. Underhill, Dianne Anderson, and Robert A. Silva

As the popularity of leadership coaching programs rapidly grows, corporations are increasingly challenged to provide consistent quality when rolling them out across organizational and international boundaries. HR sponsors struggle to manage disparate coaching approaches, questionable coach credentials, variations in pricing, and a lack of measurable results.

Recently, many brand-name organizations have responded by designing corporate-endorsed approaches that link program activities to leadership competencies and require measurable results, while delegating implementation to one or two global coaching vendors.

Agilent Technologies is a pioneer and best-practices leader in large-scale, international coaching implementation. This case study highlights the development and implementation of Agilent's APEX (Accelerated Performance for Executives) executive coaching program. APEX has served over one hundred leaders through a sixty-seven-person, worldwide coaching pool for more than five years. Based on feedback from raters, more than 95 percent of leaders demonstrated positive improvement in overall leadership effectiveness while participating in the program.

The lessons learned by Agilent in the implementation of its international coaching program serve as valuable insights for any organization committed to the continuing development of key leaders.

Establishing Context

In 1999, Hewlett-Packard (HP) announced a strategic realignment to create two companies. HP retained the computing, printing, and imaging businesses. The spin-off company, Agilent Technologies, would encompass test and measurement components, chemical analysis, and medical businesses.

Agilent was launched in November 1999. New corporate headquarters were constructed on the site of HP's first-owned research and development (R&D) manufacturing facility in Palo Alto, California. Agilent quickly declared three new corporate values to guide its future: speed, focus, and accountability. Agilent also retained the "heritage" HP values: uncompromising integrity, innovation, trust, respect, and teamwork.

The development of future leaders was, and is, one of CEO Ned Barnholt's critical priorities. The need for strong leaders, essential to building and sustaining the company, soon became articulated in a comprehensive leadership development strategy. From the outset, executive coaching, focused at further developing executives recognized as high-potential or high-performing leaders, was seen as a key component of that emerging strategy.

Executive coaching had a history at HP, but previous efforts were largely uncoordinated. Coaching had not yet been strategically integrated within the company's leadership development initiatives. Multiple vendors and individual practitioners had provided different coaching programs at various prices. A rigorous assessment of the cost and value of these early programs prompted Agilent to create an outstanding "corporately recommended" integrated coaching program with an understood price and preferred discount rate.

In 1999, Agilent's Semiconductor Products Group (SPG) engaged in a coordinated, "results-guaranteed" coaching program with Alliance for Strategic Leadership (A4SL). More than fifty of SPG's senior leaders were to receive one-year leadership effectiveness coaching. This effort attracted positive attention throughout the company and would later form the foundation of the APEX program.

In February 2000, Agilent's global program manager (and article co-author, Dianne Anderson) was charged with designing the corporate coaching solution for the company's senior managers and executives (about 750 people worldwide). She collaborated with A4SL (specifically article co-author, Brian Underhill) to design and deliver the new APEX program, based on the successful coaching model already used within SPG.

Development of the Agilent Global Leadership Profile

At the outset, there was a clear need for a new leadership behavioral profile. The profile would reflect the company's strategic priorities and core values, as well as the expectations of senior leaders. Once a leadership inventory was designed for the initial SPG coaching work, Agilent needed a company-wide profile to position the leadership behaviors throughout the whole organization in a consistent fashion.

This second-generation leadership profile was based on key strategic imperatives of top management. These included Agilent's new and heritage core values and SPG's original profile. After gathering feedback from multiple sources, the *Agilent Business Leader Inventory* was finalized.

In the spring of 2001, Agilent again updated the inventory to create a set of profiles that would span all management levels. A multi-functional team of Agilent and A4SL consultants set out to create the new profile.

An iterative process of document review, internal inputs, and refinements took place. A scalable and aligned *Global Leadership Profile* emerged for use throughout the organization. The final mid-level/first-level manager profile turned out to be largely similar to the original executive profile; there were only slight differences in some of the specific behavioral descriptions. Both profiles were reviewed by a senior manager in each of Agilent's business units and by representatives of non-U.S. divisions. Feedback from these reviews was incorporated into the final product: the *Agilent Global Leadership Profile* was ready for consistent application across all divisions. It has been in use ever since.

Initial Objectives for the APEX Program

From the outset, the Agilent desire was for a coaching program that could address multiple objectives, including:

- *Senior manager and executive focus:* Candidates for APEX participation included vice presidents, corporate officers, business unit leaders, general managers, directors, and functional managers.
- *Global reach:* Agilent is a worldwide organization with facilities in more than sixty countries. The APEX program would need to effectively serve leaders with local coaches in the respective regions or within an hour's flight. Awareness of local cultural nuances would be critical, and local language capability would be highly preferred.
- *Accountability for results:* APEX needed to provide added value for Agilent. In return for the company's investment in them, participants would have to demonstrate positive, measurable change in leadership effectiveness as seen by direct reports and colleagues.
- *Flexibility and user-friendliness:* APEX had to be user-friendly from beginning to end. A simple menu of options was created that was suitable for a range of budgets and varying levels of interest in the coaching process. Priority was also placed on creating a program that made it easy to initiate a coaching engagement and to administer payment for coaching services.

Fundamentally, APEX is a behaviorally based executive coaching approach that focuses on improving leadership behaviors on the job. APEX must not be used for career planning, life planning, strategic planning, or remedial coaching. This distinction was made clear throughout the internal marketing process.

Several months of instrument and process design ensued to meet these objectives. The structure of several coaching options was outlined. A general program description was drafted. A global coaching pool was established, mirroring locations of Agilent's key global facilities. Certification standards for APEX coaches were determined. Procurement standards were established to smooth the contracting process. Procedures to guide the 360-degree feedback and follow-up survey scoring were created. Finally, pages on the corporate intranet were developed containing the program description, pricing, coach bios, and contracting information.

In May 2000 at a corporate Leadership Development Showcase attended by business HR and leadership and development practitioners, the Accelerated Performance for Executives program was officially launched. APEX was introduced to HR managers and leadership development specialists throughout the organization. While refinements and new services were continually added, the APEX program history now reflects five years of delivering results consistent with the original program objectives.

Presenting Coaching Options Within APEX

Based on an achievement-oriented mountaineering theme, the full APEX offering includes five appropriately named coaching options:

- *Base Camp:* Executive participates in the Global Leadership Profile, receives a two-to-four hour, face-to-face coaching session to review results, select area(s) for development, and receive on-the-spot coaching, and creates a developmental action plan.
- *Camp 2:* Executive participates in the Global Leadership Profile, receives six months of face-to-face and telephone coaching, and one mini-survey follow-up measurement (see "Measurement: The Mini-Survey Process" for more on the mini-survey follow-up measurement and see Exhibit 22.1 for the Mini-Survey itself). Coach conducts telephone "check-in" with key stakeholders. Coaching work is guaranteed for results.
- *Camp 3:* Executive receives six months of face-to-face and telephone coaching and one mini-survey follow-up measurement. Coach conducts up to twelve interviews with key stakeholders (instead of 360-degree scoring) and provides write-up of results. Coach conducts telephone "check-in" with key stakeholders. Coaching work is guaranteed for results.
- *High Camp:* Executive participates in the Global Leadership Profile. Receives one year of face-to-face and telephone coaching and two mini-survey follow-up measurements. Coach conducts telephone "check-in" with key stakeholders. Coaching work is guaranteed for results.
- *Summit:* Executive receives one year of face-to-face and telephone coaching and two mini-survey follow-up measurements. Coach conducts up to twelve interviews with key stakeholders (instead of 360-degree scoring) and provides write-up of results. Coach conducts telephone "check-in" with key stakeholders. Coaching work is guaranteed for results.

Most APEX options include a unique offer: a results guarantee. That is, leaders don't pay until coaching is complete and leaders don't pay unless they improve. Improvement is determined by those working with and rating the leaders, not by the leaders themselves. This approach has proven to be popular among Agilent executives. In spite of a recent difficult market environment in the technology arena, leaders can continue their personal development efforts and delay payment for professional services for up to one year. In addition, leaders knew they would only pay for demonstrated perceived improvements in their effectiveness, as determined by a follow-up mini-survey process.

Establishing a Worldwide Coaching Pool

A recurring challenge has been assuring the availability of qualified coaches on a worldwide basis. As a virtual organization, A4SL contracts with independent coaches to deliver coaching services across the globe. This allows A4SL to add coaches to the Agilent coaching pool as needed, without incurring additional expense.

From the outset, it became evident that a set of coach certification guidelines was needed. Minimum coach requirements were established, which include significant experience working with senior executives, experience as a behavioral coach, multiple years in leadership roles, and an advanced degree. The results guarantee serves as a natural qualifier. That is, generally the quality coaches believe in their work (and have enough of it) so that they can guarantee the results, while affording a delay in compensation. Also, coaches agree to participate in company conference calls, remain current in their profession, and abide by a set of ethical guidelines. Coach bios were screened, and potential coaches were interviewed in detail.

The coaching pool has grown to more than sixty-seven coaches worldwide. Each coach participates in a telephone orientation and receives a sixty-page induction package. Agilent hosts quarterly conference calls to keep coaches informed on corporate news, to learn about the coaches' challenges in working with Agilent leaders, and to provide a forum for peer-to-peer learning.

Internal Marketing of APEX

Because APEX is a corporate-developed recommended approach, there has never been a guarantee that any of the decentralized businesses would buy in. Early on, it was agreed that an internal marketing campaign was necessary to highlight the benefits of the APEX program.

Agilent's Leadership Development Showcase served as an appropriate opening for the program. Similar presentations were then conducted in a variety of internal HR and leadership development sessions, both in person and via telephone during the summer and fall of 2000.

As the program grew, word-of-mouth became an extremely effective marketing tool. Some line executives nominated themselves and their entire reporting teams to go through the program together. Higher-profile leaders have been among some early adopters, including multiple corporate officers and vice presidents. It became apparent that the HR managers were well networked with each other as well. As a result, word of APEX spread through the Agilent HR community.

Finally, a corporate intranet site and supporting documentation were created, allowing for easy distribution of information about the program. Much time was spent crafting crisp, straight-to-the-point documentation to assist business leaders in understanding the program quickly.

Coaching Program Content

APEX begins when the program manager sends the leader three biographies based on the participant's needs, style, and location. Leaders then conduct telephone interviews with the coaches. In this way, executives have a greater sense of ownership in the process.

Once a coach is selected, the APEX process continues with in-person visits, coupled with regular, ongoing telephone and/or email contact. In practice, coaches visit participating Agilent leaders approximately every six to eight weeks (in any given APEX assignment, the number of visits may be higher or lower). Telephone and email contact during a typical month could range from one to a half-dozen contacts.

During a coaching session, any number of topics may be covered, including:

- Explore the current business context to determine what may be different/similar since the last coaching session;
- Review perceived progress toward the developmental action plan;
- Identify resources and tools to support the executive's change efforts;
- Review the executive's recent experiences with his or her behavioral goals;
- Shadow the leader and observe first-hand personal leadership tendencies (for example, staff meeting, team meeting, feedback delivery, key presentation);
- Role play (coach and Agilent executive assume roles, do a practice delivery/dry run, conduct critique, and review);
- Prepare for/review follow-up efforts with key stakeholders/feedback providers; and
- Set action items to complete for next coaching session.

Follow-Up with Key Stakeholders

The APEX program is grounded in the A4SL research regarding the impact of follow-up on perceived leadership effectiveness. In virtually every organization in which A4SL has delivered coaching services, one lesson is universally the same—*regular follow-up with key stakeholders equates with perceived improvement in leadership effectiveness.*

At least some of the Agilent executives who were seen as following up effectively likely informed raters of their development objectives during the initial debrief of the 360-degree results. The initial debriefing is ideally a focused, five-to-ten minute meeting held with each respondent immediately after the 360-degree report is received. The follow-up addresses the following: thanking raters for providing anonymous 360-degree input, relating the positive feedback, disclosing the developmental goal(s), and enlisting the rater's help in the participant's developmental efforts.

Having conducted this "initial debriefing," APEX participants are encouraged to follow up with raters at regular intervals (quarterly, on average) to pursue additional feedback on their improvement. Results regularly show better improvement among leaders who follow up versus those who do not.

Measurement: The Mini-Survey Process

APEX coaching includes up to two online "mini-surveys." Mini-surveys are short, three-to-five-item questionnaires completed by a leader's key stakeholders. Raters are asked to measure improvement in the leader's overall leadership effectiveness and specific areas for development. Raters also indicate whether the leader has followed up with them regarding his or her areas for development. Additional written comments are also requested. Aside from verifying individual improvement, mini-survey data can be aggregated to provide team, group, or corporate-level improvement data.

Results

APEX results to date (as demonstrated by aggregated mini-survey data) are impressive. Figure 22.1 depicts aggregate results regarding improvements in overall leadership effectiveness.

Aggregate Results for Overall Leadership Effectiveness

Question: "Has this person become more or less effective
as a leader since the feedback session?"
Scale: "–3" (Less Effective) to "+3" (More Effective)
N = 831 raters
73 leaders

Nearly 57 percent of respondents felt that APEX leaders had improved in overall leadership effectiveness at a "+2" and "+3" level. Over 78 percent of respondents felt that APEX leaders had improved at a "+1," "+2," and "+3" level. Nineteen percent of respondents felt that leaders did not change, while nearly 3 percent felt that leaders got worse. (See Figure 22.2.)

FIGURE 22.1. AGGREGATE RESULTS FOR OVERALL LEADERSHIP EFFECTIVENESS.

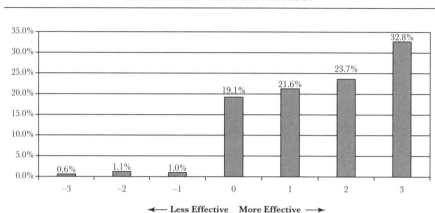

Aggregate Results for Selected Areas for Development

Improvement on specific areas for development selected by leaders.

Scale: "-3" (Less Effective) to "+3" (More Effective)
N = 2276 raters
73 leaders

Nearly 54 percent of respondents felt that leaders improved in their selected developmental goals at a "+2" and "+3" level. Nearly 77 percent felt that leaders improved at a "+1," "+2," and "+3" level. Nearly 21 percent of raters did not perceive any change, while 2 percent perceived leaders as getting worse.

Aggregate Results for Follow-Up/No Follow-Up

Figure 22.3 depicts results for those leaders who followed up versus those who did not:

73 leaders

Of the 831 raters, 530 (64 percent) believed that leaders followed up with them, versus 301 (36 percent) who perceived no follow-up. Nearly 67 percent of leaders who followed up were seen as improving at a "+2" and "+3" level, compared to 38 percent for those who did not follow up. More notably, 35 percent of leaders who did not

FIGURE 22.2. AGGREGATE RESULTS FOR SELECTED AREAS OF DEVELOPMENT.

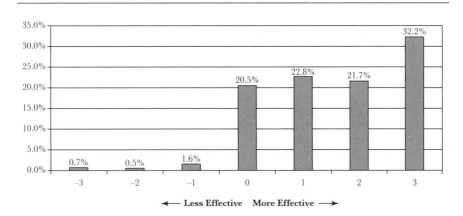

FIGURE 22.3. AGGREGATE RESULTS FOR FOLLOW-UP/NO FOLLOW-UP.

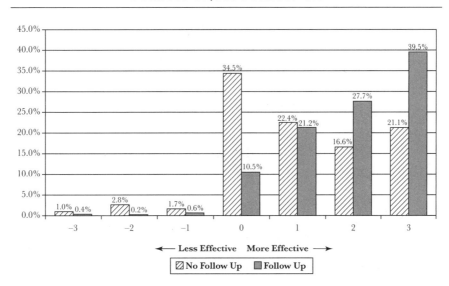

follow-up were perceived as staying the same ("0"), compared to nearly 11 percent who did follow up. Over 5 percent of those who did not follow up were perceived as getting *worse,* compared to 1.2 percent of the group who followed up.

Additionally, positive feedback was frequently reported through the qualitative remarks compiled from the mini-surveys.

Overall, APEX results to date have been very positive. Leaders are improving both in overall leadership effectiveness and in their selected areas for development, as perceived by those working with the leaders.

Key Insights and Lessons Learned

The key insights and lessons learned from the APEX experience can enable any organization to more effectively implement an enterprise-wide executive coaching program.

Senior Leadership Commitment to APEX. In recent years, the technology sector has suffered its worst downturn in recent history. Agilent's APEX program stands as a visible demonstration by senior leadership of their continuing commitment to developing leaders by sponsoring executive and personal development, even in a difficult market climate. Additionally, many "high-profile" senior leaders were early APEX adopters, inspiring many more leaders to enroll in the program.

Personal Commitment of Agilent Leaders. The vast majority of APEX participants have displayed a high level of personal commitment to self-development, as shown through their respective individual coaching partnerships. The APEX program has experienced a very low percentage of participants becoming disinterested or dropping out. Most participants have demonstrated a full commitment to completing the program. These leaders have enjoyed favorable feedback from mini-surveys administered at the program's conclusion. The investments being made in personal development are paying dividends for most APEX participants over time.

Worldwide Scope of APEX. A key challenge in the development of the program was locating and retaining quality international coaches who were willing to work under the results-guarantee clause. Early difficulties have been overcome in developing an international network of qualified coaches. Prior to this, some U.S.-based coaches traveled internationally to deliver APEX coaching services.

APEX Target Audience. Since its inception, APEX has been and remains a developmental tool targeting high-performing and/or high-potential Agilent executives. It is not intended to serve as a remedial process for an under-performing executive, nor is it intended to serve as a performance-assessment program. APEX candidates are first screened by Agilent's Leadership Development Group to ensure that APEX is a good fit.

Coach Follow-Up with Feedback Raters. APEX coaches generally keep in regular contact with a leader's key stakeholders. Coaches want to know whether raters notice the leader's new behaviors. The only APEX assignment to go full-term without achieving successful results was due partially to the coach being out of touch with raters, thereby not recognizing their continual dissatisfaction with the leader. Because raters are "customers" in the process, coaches regularly communicate with them.

Coach Mismatches. The possibility for coach mismatches appears to have been addressed and minimized. Participants beginning the program receive biographies of up to three A4SL coaches within their geographic area. Executives then contact and screen from this set of prospective coaches and ultimately select their coach. By allowing executives to largely self-select, the APEX experience has yielded very few mismatches. In those very few instances in which a mismatch has surfaced, alternative coaches have been made available.

Beyond APEX

To date, the APEX program has influenced and inspired a number of hybrid programs at Agilent Technologies. The Global 360-Degree Coaching Program provides first and mid-level leaders with Global Leadership Profile feedback and several hours of coaching using mostly APEX coaches. Agilent's LEAD program (for first-level managers) provides the profile feedback, coaching, and mini-surveys as part of its personal coaching component. The AIM program (for mid-level managers) employs both the profile and mini-surveys. Meanwhile, APEX continues to inspire many new (and renewing) senior managers.

◆ ◆ ◆

EXHIBIT 22.1. AGILENT TECHNOLOGIES MINI-SURVEY.

 Agilent Technologies

Innovating the HP Way

Agilent Technologies MiniSurvey

Follow-Up to the 360-Assessment

Follow-Up to Agilent Leadership Inventory

Company Items
C1 Since the feedback session, has this person followed-up with you regarding how
he/she can improve?
1: No
2: Yes

C2 Do you feel this person has become more or less effective as a leader since the feedback session? (Do not consider environmental factors beyond this person's control.)
-3: Less Effective
-2:
-1:
0: No Change
1:
2:
3: More Effective
N: No Information

Original 360-Degree Survey Items
Please rate the extent to which this individual has increased/decreased in effectiveness in
the following areas of development during the past several months.

2 Distills market knowledge into meaningful trends and patterns
-3: Less Effective
-2:
-1:
0: No Change
1:
2:
3: More Effective
N: No Information

2a Do you feel that change was needed in the area mentioned in the previous question?
   1: No
   2: Yes

14 Effectively communicates his/her organization's vision
   -3: Less Effective
   -2:
   -1:
   0: No Change
   1:
   2:
   3: More Effective
   N: No Information

14a Do you feel that change was needed in the area mentioned in the previous question?
   1: No
   2: Yes

30 Openly shares information
   -3: Less Effective
   -2:
   -1:
   0: No Change
   1:
   2:
   3: More Effective
   N: No Information

30a Do you feel that change was needed in the area mentioned in the previous question?
   1: No
   2: Yes

Follow-Up to Agilent Leadership Inventory

Comments
What has been done in the past several months that you have found to be particularly effective?

_____
_____
_____
_____
_____
_____

What can this person do to become more effective as a manager in the development areas noted above?

_____
_____
_____
_____
_____
_____

◆ ◆ ◆

Brian O. Underhill, Ph.D., is a senior consultant and coach with Alliance for Strategic Leadership, specializing in leadership development and multi-rater (360-degree) feedback, executive coaching, and organizational culture. Dr. Underhill designs and implements large-scale, results-guaranteed executive coaching programs at multiple organizations. His executive coaching work has successfully focused on helping clients achieve positive, measurable, long-term change in leadership behavior. His clients have included Agilent Technologies, AT&T, California Public Employees Retirement System (CalPERS), the Federal Aviation Administration (FAA), Johnson & Johnson, Sun Microsystems, and Warner Lambert. He has a Ph.D. and an M.S. degree in organizational psychology from the California School of Professional Psychology (Los Angeles). Contact: Brian@bunderhill.com.

Dianne Anderson is committed to helping individuals and organizations achieve learning, change, and growth. In her current position as global program manager for Agilent Technologies, Inc., she is responsible for all global executive coaching programs and for learning and organizational effectiveness consulting to one of Agilent's business units. Anderson's career includes leadership positions and operational experience in worldwide marketing for Hewlett-Packard (HP), as well as positions in research and development. Her more than seventeen years of operating experiences have prepared her to develop the skills, knowledge, and abilities of senior management so they can more effectively compete in the global marketplace. Throughout her career she has managed complex organizations with multi-million-dollar budgets, with experience in line and staff positions at the business unit and corporate levels, and she has had responsibility for building key marketing and sales capabilities. Contact: 650-752–5373.

Robert A. Silva has served as head of the coaching practice for Alliance for Strategic Leadership since January 2002. Prior to his current role, Silva served as one of the seven directors of Keilty, Goldsmith, & Company from 1987 to 2001. His business background includes experience in the investment field with Paine, Webber in Boston, and fourteen years in sales management with Minnesota Mining & Manufacturing Company in New England. During his sixteen years as a consultant and coach, Silva has focused on the design and delivery of training to promote leadership development, organizational values, and team effectiveness. His primary emphasis, since the mid-1990s, has been in the area of executive coaching, helping leading organizations succeed by enhancing the leadership effectiveness of key individuals.

CHAPTER TWENTY-THREE

E-COACHING

Using the New Technology to Develop Tomorrow's Leaders

Marshall Goldsmith

A technological breakthrough is occurring that will dramatically change leadership development. Within the next twenty years, instant download, television quality, audio-video transmission will be commonly available to leaders around the world. People will be connected, synchronously and asynchronously, through both wired and wireless networks.

Tomorrow's leaders will have the opportunity to learn in ways that could not be imagined in the past. They will tap into a vast network that connects almost all accumulated human knowledge. This network has been called the *global mind*. When everything works, leaders will be able to learn what they need to know, when they need to know it, from the source best able to teach it! The executive coaches of the future will be the people who can help leaders *find* the knowledge they need. They will be e-coaches.

Unfortunately, as the amount of information in the global mind increases, the challenge of accessing meaningful information grows. e-Coaching will require a balance between appreciating the potential of an incredible vision and recognizing the challenge of turning this vision into a practical reality.

To understand the future of e-coaching, it is important to realize that the development of the global mind may produce both extremely positive and extremely negative consequences for leaders. The challenge of the e-coach will be to recognize the realities that exist, maximize potential benefits, and minimize potential costs. We will begin with a brief analysis of how the global mind can become both a "fantastic opportunity" and an "incredible annoyance" for leaders. We will then discuss how e-coaching can be used to develop the leaders of the future.

The Global Mind: A Fantastic Opportunity

Accessing the "Best in Class" Thought Leaders

The executive of the future will be able to readily access thought leaders who are the world's experts on almost any relevant issue. As of this writing, many of the world's greatest thought leaders are available through videoconferencing (through ISDN networks). Within a few years, thought leaders will be available for high-quality video-conferencing that is streamed to the desktop. A library of audio and video "wisdom bits" will be available so that executives can get answers to frequently asked questions without having to directly access a thought leader. Text will be categorized so that executives can review books and articles that are aimed at their specific needs. All of these tools can help leaders learn in a very efficient way. e-Coaches will be the personal learning consultants who can access these resources (without having to be the "experts"). For example, if I have a coaching client who needs help in strategy, I may have her access Vijay Govindarajan or C.K. Prahalad. If I have a client who needs advice in developing alliances, I may have him access Jon Katzenbach or Larraine Segil.

Getting Help When and Where It Is Needed

Traditional courses can be very inefficient methods for learning. They may not be designed to fit the leader's specific need. Everyone in the room has to hear the same content, delivered in the same way, at the same time. The leader of the future will be able to take online courses that are tailored to specific developmental needs. Parts of the course that are less relevant can be "skimmed" or skipped entirely. Research has shown that course material that is quickly applied (on the job) is much more likely to be retained than course material that is not applied for long periods of time. e-Coaches can help leaders find relevant information on an "as needed" basis. They can also help leaders design a customized curriculum that meets their unique learning needs.

Learning from Around the World

Traditionally, almost all training or coaching has been done by professionals or co-workers who live in the same country. In fact, in most cases professionals who live in the same region of the country have done this work. New technology will enable expertise to come from around the world. Geographical boundaries will no longer be a constraint. As organizations become increasingly multinational, the "globalization of learning" will become increasingly important. Asynchronous learning will mean that time zones will become less and less of a constraint to development. e-Coaches will be able to help find diverse resources to deal with cross-boundary issues (that experts from one country might not understand).

Using "Push" Technology to Help Leaders Change

Research on behavioral change for leaders has shown a clear pattern. Leaders who identify desired behaviors to change, involve their co-workers in the change process, and follow up are much more likely to demonstrate long-term improvement than those who do not.[1] "Push" technology can be used to give leaders an ongoing stream of reminders and ideas for change. This type of reinforcement has been shown to dramatically increase the probability that leaders will "stick with" their change efforts. Traditional, people-centered techniques for follow-up and reinforcement tend to be very expensive and time-consuming. Technology-based tools for follow-up and reinforcement can be both more efficient and more effective. Measurement tools, such as 360-degree feedback and mini-surveys, can be administered online, at low cost, and whenever needed. e-Coaches will be able to use tailored reminders, measurement tools, and reinforcements *without* having to be physically present.

Coaching for Many Leaders, Not Just the Privileged Few

Traditional coaching is very expensive. In most cases the coach has significant in-person interaction with the leader being coached. Even in cases where the coach is local, travel time can exceed the actual time spent coaching. New technology will allow leaders to receive asynchronous coaching that is much more efficient. Coaches can work from one location and communicate with leaders from around the world. One coach, through using many of the tools mentioned above, could work with many leaders (as opposed to the few that are possible in traditional coaching).

The Global Mind: An Incredible Annoyance

Drowning in a Sea of Information

Almost all of the executives I work with report: (1) a dramatic increase in the number of emails that they receive per day and (2) a dramatic decrease in the number of these emails that are actually important. A common concern is "too much information, too fast"! Asynchronous communication, rather than leading to more "free" time, has led to a "24/7" lifestyle where executives feel they are almost always "on call." One great challenge of the e-coach will be to help leaders sort out what is most important and help them "let go" of the rest. The last thing that most executives of the future will want is more email with "To Do" lists!

Accessing Relevant Information Is Becoming More Difficult

As the total amount of information available through the global mind increases, the amount of useless information is growing much faster than the amount of useful information. Search engines are becoming increasingly irrelevant. For example, I looked up the term "coaching" on Google and found 18,700,000 references. Almost none of these would have any interest for any executive. I looked up "marshall goldsmith" and found 30,500 references about *me*. Most of these references were not even interesting to me, much less to anyone else! Getting to the useful advice and avoiding "noise" can be a real challenge. The e-coach of the future will need to be able to quickly find the *relevant* information that can help the leader being coached.

Finding *High-Quality* Leadership Development Tools Is Not Easy

Many e-learning organizations have made the mistake of trying to transfer traditional learning methodologies (classroom training or video) directly into e-learning. Unfortunately, this seldom works. Many existing e-learning tools for leaders are poorly designed. They are often too long, slow, awkward, and boring. They have not been developed with the insight required to take advantage of new technology. Leaders will not use them for any extended period of time.

The Internet does not have a "quality control" function. The "good news" is that anyone can put anything into the global mind. This is also the "bad news"! e-Coaches will not only have to help leaders find relevant content, but they will also have to help the leaders find development tools that have a real impact. The theory of doing this will be much easier than the practice!

Maintaining Attention Span for In-Depth Learning Has Become More Challenging

While short "bytes" of information can be highly efficient in helping leaders solve specific problems, they may be dysfunctional for dealing with long-term issues requiring deeper analysis. In many cases, leaders need to improve long-term interpersonal relationships. This can seldom be achieved in a short period of time, no matter how great the advice. New technology increases the danger of reinforcing a "quick fix" mentality for development. Access to the same information can lead to homogeneity of thought. It can tend to create "McLeaders." This type of training may not prepare leaders to handle deeper, more diverse, or novel issues. e-Coaches will need to help their clients know when immediate, focused information is acceptable and when longer-term, deeper understanding is needed.

The Role of the e-Coach

The e-coach of the future will be an individualized learning consultant. The e-coach will not have to *possess* the knowledge that is needed by the client. The e-coach will need to help the client *find* the needed knowledge. The process of e-coaching will involve: (1) helping clients diagnose their developmental needs; (2) assessing the resources that should be expended to meet these needs; (3) analyzing the range of learning options that are available to help meet these needs; (4) connecting leaders with the highest value-added coaching and learning opportunities (given their unique needs and resources); and (5) providing ongoing support to ensure results.

Diagnosing Developmental Needs

The e-coach will need to know the *unique developmental needs* for each client. For example, some leaders may have the need to change behavior; others may need development in strategy, while some may need functional training (for example, marketing or finance). Each of the developmental needs listed above requires a very different learning strategy.

Along with understanding the need for learning, the coach will need to understand the *depth* of learning that is desirable. In some cases general knowledge may be very sufficient (for example, "finance for non-financial mangers"). In other cases very specific deep knowledge may be needed. In general, a learning strategy aimed at deeper knowledge will require *interaction* with a thought leader. The person being coached will need to be able to ask specific questions and have a dialogue. A learning strategy aimed at more general knowledge may just require *information*.

A third factor in diagnosis is *urgency*. If the decision time is now, an immediate response may be required. If the need is long-term and developmental, a "quick fix" may do more harm than good. A longer-term strategy that may involve asynchronous communication could be optimal.

Assessing Resource Allocation

Before designing a learning strategy, the e-coach will need to understand the client's optimal resource allocation. The first factor to consider is *time*. Most executives I work with today feel busier than they have felt in their entire lives. There is little to indicate that this trend will be reversed in the future! e-Coaches will need to do an analysis to determine the benefit of the learning as compared with the cost in time for learning.

A second factor to consider is *money*. e-Coaches will need to be able to assess learning options and weigh tradeoffs. For example, would the leader be better off with a shorter video conference with the world's leading authority or a longer in-depth intervention with a consultant who has less expertise? The number of options available to leaders will increase dramatically. As the number of options grows, the e-coach will need to gain increasing expertise in evaluating these options.

A third factor in resource allocation is *bandwidth*. If the leader has access to very high bandwidth, learning options that involve full-motion video may be very desirable. If bandwidth is restricted, technological difficulties can make full-motion video more of an annoyance than a value. While access to high bandwidth is increasing rapidly, bandwidth concerns will continue to be an issue for the next several years. Anyone in the e-learning field knows that there is often a huge gap between what *should* work at a certain bandwidth and what *does* work!

Analyzing Learning Options

On one hand, leaders of the future will have more learning options (by far) than leaders of the past. On the other hand, it will become increasingly difficult to understand and evaluate all of these choices. The e-coach will need to have a broad understanding of what the learning options are and how these various alternatives can help their clients.

To illustrate this point, let us assume that our hypothetical leader of the future has decided that she needs to learn some important concepts that are best taught by (my friend) Vijay Govindarajan. She will be faced with a vast array of learning alternatives. Following are a sampling of her possible choices and some of the tradeoffs involved in each.

- *Vijay as a personal coach*—This provides a great opportunity for in-depth learning that is suited to her needs. Unfortunately, this is very expensive and time-consuming. Along with being a coach, Vijay is a professor at Dartmouth. He be may be too "booked" to be able to make this type of a commitment.
- *Vijay as a consultant*—This is more reasonable, but still very expensive. She has the advantage of in-depth, in-person dialogue. Travel time scheduling problems have to be considered as potential issues.
- *Vijay in a videoconference dialogue*—This is much more accessible and less expensive. She has the advantage of dialogue that is aimed specifically at her needs. She loses some of the in-person "touch" but has much easier access.
- *Vijay in a wireless "instant message"*—This is an option that will become more common in the future. It provides the opportunity for an immediate idea, in a specific situation, at a specific time. The closer the requirement is to "real time," the more expensive this option will be.

- *Vijay in a satellite broadcast*—She gets to hear Vijay at far less cost (because there are many other people listening at the same time). Although these claim to be "interactive," she will be lucky if he answers even one of her questions.
- *Vijay in an Internet course*—The value of this option will vary widely based on design and technology. She might get to look at pre-packaged, "frequently asked questions" that could meet her needs. She may have the option of sending an email to Vijay. She could have the chance to replay various components of the course that she needs and to skip components of the course that do not add value.
- *Vijay in text (either online or in print)*—This "generic" option can be excellent for stimulating thinking and giving ideas, but it is often not useful for answering unique questions based on specific circumstances.
- *Vijay in a "wisdom bit" or "push" reminder*—This can be an excellent, low-cost option for reinforcement or encouragement. It can help her "stay on course" when attempting to change. It will seldom solve in-depth problems or meet long-term developmental needs.

This illustration addresses only *some* of the learning options for the leader of the future. However, this shows both the opportunities and challenges faced by the e-coach. As a personal learning consultant, the e-coach will need to have a trusted network of advisors who can recommend the highest value-added resources.

Connecting Leaders with Learning Opportunities

The e-coaches of the future will be "matchmakers"! They will be the personal learning consultants who can help leaders diagnose needs, assess resource allocation, analyze learning options, and then connect leaders with the best value-added resources.

In this chapter, we have made the assumption that e-coaches are humans. Given the complexity faced by leaders and the primitive nature of the field, this is probably a safe assumption for the next several years. Ultimately, e-coaching may become much more "virtual." Trusted panels of experts and clients will assess learning options. Options will receive ratings on content, quality and resource requirements. Clients will be able to share their need and resource profiles with their virtual coaches. The virtual coach will then assess learning options and recommend the highest value-added alternatives. Human e-coaches will learn to work with virtual assistants who help them better meet clients' needs.

Providing Ongoing Coaching

The field of executive coaching is experiencing huge growth. It is highly unlikely that this trend will reverse in the next ten years. Leaders will have greater and greater needs to learn. Coaching (when done well) has been shown to be a very effective way to help leaders learn and (more importantly) to help leaders achieve positive long-term change.

As the world has become more complex, it has become increasingly obvious that no leader can "know it all." The same is true for coaches. One of the greatest challenges faced by the human e-coaches of the future will be "letting go" of ego. Traditionally the "coach" has been thought of as a wise guru whose personal counsel will help clients achieve their goals. The e-coaches of the future will be successful because of their ability to match client requirements with the resources available in the global mind. This involves a transition from "being the expert" to "finding the expert." It also means that more of the coach's time will be spent on "learning" than on traditional "teaching."

Leaders are much more likely to change if they have ongoing support and encouragement from someone who cares. This has always been true and will probably always be true. This is one role that human coaches will continue to play. Leaders will probably be busier than ever. Competition may get even tougher. Free market capitalism is evolving into the knowledge economy. Leaders need to learn more and more, but have less time to learn it! The e-coach of the future will combine "high-tech" and "high-touch" by using technology to help find knowledge and using their humanity to provide support and encouragement.

Note

1. See Leadership Is a Contact Sport, M. Goldsmith & H. Morgan. *strategy+business*, Fall 2004.

◆ ◆ ◆

Marshall Goldsmith has recently been named by the American Management Association as one of fifty great thinkers and leaders who have impacted the field of management over the past eighty years. He has been described in *The Wall Street Journal* as one of the top ten executive educators; the *Economist* as one of the most credible thought leaders in the new era of business; *Forbes* as one of five most-respected executive coaches; and *Fast Company* as America's preeminent executive coach.

Dr. Goldsmith has a Ph.D. from UCLA and is an adjunct professor at Dartmouth's Tuck School of Management. He has been asked to teach in executive education programs at Michigan, MIT, and the Wharton School. He is one of a select few consultants who have been asked to work with over seventy major CEOs and their management teams.

Dr. Goldsmith is co-editor or author of eighteen books, including *The Leader of the Future* (a *Business Week* best seller), *Global Leadership: The Next Generation*, and *The Art and Practice of Leadership Coaching*. Contact: www.marshallgoldsmith.com/; marshall@marshallgoldsmith.com.

CHAPTER TWENTY-FOUR

CAREER DEVELOPMENT

Anytime, Anyplace

Beverly L. Kaye

W hat does a manager set aside when another project or problem is piled on, and there just isn't time to do everything?

- The calculations for the annual budget process? No way, managers reason. Those have a deadline.
- The weekly meeting with the boss and other unit directors? Not on your life. The boss wouldn't stand for it.
- The negotiations with outside contractors? Not possible. Nobody else really knows how to handle them.
- The activities related to developing employees, such as performance reviews or counseling sessions? Well, maybe. After all, those can wait until things settle down.

Even though most managers readily agree that people are their most important resource, they find it easy to postpone human resource development in favor of other pressing concerns. The career counseling they have been meaning to do slips to the bottom of the mental in-box, right next to performance appraisals and requests for training. Too often, employees find their managers inaccessible. They see their managers infrequently and speak to them even less. When employees do initiate interaction, managers have a way of "tossing it off"—responding to employees' questions and concerns with palliatives like, "Hang in there!" or "Let me think about that."

This isn't because managers don't care about the developmental needs of employees. They know that companies pay a price for dissatisfied workers who find few challenges or career opportunities in their jobs. They understand the costs of having to recruit and train new employees. They understand that high staff turnover cuts productivity. They recognize that career development and counseling create a better "fit" between employees and their jobs, which increases efficiency and elevates morale. But they still don't make employee development a priority. Why? Listen to these typical comments:

- "I know I should sit each employee down for a chat about his or her future here and career in general. That would be ideal. But I have twelve people who report to me directly; then there are dozens under them. We're talking about an enormous task."
- "I guess I'm really wary about raising expectations that we just can't meet, like pay raises and promotions. If we start talking about career goals, we could be opening a Pandora's Box."
- "Those sessions on 'Let's spend an hour talking about you' seem so forced. To really counsel my employees, I'd have to be much more skilled in that area. I'm a planner and an organizer, not a counselor."
- "If we're going to get into career development, it has to include everyone. And that would take a lot more time than we have right now. So at least for the foreseeable future, employees are going to have to deal with career issues on their own."

Just Do It

Contemporary organizational practices rely heavily on managers' abilities to get the most from their employees. But with the ranks of middle managers shrinking, those who remain have more responsibilities and less time to devote to employees' critical developmental needs.

Employees can't put their career needs on hold until managers accumulate the time and talent to offer them comprehensive career guidance. HRD specialists can help managers substantially meet employees' needs by teaching managers to incorporate career development into their day-to-day routines.

Some managers do this naturally—they recognize employees' interests through casual conversation or by observing how employees work. They give feedback that can help workers develop professionally. These managers take advantage of "coachable moments"—opportunities that occur in the context of ongoing work and open the door for valuable, if brief, career counseling. "Coachable moments" help managers address career development within the small amount of time available.

Coachable moments represent an informal, spontaneous opportunity for career development. Coachable moments do not substitute for formal programs and in-depth counseling, but they can produce important results.

To take advantage of coachable moments, managers first need to understand and commit to the need for career development as a way to use human resources productively. To act on that commitment, managers must take three steps: recognize, verbalize, and mobilize.

- Managers need to *recognize* opportunities for coachable moments when they occur, picking up on cues from employees whose words and actions indicate an openness to immediate developmental feedback.
- Managers need to *verbalize*. They have to take time to talk to employees in a way that helps both parties understand and "check out" developmental options.
- Last, managers need to *mobilize*. They should suggest, on the spot, next steps that can help employees develop their careers.

With those three steps, in just a few minutes, a manager can serve as a catalyst for an employee to undertake his or her own enrichment and developmental activities.

Recognize Opportunities

The following common cues from employees can tip off managers to opportunities for "coachable moments."

An Employee Demonstrates a New Skill or Interest. Lynne, a secretary in the word processing pool, hands her manager a flyer she produced on her computer. It looks almost as good as one that might have come from the company's graphics department. Lynne mentions, "I've been doing some fiddling with that new graphics program and the laser printer."

This type of cue indicates that an employee is taking a crucial step in career development: self-assessment. Most who take this step will not end up in an entirely new career or different job. But with help, by broadening their skills, they can expand their contributions to the organization and gain more satisfaction from their work.

An Employee Seeks Feedback. Marc, a new supervisor, has drafted a detailed proposal for reorganizing tasks in his purchasing unit, including a budget that demonstrates annual cost reductions. Several days after submitting it to his boss, he asks her: "Did you get a chance to check out those figures in the budget I gave you for the new organization?"

An employee who asks for feedback or evaluation might be examining strengths and weaknesses, not just fishing for a pat on the back. This type of cue indicates that an employee is conducting a reality check, the second critical step in career development. When managers recognize these coachable moments, they should relate feedback on the activity to the employee's potential; this helps the employee discover areas to enhance and develop.

An Employee Is Thinking About Change in the Organization. Lindsey, a computer programmer, mentions to her manager, "I heard that the advertising office might develop a slot for its own network-management person. Is advertising growing that fast, or do a lot of departments already have their own network managers?"

When employees show interest in better understanding the organization's structure and development, they might need an opportunity for organization study. Managers can help employees see how their aspirations fit with organizational realities and directions. Employees might use this information to develop career paths that eventually could take them outside their current units; in the meantime, they will add value to their present positions.

An Employee Is Experiencing a Poor Job Fit. Barry, a payroll supervisor, recently has become the subject of complaints about sloppy work in his unit. When his manager points out an error, Barry responds, "I guess that one just slipped by. The only way to make sure nothing slips is for me to monitor my people more closely, and I really don't want to do that. That's not my job."

When an employee sends cues about poor job fit, it might mean the employee is considering his or her options and goals, a vital aspect of the career development process. An employee might have outgrown the job, or the job might not match his or her interests or abilities. If managers recognize these signals as opportunities for coachable moments, they might be able to help unhappy employees find better matches.

An Employee Is Searching for Development Opportunities. Julie, who deals with new-client prospecting for a large construction-management firm, tells her manager, "You can probably count on me being here in this job forever. I thought I might be good at project planning, but those people are all hired from outside with previous experience."

Most employees who have clear goals in mind but don't know how to achieve them need only minimal encouragement and suggestions to help them map out career plans. But typically, they don't ask for help outright. Instead, they vent frustration.

Managers must recognize that these employees are not just asking for empathy; they want help in planning the actions they should take to attain their goals.

Verbalize Support

This step opens a dialogue and establishes a rapport that says, "I noticed; I care." By verbalizing, managers confirm that they have read employees' cues correctly, and they demonstrate their interest.

For some employees, a coachable moment requires only a brief verbal response—assured of support from above, they are motivated to pursue their own career development. Other employees need more help in sorting out how they want to direct their energies and develop their careers. In either case, the verbalization step is not meant to provide solutions, but to help employees define their goals and needs. Let's look at some examples of verbalizing that might follow the cues offered in the previous cases.

New Skill or Interest. When Lynne showed her boss the flyer and mentioned that she had produced it with new software, her manager could have taken advantage of the coachable moment by saying, "This is really good. Is it something you'd like to do more of?" or "Nice job. I had no idea you were interested in graphics." This type of brief response shows approval and opens the door for the employee to discuss a new area of skill or interest. It goes beyond the disinterest of, "Thanks. We can use that."

Evaluation or Feedback. When Marc asked his boss if she had checked the budget figures in his reorganization proposal, his manager could have responded, "I like your use of a program budget rather than an expenditure budget. How did you decide that would prove your point best?" or "Budgeting really seems to be a strong point for you."

This opens a dialogue that might prompt Marc to talk about specific job interests—the skills he might want to enhance and develop in his work. Dialogue would be cut off if the manager had simply responded, "I've only skimmed the report, but it looks fine."

Change Within the Organization. When Lindsey asked if many departments have their own network managers, her manager could have said, "Sales and research have their own network managers, and I think we'll be seeing more departments going that route" or "We're growing in that direction. Is it something you'd be interested in?" This kind of response provides the desired information and the opportunity for the employee to confirm his or her interest in a different area of the organization. If Lindsey's manager had simply said, "I'm not sure; you might check with personnel," the coachable moment would have been lost.

Poor Job Fit. When Barry said it was not his responsibility to prevent errors by supervising his staff more closely, his manager could have asked, "What do you see as the critical functions of your job?" or "Why don't you want to monitor your people more closely?"

The key is to open a dialogue that can help identify the source of the problem. Is the employee bored or disinterested? Does the employee lack training or knowledge? Managers need to confront these situations, not just shrug them off with a vague directive ("You're going to have to try to eliminate those continuing errors").

Searching for Development Opportunities. When Julie told her manager that she believed her lack of experience would prevent her from ever trying project planning, her manager could have suggested, "Some of your experience in our area could be applicable, with just some additional training" or "If you're serious about it, there might be some ways you can get similar experience here." Such a response lets Julie know her manager supports her development desires and has ideas that can help.

Verbalizing requires a commitment on managers' parts to keep the conversation going, but it does not require a lengthy interaction that seeks to explore and solve all issues. Even if a manager decides to stop at this step, verbalizing can make a valuable contribution to an employee's pursuit of career development.

Mobilize the Employee

Once a manager has recognized a cue and opened a conversation with an employee, the manager can "mobilize" the employee by suggesting steps the employee can take to develop his or her career. At this stage, the key for managers is to be candid and specific. Mobilizing still leaves the responsibility for career development with the employee, but it helps the employee focus on realistic, doable steps. Here are ways in which managers in the previous examples could mobilize their employees.

- After recognizing Lynne's new skill at computer graphics and confirming her interest, Lynne's manager could say: "You might want to take a shot at the invitations for Steve's retirement party" or "Why don't you ask Michele down in graphics what other new programs are available that you might want to learn?"
- After Marc has requested and received feedback on development of a budget proposal, his manager could suggest: "Let's put this on the agenda of the next administrative meeting so you can show the other supervisors how performance budgeting might help them" or "This year, why don't you draft your unit's budget for my review, instead of me doing it?"
- After Lindsey has expressed an interest in computer-network management positions within the organization, her manager might mobilize her by saying, "If it's something you're thinking about for yourself, you might want to talk to Jane Hunter, who does computer personnel work, about the kinds of training those positions require" or "A computer-network manager is something our division might

eventually need, too. Why don't you talk to some of the network managers in other divisions and work up a proposal for me about when and how our unit might phase into that?"

- After confirming Barry's poor job fit, Barry's manager might say, "You have some valuable skills, but we might not be using you in a way that fits your interests. If you make a list of your skills and interests, I'll look at it with you to see what we can do to improve the situation."

- After Julie has indicated that she can't identify strategies to develop the opportunities she seeks, her manager could suggest: "You got to know Alan pretty well when he was planning the university project. Why don't you talk to him about courses and projects that might help you learn the ropes; then bring a list of them to me so that we can see what we can do" or "If I were you, I'd review some of the job descriptions for planning positions to check out qualifications. Then you'll have an idea of exactly what gaps you might need to fill and what you already have to offer."

Mobilizing employees takes more creativity and awareness than time on a manager's part. This step leaves an employee with concrete suggestions he or she can act on and demonstrates that managers are interested in employees' developmental needs and willing to be involved.

Seize the Moment

With practice, acting on coachable moments can become routine and almost instinctive for managers. Seizing the opportunity for "coachable moments" creates a caring environment that can alleviate many employee frustrations about development on and beyond the current job.

Coachable moments can go a long way toward meeting employees' needs for job satisfaction and the organization's need for effective use of employee talent. These brief encounters enable managers to seize the moment for employee development when lengthier discussions and planning sessions aren't possible.

Acting on a coachable moment might add up to only a five-minute discussion, but that discussion can initiate important partnerships between caring (but extremely busy) managers and employees who need help and encouragement to focus on career goals.

◆ ◆ ◆

Beverly L. Kaye is president of Career Systems International, Inc. Her cutting-edge management and career-development programs are used by leading international corporations. Kaye is a prolific writer, popular lecturer, and management consultant.

In the early 1980s, she published the classic *Up Is NOT the Only Way,* which forecast how individual careers would be affected by the move to leaner and flatter organizations. More recently she co-authored *Love 'Em or Lose 'Em: Getting Good People to Stay.* Kaye's honors and awards include the National Career Development Award of the American Society for Training and Development (ASTD) and the Best Practice Award from ASTD. Her career development materials are produced by Career Systems International. Contact: www.careersystemsintl.com; www.keepem.com; www. loveitdontleaveit.com; Beverly.Kaye@csibka.com.

CHAPTER TWENTY-FIVE

COACHING IN THE MIDST OF DIVERSITY

R. Roosevelt Thomas, Jr.

Coaching frequently receives rave reviews as a developmental tool. In fact, successful people in organizations often credit a coach or mentor who guided them to or through the attainment of critical experiences or helped them develop required competencies or pay appropriate dues.

Yet in the past, this tool has been used most frequently by white men to help white men. As the workforce continues to become more diverse, and minorities and women continue to report coming up against glass ceilings in many environments, the question becomes: Can coaching enhance a manager's ability to access talent from a workforce characterized by diversity?

This chapter explores how leaders and managers of an increasingly diverse workforce may offer this developmental tool to those whose attributes and behaviors differ from their own. It first defines coaching and analyzes the dynamics of effective coaching relationships. Then it addresses the impact of diversity on the coaching process.

Because most organizational settings require collective efforts for success, this chapter focuses on coaching in the context of teams as opposed to individual efforts. Similarly, while workforce participants can differ along an infinite number of dimensions, the discussion here centers around two that receive enormous attention: race and gender. However, the reader likely will find it possible to extrapolate to other dimensions of interest.

What Is a Coach?

A coach is an individual who enables others to achieve collective objectives. Through a variety of activities, coaches seek to foster individual and team achievement. Coaches relish achieving through others and serve in a variety of roles, some of which are described in the following paragraphs.

Mentors (Teaches). A basic coaching function is that of teaching or mentoring. Comments about great coaches often begin by acknowledging the individual's teaching capacity. This function is probably the cornerstone of the coaching role.

Sponsors (Advocates). On and off the field, coaches sponsor, advocate, or run interference for their players. This could mean pleading the player's case with an umpire or referee, or it could involve helping to access necessary resources or a promotion or reward for a participant. The coach can perform this function openly or behind the scenes. Players are often unaware of the coach's intervention.

Counsels. The coach provides a sounding board for players desiring to test or refine their thinking about some aspect of their game. In the coach, players ideally find an individual who cares enough to be open and honest in his or her responses.

Creates a Motivational Environment. The coach does not motivate, but rather provides an environment that allows each player's personal motivation to come to its full potential. This may require the coach to respond to different players differently, given his or her understanding of each individual.

When players are motivated to satisfy an authority figure, the effective coach assumes the role of a demanding authoritarian. When players are motivated to satisfy an inner drive for excellence and perhaps perfection, the effective coach becomes a facilitative counselor. Phil Jackson, former coach of the Chicago Bulls basketball team, provides an interesting example of creating a motivational environment (Jackson & Delehanty, 1995).

Because Jackson believed that all players sought to connect to something bigger than themselves, he focused on fostering spirituality for team members. Drawing from a variety of spiritual traditions, he created an overarching metaphor that framed basketball seasons as "sacred journeys." His goal was to provide an environment in which the spiritual motivations of his players could manifest themselves and become sources of cohesiveness and collective achievement.

Communicates the Rules. Coaches convey to players how the game is played. They help them to understand the formal and informal (unwritten or not talked about) success requirements. Key to their ability to do so is a sense of timing. They must convey the rules when opportunity knocks. Setbacks or defeats, for example, can provide opportunities to convey lessons about winning that would be difficult to "hear" in the midst of success.

Provides Perspective. In the heat of competition, a participant can lose perspective and focus. From the sideline, coaches often can see things that players cannot. The ability to help players stay in touch with the "big picture" can make the difference between failure and success.

Characteristics of Effective Coaching Relationships

Effective coaching relationships share several characteristics. One key characteristic is affirmation by the organization that coaching is a legitimate activity. In many settings, the prevailing culture excludes coaching as a requirement or an expectation. If coaching exists, it is because of the preferences of the coach and it is viewed not as an organizational necessity, but as a quirk of a nice, "people-oriented" individual.

Acceptance of coaching responsibility is another shared characteristic of effective coaching relationships. Yet even in cultures that encourage coaching, leaders and managers can be reluctant to do so.

Several things contribute to this reluctance. Many managers prefer "doing the work" rather than coaching. Others may believe in "rugged individualism." Within organizations, this translates as "the cream will rise to the top" and "the really good don't need help."

A related hindrance to accepting responsibility for coaching is meritocracy. Some view coaching as an activity that compromises the notion of merit-based success. They contend that recipients of coaching have availed themselves of improper help and cannot claim to be self-made.

Successful coaching relationships also rely on the potential beneficiary's willingness to be coached. Great athletic coaches frequently credit their success to having coachable players. In organizations, the factors that inhibit managers from wanting to coach can make potential beneficiaries unwilling to be coached. For example, rugged individualism, meritocracy, and a desire to be self-made can cause individuals to forge ahead alone, depriving themselves of the benefits of any proffered coaching.

There is irony here. Because coaching often occurs behind the scene, individuals who refuse to be coached are often misinformed. They fail to realize that the "self-made successes" they admire have benefited from effective coaching.

Intimacy is part of successful coaching relationships as well. Coaches serve before, during, and after games. Coaches and players spend an enormous amount of time together. The more intimate the relationship is, the greater the potential for effective coaching; the more effective the coaching is, the greater the intimacy that is likely to be shared.

Trust, which grows with intimacy, is also necessary for coaching success. Trust both accompanies intimacy and makes it possible. A by-product of trust and intimacy is caring.

Coaches care for players; players care for coaches and other players. Often, successful professional sports teams and high-achieving businesses refer to themselves as "family" or as having a "special kind of chemistry." Recently, a commentator noted that the chemistry of the Atlanta Falcons was especially good. In response, Coach Dan Reeves noted: "That's been true on all the winning teams I have seen. Football is a team sport. And players have to come to care deeply about each other." This caring reflects the trust and intimacy required for effective coaching.

Effective coaching also requires shared commitment and ownership. Coaches and players share a commitment to collective objectives, and while the coaches cannot play, they share ownership in any success or failure that may be realized. This is why coaches frequently accept responsibility for a team's failure.

Presumptions of fairness and equal treatment are essential to quality coaching relationships as well. Effective coaches strive to treat people fairly and equally within the context of collective objectives. However, in quality coaching relationships, both coaches and players know that treating people fairly and equally does not necessarily mean treating them the same. Unless this understanding exists, coaches risk being accused of favoritism as they respond to their players' different needs.

Who Are the Coaches?

How can we identify coaches within organizations? Some believe that mentors are coaches, but not all mentors are coaches. Mentors may agree to teach without sharing ownership or responsibility for outcomes, or without accepting the intimacy that characterizes effective coaching.

The same can be said for sponsors. All effective coaches are sponsors, but not all sponsors are coaches. Some sponsors maintain a distance that precludes intimacy or shared ownership of results.

Organizational coaches are likely to be leaders and managers. Leaders are responsible and accountable for organizational results. They may be formal heads of organizational units, such as divisions, functions, or departments, or individuals chairing cross-functional teams, task forces, or special projects.

But coaches also can be those with informal influence. A valued individual contributor can provide coaching to a network (team) without having formal authority. Alliances such as these may exist around points of view, shared interests, or professional experiences. Within a company, for example, a group of chemists committed to a particular school of thought might be headed informally by one of its colleagues.

This individual can influence associates through coaching efforts centered in mutual respect and trust, professional intimacy, shared commitment and ownership, mentoring and sponsoring—all without formal authority or responsibility. As individuals experience success or failure, so do the coach and fellow practitioners.

Impact of Diversity

My research and work with organizations has convinced me that diversity can play havoc with developmental processes such as coaching, mentoring, and sponsoring. A consequence has been less-than-optimal development, opportunity, and utilization of talent with respect to minorities and women. Some issues that the presence of diversity can raise are examined below.

Social Allegiances. White males coach white males best because of social allegiances and relatively high comfort levels, compared to those that they experience with minorities and women. As one white male manager commented, "Mentoring is very important here, but minorities and women don't get the guidance they need, so they walk on land mines that could be avoided." When asked why the guidance was not forthcoming, he replied, "Social allegiance. We don't know how to relate to women and minorities as subordinates or peers. We're more comfortable with white males. Lately, we've made some progress with women, but we're nowhere with minorities."

Another indicator of this "social allegiance gap" is the way in which mentoring and coaching relationships evolve. White males typically report having been chosen, whereas minorities, in particular, describe themselves as having acted proactively to initiate a mentoring relationship. One black woman noted, "I selected the white male I wanted as a coach and approached him. He was reluctant at first and appeared to be uncomfortable, but it has worked out well."

Preferential Treatment. Concerns about reverse discrimination and preferential treatment can block the establishment of coaching relationships with minorities and women. The desire of minorities and women to avoid being labeled an Affirmative Action hire or promotion can deter them from entering into the informal developmental coaching arrangements that can be pivotal to one's career. Some fear that asking for a coaching relationship will be viewed as a request for favoritism or a sign of weakness, so they wait to be approached.

White males worry that offering coaching to those individuals might spill over into preferential treatment, or be seen as an insulting suggestion that minorities and women need special help to be successful. The fact that coaching relationships in many organizations do not operate in the open, but rather in a shroud of mystery, means that whispers and rumors further complicate matters.

Lack of Confidence. Many white males possess only a limited history of interacting with minorities and women as colleagues and peers. As a result, they often feel inadequate to the task of creating a motivational environment or providing perspective for minorities and women.

One white woman manager relied primarily on a white male for coaching and developmental assistance, and indeed, he performed well in this role. Her undoing, however, came from being blindsided by women's issues. In retrospect, she feels that she lost touch with the challenges of being a woman in an organization. Her white male mentor lacked experience and knowledge in that arena. Had she had an additional relationship with a more experienced woman manager (who were scarce in her company at that time) or with a network of women, she might have avoided being blindsided.

Lack of Trust. Trust facilitates effective coaching. When minority and women employees enter a company and see people like themselves clustered or at the bottom of the pyramid, they may find it difficult to trust the organization's process.

In one corporation, a black male learned that effective social relations with white males were required to receive a promotion. Although he perceived some of what was suggested as personally demeaning, he stood ready to do what was necessary. But he did not act on the counsel he received. He realized that the advice had worked for white males seeking promotions, but he did not trust that it would work for him as a black male. His fear was that he would do something he found distasteful, only to have it fail to make a difference for him. Subsequently, he left the corporation in search of another setting, one in which he had more trust.

Fear of Intimacy. Coaching requires intimacy. Some white males worry about establishing such intimacy. One white male remembers, "When women first arrived in numbers, white males here feared closing their doors when they met with a woman."

Minorities, too, can be uncomfortable with intimacy, particularly if they come to the workplace with no history of intimacy with whites. One black woman manager recalls hearing her grandmother, who prospered as an entrepreneur, say repeatedly, "I would just never work for a white person." Now this black female works in a corporation with white males and white females. Her grandmother's voice lingers, making it difficult for her to be intimate with her white colleagues.

Faulty Presumptions of Fairness and Equal Treatment. Because many companies do not define coaching as legitimate, individuals can presume that it constitutes an unfair practice and fosters inequality. With diversity, perceptions of lack of fairness and equal treatment can quickly evolve into charges of racism and sexism. This reality can lead managers with significantly diverse workforces to avoid coaching out of a belief that doing so could lead to charges of some "ism."

Recommendations

Executives who wish to foster effective coaching in the midst of diversity must begin by legitimizing coaching. They can do this by encouraging potential coaches to accept the responsibility and by encouraging potential recipients to be coachable. They must posit coaching as a necessity that is critical to the organization's viability. In particular, facilitating executives must take care to sanction and reward coaching across racial and gender lines.

Facilitating executives must also encourage potential coaches and recipients to accept responsibility for addressing diverse coaching relationships—for making the coaching experience effective. A critical step here will be to prepare both parties to respond to diversity appropriately.

They must also encourage both potential coaches and recipients to be open to differences that might be uncomfortable, but do not compromise achievement of personal and organizational objectives. They can do this by helping the coaching parties identify and focus on the requirements for success, as opposed to personal preferences or traditions.

Facilitating managers must also help the coaching participants become comfortable with the diversity tension that can characterize relationships in which people have significant differences. They can do so by helping them to accept the reality of the tension, and therefore avoid undue stress when it appears. They can also do this by helping them to maintain a focus on requirements.

Facilitating managers can also help coaches and recipients to become skilled in responding appropriately to diversity issues. In *Redefining Diversity* (Thomas, 1996), I detail action options for coping with diversity. The coaching partners will benefit from familiarity with these options and the ability to select the option or blend appropriate for their relationship.

Clearly, coaching in the midst of diversity requires preparation. Unlike coaching relationships between relatively homogeneous pairs, it cannot be left to chance. It is equally clear that, although the discussion here has focused on the dimensions of race and gender, it could be generalized to include other variables, such as age, tenure with the organization, sexual orientation, and functional background. As workforce participants become more diverse, executives and managers desiring to access talent will need to become effective in fostering coaching across diversity lines or risk not tapping potential to the degree required for success.

◆ ◆ ◆

R. Roosevelt Thomas, Jr., has been at the forefront of developing and implementing innovative concepts and strategies for maximizing organizational and individual potential through diversity management for the past twenty years. He currently serves as CEO of Roosevelt Thomas Consulting & Training, Inc., and as president of The American Institute for Managing Diversity (AIMD). Dr. Thomas is the author of five published books; his most recent is *Giraffe and Elephant—A Diversity Fable.* Dr. Thomas has been active for more than twenty years as a consultant to numerous Fortune 500 companies, corporations, professional firms, government entities, non-profit organizations, and academic institutions, and he has served as a frequent speaker at national conferences and industry seminars. He has also served as secretary of Morehouse College, dean of the Graduate School of Business Administration at Atlanta University, assistant professor at the Harvard Business School, and instructor at Morehouse College. Further, Dr. Thomas has been recognized by *The Wall Street Journal* as one of the top ten consultants in the country, elected as a Fellow in the National Academy of Human Resources, and cited by *Human Resource Executive* as one of HR's Most Influential People. Contact: www.rthomasconsulting.com; rthomas@rthomasconsulting.com.

CHAPTER TWENTY-SIX

COACHING EXECUTIVES

Women Succeeding Globally

Nancy J. Adler

I used to question what executive coaches brought to clients that the executives themselves didn't already know from their own experience. Having had the privilege of coaching many executives, I now understand that the answer is perspective—a perspective beyond that of their own experience, organization, and culture. In particular, given my background, I almost always have the opportunity to reframe issues in a broader, global perspective. More frequently today, I have the opportunity to reframe business realities that have previously been appreciated primarily from a man's perspective into broader possibilities as seen from both men's and women's perspectives.

Part of bringing a broader perspective is to offer a context of meaning beyond each executive's unique position, organization, and industry. By quietly asking questions that are beyond the bottom line, coaching dialogues offer opportunities for executives to consider more consciously the types of contributions they are making to their companies and to choose the kinds of contributions they would like to be making more broadly for the betterment of the world. Examples of these questions include:

- "What does success mean to you?"
- "In which ways does your work lead to your company doing well financially and simultaneously doing good for society?" and
- "Why would your daughter be proud to tell her daughter about what you are accomplishing?"

These questions often appear illegitimate when taken out of the privacy of the executive coaching dialogue. In the public glare of business-as-normal, such questions frequently fail to appear sufficiently pragmatic to warrant executive time. And yet the conversations, reflection, and learning that such questions generate often bring soul, along with deep, personal motivation, back into the pragmatism of professionalism. Context, significance, and purpose are without counterparts in the pragmatism of successful careers, successful lives, and successful societies.

How Does Coaching Women Executives Differ from Coaching Men?

While few people question that the economy has gone global, most assumptions about building a global career and succeeding as a global executive remain based on the experience of men. Many of the most fundamental assumptions about executive success remain parochial—limited not only to the experience of men, but often to the experience of men working within their own home countries. If companies continue to believe current parochial assumptions about business success, few, if any, women will venture out into the world beyond their national borders, and even fewer will succeed once there. In these opening years of the 21st century, one of my roles has become coaching executive women to succeed in a global economy by going beyond the myths and erroneous assumptions of history.

Because so few women worked as global managers in the 20th century, let alone as global executives, ignorance and misleading myths abound. Not surprisingly, many women, especially in such English-speaking cultures as the United States, have been led to believe that they must emulate men to succeed. Fearing to differentiate themselves in any way from their successful male predecessors and contemporaries, many women become reticent to challenge openly the abundant myths about the barriers women supposedly face when attempting to conduct business abroad. One of the most valuable aspects of executive coaching, therefore, has become the private space it creates for women managers and executives to ask such societally unacceptable questions as:

- "Is it true that businesswomen can't succeed in the Middle East?"
- "Will I insult the Arabs if I lead the negotiating team in Saudi Arabia?"
- "Is it true that our company's expansion into South Asia will be jeopardized if I head up the project?"
- "Even if I succeed in getting the CEO to send me to Korea, will I fail once I'm there? I've heard that Korean businessmen just ignore women. Is it true that they never take a businesswoman seriously?"

- "Will our joint venture partners be annoyed when they see that my company has sent me as the lead engineer?"
- "Will men in Latin America really think that my company has sent me as some kind of sexual plaything? What do I need to do to get them to respect me?"

As I listen to women telling their stories and asking their "unaskable" questions, my most frequent response is, "Why?" Why do you think that might happen to you? What reality do you want to be true for you? How can you go beyond all the negative scenarios of what you and others in your company imagine will occur? Why do you think foreigners will be more prejudiced against you than are some of the executives you have already successfully dealt with here at home? How can you go beyond history's erroneous assumptions to create your own reality? In the privacy of executive coaching dialogues, we laugh, question, and explore a world that has literally been foreign to all too many women and companies. In the process, we lay to rest the misleading belief that women cannot succeed abroad or that, in order to succeed, they must act like men. Let me give a few examples.

Myth One: Global Experience Is Not That Important

Lisette, an executive in a major consumer products company with two teenagers in high school, recently turned down an assignment in Brussels. Annoyed with her, Lisette's boss told her that he would not consider her for a senior vice presidency because she was not mobile. He emphasized that her promising career would plateau if she did not willingly move abroad to take the expatriate assignment.

Lisette challenges the importance of international experience. She knows that neither her boss, nor his boss—the CEO—have had much experience abroad beyond regularly boarding airplanes. Given that she is currently the highest ranked woman in the company, the requirement that she gain international experience looks suspiciously like another hurdle her boss is putting in the way of her career progress—the latest hurdle defining the glass ceiling.

My response to Lisette's angry phone call is a resounding, "No!" Business has gone global. Requiring international experience reflects neither sexism nor a new variant of the glass ceiling. "Your boss is right. If you choose not to get international experience, it is you who are choosing to remain well below the glass ceiling. No man or woman should be promoted into the executive ranks of a major 21st-century company without having a profound understanding and appreciation of global business dynamics. Your boss and the CEO grew their careers in another era, an era of domestic or, at most, multi-domestic business. Unless your aim is to progress backward through history and to attempt to have a parochial 19th- or 20th-century career, you don't dare consider limiting your experience to domestic, stay-at-home assignments."

Lisette doesn't like what I am saying, but she believes me. As an executive coach, an outsider, she knows that I am on her side and that I will tell her the truth—even if it is an inconvenient truth that she would rather not hear. Recognizing the truth, however, does not imply resignation to a career stopped by a seemingly impenetrable global glass ceiling. The outwardly paradoxical question I raise with Lisette is: "How can you acquire significant global experience while simultaneously keeping your commitment to not move abroad during your children's formative high school years?" Asking such paradoxical questions as: "How can you both move abroad and not move abroad?" and then helping executives resolve them is a significant part of my executive coaching role.

Myth Two: Given Family Commitments, I Can't Take a Global Assignment

In reflecting on her dilemma, Lisette realized that expatriation, while a very powerful way to gain global experience, was not the only alternative open to her. As we brainstormed options, Lisette discovered that she could increase her global experience significantly by participating on global task forces, increasing her international business travel, and—her most creative idea—taking short-term assignments in Europe and Asia while her two teenagers were away each summer at camp. For Lisette, as well as for many other executive women, the problem is the form in which global experience has traditionally been offered (expatriate assignments), not the requirement for global experience itself. The trap for Lisette would have been to reject global experience because it was offered in its traditional, and to her unacceptable, form—as a three-year to five-year expatriate assignment. The trap for me as a coach would have been to accept her boss's definitions of reality, rather than helping Lisette to think beyond the mythology surrounding the corporation's increasingly anachronistic requirements. As Lisette's subsequent discussions with the CEO revealed, expatriation as a developmental strategy was a better fit for the company's needs in the past, when their business strategy required key executives to have an in-depth knowledge of only one foreign culture. By contrast, today's globally integrated transnational business strategies require key executives to understand multiple cultures and their interactions. The very option that Lisette was suggesting for herself—shorter-term exposure to multiple countries—has actually become preferable in many cases to the company's traditional emphasis on a single, longer-term expatriate assignment.

Myth Three: Being a Woman Is a Disadvantage for Global Managers Because Certain Cultures Make It Impossible for Women Executives to Succeed

This is a pervasive and erroneous myth that finds its way into the thinking of the vast majority of today's executives, both male and female. Valana, a senior financial analyst for a major pharmaceutical company, was offered a regional vice presidency in Japan.

Given the company's new startup operations in Pakistan, the position in Japan would involve considerable travel to this Islamic country. Valana felt simultaneously excited and cautious. As a woman, would she be able to succeed in Japan and Pakistan, both countries reputed to act with hostility toward women managers and executives? She worried that if she openly raised her fears with her boss, he would change his mind and that, once again, the company would assume that it could not send women abroad. To make sure that she did not ruin the opportunity to work abroad for herself or for other women, she chose not to raise her concerns inside the company, but rather relied on the confidentiality inherent in the executive coaching relationship. She called me.

Valana's initial fear was that no woman could succeed in Japan or Pakistan. Her real fear was that if she accepted the position, she would be setting herself up for failure. When I asked her why she believed she would fail in either of these two Asian countries, she immediately cited the cultural limitations placed on most women in Japan, as well as in most Islamic countries. Unconsciously, yet understandably, Valana had fallen into the *Gaijin Trap*. She had assumed that, as a woman, she would be treated similarly to the local Japanese and Pakistani women, few of whom are given the cultural latitude to succeed as executives in major multinational businesses. Her mistake was not in her statistics; she was right that there are still very few women executives in either country. Rather, her mistake was in overemphasizing the salience of being a woman. Based on the actual experience of women executives who have worked abroad, we know that American women are treated as foreigners who happen to be women. They are not treated in the same way as local women. While both the Japanese and Pakistanis limit the roles that local women can take in business, neither culture confuses foreign women with local women. Valana's freedom to succeed lies in the fact that she is visibly foreign. The mistake for Valana would be to assume that the Japanese could not tell that she is not Japanese (or that the Pakistanis could not tell that she is not Pakistani); they can.

To get accurate tips on how to succeed in such cultures, I suggested that Valana restrict her advice gathering to conversations with other North American and European women who have worked for major global companies in Japan or Pakistan. From them she could learn the nuances of showing respect in each culture without limiting her own success. I strongly advised that she disregard suggestions made by both men and women who had not had direct experience with women working in the particular countries in which she would be working. Without direct experience, even the best-intentioned colleagues unconsciously pass on myths disguised as advice. The only thing that eradicates the myth that women cannot succeed abroad—and, simultaneously, the fear that such myths engender in both women executives and the companies that hesitantly consider sending them on global assignments—is learning about the actual experiences of women executives who have worked abroad—the majority of whom have succeeded. (See Adler, 1994, for further research on this topic.)

In the next couple of weeks, Valana did talk with many such women, coming back to me frequently to ask whether I thought their suggestions would be relevant for her. Among her many questions, Valana asked if it were true that women executives did not have to stay up drinking until late into the night in order to do business with Japanese firms. My answer: "Absolutely true." Whereas male business behavior in Japan is fairly codified and usually includes a lot of business entertainment and drinking, the newness of women conducting significant business in Japan means that male/female business behavior has yet to become rigidly codified. Given the ambiguity at this point in history, women have more latitude than do men to conduct business in ways that feel most comfortable to them. As one highly successful American woman executive, who had been based out of Tokyo for years, laughingly related to me, "Among all of my male colleagues, I am the only one who has consistently maintained great relationships with Japanese clients without needing to put my liver in jeopardy! I can get away with conducting business over lunch and a Perrier; the men can't."

Myth Four: Public Is Public, and Private Is Private; to Be Taken Seriously, a Woman Executive Must Hide Her Role as a Wife and Mother

The myth, albeit false, is that foreigners will not take a businesswoman seriously unless she is completely focused on work. American women, who come from one of the most task-oriented cultures in the world, often fall into the trap of attempting to emulate American businessmen. They try to focus almost exclusively on business—to the detriment of both their worldwide business success and their private lives.

Perhaps one particularly successful businesswoman's experience says it all. On a business trip to Hong Kong, Katia, a marketing vice president for a global telecommunications firm, was negotiating her first major contract with a consortium of Thai, Malaysian, and Chinese companies. The negotiations were not going very well and looked to be in jeopardy. At a particularly tense moment in the deliberations, Katia glanced at her watch, stood up, and apologized for needing to take a ten-minute break. While receiving quizzical looks from the group of men, she explained that it was bedtime for her seven-year-old daughter, back home in Chicago, and that she always called to say good night to her daughter, no matter where she was in the world.

Returning ten minutes later, Katia was surprised to discover that the tension around the negotiating table had melted. As she entered the room, the Thai executive asked how her daughter was doing, the lead Chinese negotiator asked Katia if she had a picture of her daughter, and the other negotiators expressed how difficult they imagined it must be for a mother to be so far away from her daughter. After this brief exchange of warm interest and concern, the negotiations continued, now clearly with a focus on efficiently finding a mutually beneficial agreement. At noon the following day, the negotiation that had appeared irreversibly stuck came to a successful conclusion.

Most women from Anglo-Saxon cultures, and especially those from the United States, have been coached by their colleagues to separate their private lives from their professional lives. To succeed abroad, however, these same women need to unlearn the advice they have received from their Anglo-Saxon colleagues. Unlike the task-orientation of Anglo-Saxon countries, most countries in the world emphasize relationship building. In countries such as China, Malaysia, and Thailand, people will only conduct business with people they know, like, and trust. Revealing who you are as a whole person—including unmasking some aspects of your private life—allows colleagues from relationship-building cultures to get to know you, and, therefore, to want to do business with you. It is not that people from relationship-oriented cultures aren't concerned about accomplishing the task; they are. It's just that relationships must precede task. Katia's relationship with her daughter added the dimension of wholeness that she needed to succeed.

Katia laughs today that a number of her women friends, who are also global executives, now carry pictures of their children very visibly in their business-card cases. Why? Because from the first moment of contact, clients know that they are whole people—wives, mothers, and businesswomen.

Executive Coaching: Reaching Beyond the Myths of History

The privacy of coaching sessions makes it easier for executives to say, "I'm not certain. . . . I just don't know. . . ." Privacy and supportive advocacy legitimize moments of not knowing. Premature certainty and commitment extinguish innovative possibilities. For both women and men, coaching dialogues can foster a depth of questioning that allows executives to escape the bounded thinking of their own professional, organizational, and national cultures. For women, coaching sessions encourage exploring alternatives that reach beyond the accepted "wisdom" of successful men who have worked worldwide, primarily with other men. At their very best, coaching sessions provide the time, space, and learning opportunities that allow executives to offer profound and wise counsel to themselves.

◆ ◆ ◆

Nancy J. Adler is a professor of organizational behavior and international management at the Faculty of Management, McGill University, in Montreal, Quebec, Canada. She received her B.A. in economics and her M.B.A. and Ph.D. in management from the University of California at Los Angeles.

Dr. Adler consults and conducts research on global leadership, strategic international human resource management, international negotiating, culturally synergistic problem solving, and global organization development. She has authored more than one hundred articles, produced the film *A Portable Life*, and published four books: *International Dimensions of Organizational Behavior*, *Women in Management Worldwide*, *Competitive Frontiers: Women Managers in a Global Economy*, and *From Boston to Beijing: Managing with a Worldview*.

Dr. Adler has consulted to global businesses, government agencies, and civil-sector organizations on projects in Asia, Africa, Europe, North and South America, and the Middle East. She has taught Chinese executives in the People's Republic of China, held the Citicorp Visiting Doctoral Professorship at the University of Hong Kong, and taught executive seminars at INSEAD in France, Bocconi University in Italy, and Oxford University in England. She received McGill University's first Distinguished Teaching Award in Management and has subsequently been awarded it for a second time.

She has served on the Board of Governors of the American Society for Training and Development (ASTD), the Canadian Social Science Advisory Committee to UNESCO, the Strategic Grants Committee of the Social Sciences and Humanities Research Council, and the executive committees of the Pacific Asian Consortium for International Business, Education and Research, the International Personnel Association, and the Society for Human Resource Management's International Institute, as well as having held leadership positions in the Academy of International Business (AIB), the Society for Intercultural Education, Training, and Research (SIETAR), and the Academy of Management. Dr. Adler received ASTD's International Leadership Award, SIETAR's Outstanding Senior Interculturalist Award, the YWCA's Femme de Mérite (Woman of Distinction) Award, and the Sage Award for scholarly contributions to management. She was selected as a 3M Teaching Fellow, honoring her as one of Canada's top university professors, and elected to both the Fellows of the Academy of International Business and the Academy of Management Fellows. She was recently inducted into The Royal Society. Contact: nancy.adler@mcgill.ca.

Index

Pfeiffer Publications Guide

This guide is designed to familiarize you with the various types of Pfeiffer publications. The formats section describes the various types of products that we publish; the methodologies section describes the many different ways that content might be provided within a product. We also provide a list of the topic areas in which we publish.

FORMATS

In addition to its extensive book-publishing program, Pfeiffer offers content in an array of formats, from fieldbooks for the practitioner to complete, ready-to-use training packages that support group learning.

FIELDBOOK Designed to provide information and guidance to practitioners in the midst of action. Most fieldbooks are companions to another, sometimes earlier, work, from which its ideas are derived; the fieldbook makes practical what was theoretical in the original text. Fieldbooks can certainly be read from cover to cover. More likely, though, you'll find yourself bouncing around following a particular theme, or dipping in as the mood, and the situation, dictate.

HANDBOOK A contributed volume of work on a single topic, comprising an eclectic mix of ideas, case studies, and best practices sourced by practitioners and experts in the field.

An editor or team of editors usually is appointed to seek out contributors and to evaluate content for relevance to the topic. Think of a handbook not as a ready-to-eat meal, but as a cookbook of ingredients that enables you to create the most fitting experience for the occasion.

RESOURCE Materials designed to support group learning. They come in many forms: a complete, ready-to-use exercise (such as a game); a comprehensive resource on one topic (such as conflict management) containing a variety of methods and approaches; or a collection of like-minded activities (such as icebreakers) on multiple subjects and situations.

TRAINING PACKAGE An entire, ready-to-use learning program that focuses on a particular topic or skill. All packages comprise a guide for the facilitator/trainer and a workbook for the participants. Some packages are supported with additional media—such as video—or learning aids, instruments, or other devices to help participants understand concepts or practice and develop skills.

- *Facilitator/trainer's guide* Contains an introduction to the program, advice on how to organize and facilitate the learning event, and step-by-step instructor notes. The guide also contains copies of presentation materials—handouts, presentations, and overhead designs, for example—used in the program.

- *Participant's workbook* Contains exercises and reading materials that support the learning goal and serves as a valuable reference and support guide for participants in the weeks and months that follow the learning event. Typically, each participant will require his or her own workbook.

ELECTRONIC CD-ROMs and web-based products transform static Pfeiffer content into dynamic, interactive experiences. Designed to take advantage of the searchability, automation, and ease-of-use that technology provides, our e-products bring convenience and immediate accessibility to your workspace.

METHODOLOGIES

CASE STUDY A presentation, in narrative form, of an actual event that has occurred inside an organization. Case studies are not prescriptive, nor are they used to prove a point; they are designed to develop critical analysis and decision-making skills. A case study has a specific time frame, specifies a sequence of events, is narrative in structure, and contains a plot structure— an issue (what should be/have been done?). Use case studies when the goal is to enable participants to apply previously learned theories to the circumstances in the case, decide what is pertinent, identify the real issues, decide what should have been done, and develop a plan of action.

ENERGIZER A short activity that develops readiness for the next session or learning event. Energizers are most commonly used after a break or lunch to stimulate or refocus the group. Many involve some form of physical activity, so they are a useful way to counter post-lunch lethargy. Other uses include transitioning from one topic to another, where "mental" distancing is important.

EXPERIENTIAL LEARNING ACTIVITY (ELA) A facilitator-led intervention that moves participants through the learning cycle from experience to application (also known as a Structured Experience). ELAs are carefully thought-out designs in which there is a definite learning purpose and intended outcome. Each step—everything that participants do during the activity— facilitates the accomplishment of the stated goal. Each ELA includes complete instructions for facilitating the intervention and a clear statement of goals, suggested group size and timing, materials required, an explanation of the process, and, where appropriate, possible variations to the activity. (For more detail on Experiential Learning Activities, see the Introduction to the *Reference Guide to Handbooks and Annuals*, 1999 edition, Pfeiffer, San Francisco.)

GAME A group activity that has the purpose of fostering team spirit and togetherness in addition to the achievement of a pre-stated goal. Usually contrived—undertaking a desert expedition, for example—this type of learning method offers an engaging means for participants to demonstrate and practice business and interpersonal skills. Games are effective for team building and personal development mainly because the goal is subordinate to the process—the means through which participants reach decisions, collaborate, communicate, and generate trust and understanding. Games often engage teams in "friendly" competition.

ICEBREAKER A (usually) short activity designed to help participants overcome initial anxiety in a training session and/or to acquaint the participants with one another. An icebreaker can be a fun activity or can be tied to specific topics or training goals. While a useful tool in itself, the icebreaker comes into its own in situations where tension or resistance exists within a group.

INSTRUMENT A device used to assess, appraise, evaluate, describe, classify, and summarize various aspects of human behavior. The term used to describe an instrument depends primarily on its format and purpose. These terms include survey, questionnaire, inventory, diagnostic, survey, and poll. Some uses of instruments include providing instrumental feedback to group members, studying here-and-now processes or functioning within a group, manipulating group composition, and evaluating outcomes of training and other interventions.

Instruments are popular in the training and HR field because, in general, more growth can occur if an individual is provided with a method for focusing specifically on his or her own behavior. Instruments also are used to obtain information that will serve as a basis for change and to assist in workforce planning efforts.

Paper-and-pencil tests still dominate the instrument landscape with a typical package comprising a facilitator's guide, which offers advice on administering the instrument and interpreting the collected data, and an initial set of instruments. Additional instruments are available separately. Pfeiffer, though, is investing heavily in e-instruments. Electronic instrumentation provides effortless distribution and, for larger groups particularly, offers advantages over paper-and-pencil tests in the time it takes to analyze data and provide feedback.

LECTURETTE A short talk that provides an explanation of a principle, model, or process that is pertinent to the participants' current learning needs. A lecturette is intended to establish a common language bond between the trainer and the participants by providing a mutual frame of reference. Use a lecturette as an introduction to a group activity or event, as an interjection during an event, or as a handout.

MODEL A graphic depiction of a system or process and the relationship among its elements. Models provide a frame of reference and something more tangible, and more easily remembered, than a verbal explanation. They also give participants something to "go on," enabling them to track their own progress as they experience the dynamics, processes, and relationships being depicted in the model.

ROLE PLAY A technique in which people assume a role in a situation/scenario: a customer service rep in an angry-customer exchange, for example. The way in which the role is approached is then discussed and feedback is offered. The role play is often repeated using a different approach and/or incorporating changes made based on feedback received. In other words, role playing is a spontaneous interaction involving realistic behavior under artificial (and safe) conditions.

SIMULATION A methodology for understanding the interrelationships among components of a system or process. Simulations differ from games in that they test or use a model that depicts or mirrors some aspect of reality in form, if not necessarily in content. Learning occurs by studying the effects of change on one or more factors of the model. Simulations are commonly used to test hypotheses about what happens in a system—often referred to as "what if?" analysis—or to examine best-case/worst-case scenarios.

THEORY A presentation of an idea from a conjectural perspective. Theories are useful because they encourage us to examine behavior and phenomena through a different lens.

TOPICS

The twin goals of providing effective and practical solutions for workforce training and organization development and meeting the educational needs of training and human resource professionals shape Pfeiffer's publishing program. Core topics include the following:

> Leadership & Management
> Communication & Presentation
> Coaching & Mentoring
> Training & Development
> E-Learning
> Teams & Collaboration
> OD & Strategic Planning
> Human Resources
> Consulting

What will you find on pfeiffer.com?

• The best in workplace performance solutions for training and HR professionals

• Downloadable training tools, exercises, and content

• Web-exclusive offers

• Training tips, articles, and news

• Seamless on-line ordering

• Author guidelines, information on becoming a Pfeiffer Affiliate, and much more

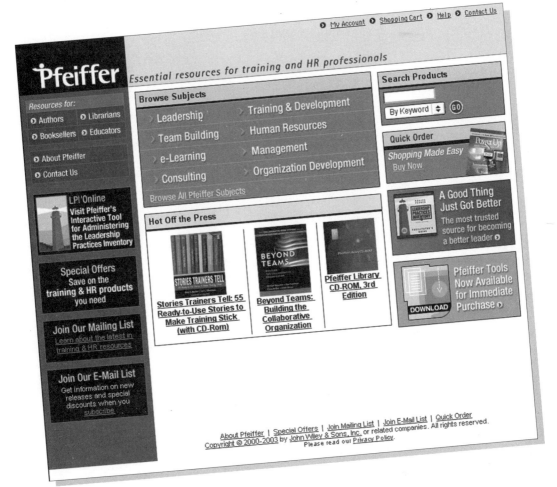

Discover more at www.pfeiffer.com